THE WRITER of these facinating
letters was the wife of the Hon.
Edward Boscawen, Pitt's
favourite Admiral. During her
lifetime, her friends compared
her letters to those of Mme. de
Sevigné, and even in France she
was described as "*La Sevigné
d'Angleterre.*"

No previous biography of
Fanny Boscawen has ever been
written, and the publication of
the present volume, with its
charming selection from the
letters she wrote during the first
half of her life, is an event in the
world of books. Possessing a
quality of rare freshness and
spontaneity, the letters touch
every note in the scale of human
emotions ; and linked together
with a running commentary by
the editor, whose wife is Mrs.
Boscawen's great - great - great
grandaughter, they paint an
unforgettable portrait of a really
lovable character all the more
engaging because of its complete
lack of self-conciousness.

ADMIRAL'S WIFE

The Rt. Hon. Edward Boscawen, P.C., M.P.
Admiral of the Blue
Aet 49
(*From the painting by Sir Joshua Reynolds in the National Portrait Gallery*)

ADMIRAL'S WIFE

Being the life and letters of The Hon.
Mrs. Edward Boscawen from 1719 to 1761

By
CECIL ASPINALL-OGLANDER

WITH ILLUSTRATIONS

LONGMANS, GREEN AND CO.
LONDON ❖ NEW YORK ❖ TORONTO

LONGMANS, GREEN AND CO. LTD.
39 PATERNOSTER ROW, LONDON, E.C.4
17 CHITTARANJAN AVENUE, CALCUTTA
NICOL ROAD, BOMBAY
36A MOUNT ROAD, MADRAS

LONGMANS, GREEN AND CO.
55 FIFTH AVENUE, NEW YORK
221 EAST 20TH STREET, CHICAGO
88 TREMONT STREET, BOSTON

LONGMANS, GREEN AND CO.
215 VICTORIA STREET, TORONTO

First Published 1940

PRINTED IN GREAT BRITAIN
BY WESTERN PRINTING SERVICES LTD., BRISTOL

TO THE MEMORY

OF

FANNY BOSCAWEN

IN ADMIRATION

AND TO

ALL HER DESCENDANTS

I LOOK upon it as a fortunate omen to begin my New Year in Mrs. Boscawen's company. She is in her conversation everything that can make the hours pass agreeably. I must be happier, and I should be better for her friendship.

Elizabeth Montagu.

PREFACE

THE HONOURABLE MRS. EDWARD BOSCAWEN, great-great niece of John Evelyn the diarist, and wife of Pitt's favourite admiral, was one of the best-known figures of eighteenth-century London. It was of her that Boswell wrote, in his *Life of Johnson*: "If it be not presumptuous of me to praise her, I would say that her manners are the most agreeable, and her conversation the best, of any lady with whom I ever had the happiness to be acquainted." Frequent allusions to "the attractive," "the agreeable," or "the accomplished Mrs. Boscawen" are also to be found in most of the well-known volumes which describe the social life of the eighteenth century. Hannah More compared her letters to those of Madame de Sevigné; even in France she was described as "La Sevigné d'Angleterre"; and Elizabeth Montagu, Doctor Johnson, David Garrick and Sir Joshua Reynolds were amongst her many friends.

It is therefore remarkable, and indeed a public loss, that outside the various family circles of her descendants, where the tradition of her many virtues is kept for ever green, so little is known to-day of this outstanding English personality. True, a number of her letters, covering the period 1769–87, are included in the last three volumes of Mrs. Delany's *Life and Correspondence*, and a few in the various biographies of the brilliant Elizabeth Montagu; but that, in effect, is all. The present volume is an attempt to fill the gap and to tell the story of the earlier portion of her life, as nearly as possible in her own words. Nor has the task been difficult, for in the

large number of her letters which fortunately still exist she
has left us not only a detailed account of long periods of her
life, but also an unconscious and therefore all the more vivid
delineation of her own fascinating character.

A few words must here be said about the history of the
letters used in this volume. Those addressed by Mrs. Boscawen
to her husband have been copied from the original documents
in the possession of the Admiral's direct descendant, the
present Lord Falmouth. Some of these unique documents
travelled to India and back again in the days when Robert
Clive was still an ensign, and gladdened the heart of the
Admiral at the siege of Pondicherry, and I take this opportunity
of thanking Lord Falmouth once again, both in my own name
and in that of my readers, for so kindly allowing me to publish
them. Of the other letters in this volume a few have been
copied from the correspondence of Elizabeth Montagu, but
the great majority belong to a voluminous collection of
Mrs. Boscawen's letters, never before published, the existence
of which is due to a chain of rather unusual circumstances.

Early in youth a warm friendship sprang up between the
future Fanny Boscawen and her cousin Julia, the daughter of
Edward Evelyn of Felbridge, whose wife was a natural
daughter of the Duke of Ormond. Julia married James Sayer,
of Old Palace Yard, Westminster; the two friends wrote to
each other regularly till Mrs. Sayer died in 1777; and thereafter
Mrs. Boscawen continued the correspondence with Julia's
daughter, Fanny Sayer, who had become her favourite god-
child. After Mrs. Boscawen's death, in 1805, Fanny Sayer
married, and went to live in France, and there she collected,
and bound into three large volumes, all the letters from her
godmother which she and Mrs. Sayer had saved. She indexed
all the letters with loving care; and when she died, in 1854,
in her ninety-fifth year, she bequeathed them to Mrs.

Boscawen's granddaughter, Elizabeth Boscawen, who had married Lord Arthur Somerset, himself another of Mrs. Boscawen's grandchildren. From Lady Arthur the volumes descended in turn to her granddaughter Florence Somerset, who married the late John Oglander of Nunwell; and here at Nunwell they have remained for the last fifty years.

It was during the lifetime of the Admiral that Mrs. Boscawen shared with her friend, Elizabeth Montagu, the distinction of originating the famous "Blue-Stocking Assemblies," the main object of which was to substitute the delights of conversation and discussion for the almost inescapable rubber of whist. But though, in the words of Sir William Forbes, "the strength of her understanding, the poignancy of her humour and the brilliance of her wit" made her always a sought-after guest, her real interest lay in her own home. To her husband she was not only a loving wife, but a counsellor and adviser, and a friend for every mood. To her children she was an adored playmate as well as a wise mother; and her servants learnt that she was not only their kind mistress but also their sure friend.

Though many people are apt to say to-day that they wish they had had the luck to live in the eighteenth century, a study of Mrs. Boscawen's letters is enough to persuade us that in her case at least there was little of human sorrow that did not come her way. For the greater part of her life her country was always at war. She witnessed in turn the war with Spain and France, the Seven Years War, the American War of Independence, the French Revolution, the resulting wars with France, the incessant scares of invasion, and, in her closing years, the vaunting ambitions of Buonaparte. Out of the eighteen years of her married life, at least ten were spent in ceaseless, gnawing anxiety while her husband was on active service; and at long last, three months after the Admiral's final return to England in the proud position of a national hero, he died at their new home at Hatchlands, in January 1761, at the very early age of 49.

This volume deals only with the married life of Mrs. Boscawen, and ends at the moment when, mourning the death of her husband, she felt for a time that her own life was over. Yet in point of fact a long and eventful life still lay ahead. She survived the Admiral for forty-four years, and throughout this time she continued to spend the greater part of the year at 14 South Audley Street, where her salon always attracted the literary talent of the day. Of trials and bereavements and anxieties she had more than her full share, for her eldest son died at the age of 27, her second boy, a lieutenant in the Navy, was drowned while bathing at the age of 17, and many of the political anxieties of the present time had almost their exact parallel at the end of the eighteenth century. Her third and youngest son was serving with his regiment at Boston at the outbreak of the American Revolution, and her heartbroken cry, when she first heard the news of Bunker Hill—"Pray God send us peace and reconciliation, and to me, in His mercy, the comfort of seeing my poor child again"—will find an echo in many hearts to-day. This son survived, and eventually succeeded his uncle as 3rd Viscount Falmouth.

In 1766 Mrs. Boscawen's younger daughter, Elizabeth, became the wife of the 5th Duke of Beaufort, and a few years later her elder daughter, Frances, was married to Admiral the Hon. John Leveson-Gower. Mrs. Boscawen herself never re-married, but to the end of her life her house remained the centre of an ever-widening circle of devoted friends, for her heart never grew old. Even in her frail old age her spirit was buoyant and gay, and when the end came, in her eighty-sixth year, she was universally regretted by all who knew her.

I am greatly indebted to Mrs. Hodgson, the great-great-granddaughter of Admiral Leveson-Gower, for allowing me to reproduce the portraits of Mrs. Boscawen, the Duchess of Beaufort, and the 3rd Lord Falmouth, which still hang in the place where Mrs. Boscawen used to see them, at Admiral Levenson-Gower's old home at Bill Hill, near Wokingham. My sincere thanks are also due to Mr. Montagu Norman for the photograph of St. Clere, Mrs. Boscawen's birthplace and the home of her childhood; and to Mr. Goodhart-Rendel, the present owner of Hatchlands, for the picture of that house. It was Hatchlands that Admiral Boscawen erected, as his wife characteristically expressed it, "at the expense of his country's enemies"; and its exquisite Adam decorations are a lasting tribute to Mrs. Boscawen's perspicacity in giving Robert Adam his first commission for interior decoration.

C. F. ASPINALL-OGLANDER.

Nunwell,
August, 1939.

CONTENTS

PART I

SPRING

PART II

SUMMER

ILLUSTRATIONS

PART I

SPRING

But happy they, the happiest of their kind
Whom gentle stars unite, and in one fate
Their hearts, their fortunes, and their beings blend.

JAMES THOMSON.

CHAPTER I

BIRTH AND MARRIAGE
1719–1742

FRANCES EVELYN GLANVILLE, the Mrs. Boscawen of this story, was born at St. Clere, near Wrotham, a charming house with the fairest view in Kent, on 23rd July 1719.

By birth she was purely an Evelyn, for the name Glanville was merely her mother's name. Her father, William Evelyn, a Member of Parliament and High Sheriff of Kent, was a grandson of Sir John Evelyn of Godstone, whose life-size effigy, with that of his wife, Thomasine, surmounts their massive tomb in Godstone Church. Her mother Frances Glanville, the daughter and sole heiress of William Glanville, of Devon, was a granddaughter of Jane Evelyn, who was a sister of John Evelyn of Wotton, the author of the Evelyn Diary. Fanny Glanville was therefore the great-great-niece of the diarist, and it was doubtless from him that she inherited her love of nature and much of her literary skill.

Fanny's mother died in giving birth to her only child, and all that is known of her to-day can be read on a tablet on the north side of the communion table in Godstone Church, which tells the passer-by that "With a very plentiful estate, she enjoyed a pure charitable and noble mind, free of all passions, and possessed of every virtue," and that she died on 23rd July 1719, at the age of 22. Fanny's father, who had assumed, by special Act of Parliament, the name of Glanville on marrying the Glanville heiress, and had invested a large portion of his wife's fortune in the purchase of St. Clere and other

3

lands in Kent, was married a few years later to a lady called
Bridget Raymond, who gave him a second family. It was
possibly for this reason that much of Fanny's girlhood was
spent away from home, sometimes with an aunt called Mrs.
Gore, who lived at Boxley, near Maidstone, sometimes at
Wotton with Sir John Evelyn, grandson of the diarist, whose
wife was a Cornish lady named Anne Boscawen, and sometimes with Sir John's son, another John Evelyn, who had
married his first cousin, Mary Boscawen, a daughter of
the first Lord Falmouth. It was while staying with the
younger John that Fanny first met and fell in love with her
future husband, Mary Evelyn's brother, the Honourable
Edward Boscawen, already a promising captain in the Navy.

In the early days of the eighteenth century, when country
roads were so impassable that most people travelled on horseback, and the average speed of a coach would rarely exceed
some four miles an hour, a journey from Cornwall to London
was a formidable undertaking; and the first Evelyn-Boscawen
marriage probably owed its origin to the fact that Anne
Boscawen used sometimes to live in London with her mother's
brother Sidney, Lord Godolphin. Sidney Godolphin was
well known to the diarist, for his wife, the saintly Maid of
Honour at Charles II's Court, had won John Evelyn's lasting admiration before her marriage, and her many virtues
have been described in the account he subsequently wrote of
her. For many years, moreover, the Boscawen family had
been closely connected with the Court. Lord Falmouth had
been Comptroller to the Household, his daughter Lucy was
Maid of Honour to the Princess of Wales, and his son John
was Equerry to the Duke of Cumberland.

In the vicinity of London, travelling was not so difficult,
and as Fanny's numerous relations lived within a radius of
twenty-five miles of each other, her journeys to and fro will

have been accomplished without much trouble. Yet even she describes, in one of her letters, an instance of the coachman being jolted off his box by a hole in the road, and—as an unconscious commentary on the speed they were travelling—she adds that luckily the horses were stopped before the hind wheels had. run over him.

Little can be told of Fanny's early girlhood, for only one letter has been discovered which she wrote before she was married. Fortunately, however, this one letter throws a light on Fanny's early character. Written at Boxley, when she was 17 years old, the handwriting, already completely formed, is a prettily rounded hand, full of determination, and so modern in shape that it well might belong to the twentieth instead of the eighteenth century. Nor did her writing ever change. In her eighty-fifth year it was still the same beautiful, steady hand, with never an erasure, and never a word that was not triumphantly clear.

This first letter, the first of the collection made by Fanny's goddaughter, was addressed to her cousin and lifelong friend, Julia Evelyn. Julia was recovering from a recent illness, and the letter, an invitation to Boxley, is full of affection and warm-hearted enthusiasm.

BOXLEY,
August ye 10th, 1737.

I hardly know in what manner to frame an epistle, upon the success of which depends no less than the present enjoyment and satisfaction of my life!

You are impatient, my dearest *cousine*, to know *de quoi il s'agit*. Peremptorily this. That since, on receipt of your very kind letter, I was bemoaning to my Aunt your ill state of health, it immediately occurred to her that change of air would undoubtedly be of service to you. My opinion agreed exactly with hers, for indeed I had before thought of it. Upon which she ordered me to present her service to my Uncle and Aunt and assure them that you cannot change for a better air than this is, nor for a place where you will meet with sincerer welcome.

Here give me leave to put in my oar to vouch this assertion, and depone that I have passed 4 or 5 months here every year, and that I have never had a day's illness here since I can remember. And this deponent sayeth further that here are physicians (called milch asses) which have often made her fat and well liking by the use of some restorative medicines very proper in your case.

But jesting apart, be assured dear *Cousine*, that tho' the desire I have to see you is great beyond all expression, yet my concern and regard for your health would not permit me to entertain a thought that I did not believe beneficial towards restoring it.

What shall I say more to entice you, dear *Cousine*. Shall I tell you that your cousin, my aunt, is a very good woman; that she has a sort of old fashioned (as Mr. Pope says) kindness and regard for your family; and that your incomparable letters have ranked her amongst your greatest admirers. Shall I tell you that the house stands very high, but not bleak, and that the place is so famous for health that tender mothers send their only children to be nurs'd by wholesome dames of Boxley. Shall I endeavour to *faire valoir* my own qualifications for this trust by telling you that I'll nurse you night and day, and that when I've got you—O would to God I had—I'll make it my whole care and study to render the place as agreeable to you as possible. I have done; for I find that to fill a quire of paper with reasons and inferences and what not would but ill express the vehement desire I have to see you. 'Tis an easy day's journey. *Faites-moi savoir mon sort aussitôt, je vous en prie.*

Papa and Mama set out for Ireland last Wednesday. I've not been able to hear from them since, and believe I shan't till they get to Chester. We expected yr family at St. Clere to take leave of them. You owe me something for disappointing me of that happiness. Let your next letter be as long as you can make it, though in one line you'll fix my doom. If you come you'll make me prodigiously happy. If not, be assured no distance or absence will ever be able to diminish the sincere

devotion with which I am dear Miss Evelyn's most affectionate
Cousine

and faithful friend,

F. G.

To MISS EVELYN, Felbridge, near East Grinstead, in Sussex.

Edward Boscawen, whom Fanny eventually married, sprang
from a very ancient family, which derived its name from
the manor of Boscawen-Rose, in Cornwall, of which it
had been in possession since the days of King John. One of
his forebears, John de Boscawen, married the heiress of John
de Tregothnan, whose estate of Tregothnan subsequently
became and still remains the principal seat of the Boscawen
family. Edward's grandfather, another Edward, was a member
of the Restoration Parliament, and married Jael, daughter of
Sir Francis Godolphin. By her he had three children: Hugh,
the father of the Edward of this story; Anne, who married
Sir John Evelyn; and Dorothy, the wife of Sir Philip Medows,
Knight-Marshal. This Hugh Boscawen, Edward's father, was
one of the leading politicians of his time in the Whig interest.
With two Cornish boroughs in his pocket, he sat in Parliament
for eighteen years, and in 1720 was raised to the peerage as
Viscount Falmouth. He was Comptroller of the Household
to Queen Anne and George I, and for many years was Vice-
Treasurer of Ireland. He was married, in King Henry VII's
Chapel, to Charlotte, the daughter and co-heir of Colonel
Charles Godfrey, Master of the Jewel Office, and by her he
was generously provided with a family of eighteen children,
of whom Edward, our future Admiral, born on 19th August,
1711, was the second surviving son.

On his mother's side, too, Edward Boscawen could claim
a notable pedigree, for his mother, Charlotte Godfrey, Maid
of Honour to Queen Anne, was the daughter of the famous

Arabella Churchill. This Arabella, it will be remembered, was not renowned for her beauty, but in 1665, at the age of 17, shortly after her arrival at Court as Maid of Honour to the Duchess of York, there was a momentous accident at a riding picnic. Arabella, who apparently was no horsewoman, was suddenly thrown from her horse; there was a certain disarray of her attire; and, as she lay fainting on the ground, the onlookers "could scarcely believe that a body of such loveliness had any connection with Miss Churchill's face." Be that as it may—the story is Comte de Grammont's[1]—the Duke of York was captivated, and a few months later it was obvious that "she had neither tyrannized over his passion nor let his desires languish long in suspense." The liaison lasted for eight years, and she had presented her Royal lover with four children before she settled down as the faithful and virtuous wife of Colonel Charles Godfrey. Edward Boscawen, therefore, was a great-nephew of the great Duke of Marlborough, and a nephew of James FitzJames, Duke of Berwick, Marshal of France and victor of Almanza; nor can there be any doubt that he inherited a full share of the military genius and dauntless bravery of the Churchills.

In the days when Edward Boscawen first went to sea, the life of a naval apprentice was almost unendurable except to a lad of sterling pluck and iron constitution. For a boy with the necessary grit to survive his first experiences, and the essential heart and head to make a good commander, the profession, however, was very literally the road to fame and fortune. The English people were so conscious of their dependence upon a strong navy, and so proud of its successes, that no honour was too high for its successful commanders; and, in time of war, all prizes captured by men-of-war were the undisputed property of the officers and crews who captured

[1] Peter Quennell's translation of Hamilton's *Comte de Grammont*.

them. The sums thus realized by a lucky ship's company were often very remarkable. True, the flag-officers and captains came in for the lion's share, but the ordinary seaman had often more than was good for him. In one well-known, and probably record, instance, when the Spanish treasure ship *Hermione* was captured off Cadiz by two British ships in 1762, the share of the Admiral and two captains was £65,000 apiece; the share of each commissioned officer was £12,000, and every ordinary seaman received £40.

Commodore Edward Thompson, writing to a young naval aspirant in 1752, warned him what to expect when he first went to sea. He would live and sleep, he told him, "where day never enters, and where fresh air only comes when forced. . . . Your light for day and night is a small candle . . . your victuals salt and often bad. . . . Low company is the bane of all young men, but in a man-of-war you have the collected filth of the gaols. Condemned criminals have the alternative of hanging or entering on board. . . . You will see some little outward appearance of religion, and Sunday prayers; but the congregation is generally drove together by the boatswain, like sheep by the shepherd, who neither spares oaths or blows." He ended, however, with the encouraging remark that for the young man who could win through, and pass his examination for lieutenant, the change would be "from a filthy maggot to a shining butterfly."

Boscawen's first experiences can have differed very little from those described by Thompson. In April 1726, when not quite 15 years of age, he sailed for the West Indies in the *Superbe*, sixty guns, forming part of Admiral Hosier's squadron. The size of the *Superbe* was about 900 tons, her length about twice the length of a cricket pitch, her extreme breadth about forty feet; and into this confined space, with no corner, except his sea-chest, which the young naval apprentice could call his own, was crowded a crew of 400 men, many of them the scum of the streets and the pressed refuse of the gaols.

England at that moment was not at war, but her relations with Spain were strained, and the Admiral's instructions were that, without committing a definitely hostile act, he was to do what he could to hamper Spanish trade. Admiral Hosier put these rather difficult orders into action by blockading Puerto Bello, on the isthmus of Panama, and preventing the sailing of any Spanish ships. Here, in the sweltering tropics, penned up in their fetid quarters, devoid of ventilation, the British crews remained for six months, on a ration of salt meat and warm water, with never a change of diet, and never so much as a sight of a green vegetable. Scurvy and fever were rife; the men died like flies; and when, in the following December, the strain could be borne no longer, and the squadron was ordered to Jamaica to refit, the ships' crews were so rotten with disease that their officers had great difficulty in navigating them into harbour. Two months later, they were off again to sea, this time to blockade Cartagena; and there, in August, the Admiral himself died. His successor shared the same fate, and at the end of two years of this gruelling service, out of a maximum complement of 4,750 men, the squadron in which young Boscawen was learning his hard profession had lost 2 admirals, 7 captains, 50 lieutenants and 4,000 men. Edward Boscawen had already learnt a lot, and had resolved to mitigate some of the hardships endured on the lower deck if ever he rose to authority.

After a third year in the West Indies, Boscawen returned to England, and then followed three uneventful and less strenuous years, first in the Channel and then in the Mediterranean. He became a lieutenant in 1732, and was promoted captain in 1737.

In 1738 he was again in home waters, and during this

period he occasionally stayed in Kent with his eldest sister Mary, her husband, the young John Evelyn, and their little daughter, Lucy. It was here that he and Fanny Glanville first met, when he was a rising captain of 27 and Fanny was 18. Thenceforward, we may imagine, he found that Kent was not so far from Portsmouth as he used to call it, and his visits to his sister's house increased in frequency. Fanny began to look forward to the visits of this bronzed young sailor, who was so much more of a man than anyone else she had met. The friendship gradually ripened; and in a letter which she wrote to him six years after their marriage there is a charming allusion to one of these meetings—"when you and I loved one another and told it only by our eyes."

At this moment, however, he and his ship (the *Shoreham*, twenty guns) were warned for foreign service, and in January 1739, before, apparently, there had been any talk of an official engagement, he sailed for the second time to the West Indies. There, soon after his arrival, he at last found himself on active service, and there he remained till 1742.

This war of 1739 has a very familiar ring, particularly to us in 1939, for more than one reason. Not only was it, as every child learns in his early school books, the war of Jenkins's ear, and of Walpole's warning to the bell-ringers that they soon would be wringing their hands. It has yet another significance. In 1738, when Edward and Fanny Boscawen first met at Wotton, there had for some years been a growing tension with Spain—then a great European Power—and the dispute was largely connected with the Spanish colonies. Spain, moreover, had interests in common with France and, though no one in England realized it at the time, there was already in existence what we might call a Paris–Madrid axis.

Many people in England, and especially the opposition, had felt that England's only safe course was to go to war with

Spain. But Sir Robert Walpole, the English Prime Minister, and the first English Peace Minister, holding that war was the greatest imaginable evil, had resisted this advice. Almost single-handed, he had kept his country at peace, and in 1738, when the strain between the two nations had almost come to breaking-point, he suddenly made up his mind to enter into negotiations with Spain, in the hope that a frank discussion would be the best means of settling the matters in dispute. For a moment he averted the crisis. But his hopes of a lasting peace were built on sand. Taking advantage of her respite, Spain soon began to multiply all her demands and gave yet further proof that her word could not be trusted. In these circumstances, the agitation against the English Prime Minister's policy was once more renewed. The opposition gained enormous strength from the adherence of a young man called William Pitt, the future Earl of Chatham. In certain quarters Walpole was vilified as the cur-dog of England; a cry went up that the honour of England had been sullied, and at this moment the story of Jenkins's ear stirred the imagination of the people and swept like a flood from one end of the country to the other. Walpole could resist no longer, and in 1739 England and Spain were at war.

In the West Indies, when orders reached Jamaica for retaliatory measures against the Spanish American coast, Captain Boscawen's ship was undergoing a refit, and could not be made ready for sea. He accordingly begged to be taken as a volunteer in Admiral Vernon's flagship. In that capacity he was present at the attack on Puerto Bello, and after the capture of the town he was entrusted with the task of destroying the enemy's defences. Thereafter, for the next year, he had no chance of distinguishing himself, but in March 1741 he was present with his ship at the unsuccessful attack on Cartagena, and in a gallant episode at the head of a landing party of 500 sailors and marines, he attacked and destroyed two forts, spiked their guns, and burnt their military stores and ammunition. This action marked him out for preferment, and three days later he was promoted to the command of the *Prince Frederick*, seventy guns, in the place of Lord Aubrey Beauclerc, killed in action. In 1742 he returned to England in that vessel, and after a voyage of nine weeks from Jamaica, dropped anchor at St. Helens on 14th May.

Arrived in England, he was elected Member of Parliament for what might in those days have been called the Boscawen family seat of Truro, and in June he was placed in command of the *Dreadnought*, sixty guns, and posted to the Channel Fleet. Meanwhile, however, there was time for a short visit to his sister's home in Kent, where Mary Evelyn, with sisterly understanding, had invited Fanny Glanville to join the party. The homecoming was indeed a happy one. Fanny, since first she met this unusually attractive and distinguished looking sailor, with his lithe well-knit figure, his stern yet kindly mouth, his fearless intelligent eyes, his whimsical smile, and his head always carried a little on one side, had never bestowed a glance on another man. Edward, too, had never thought, and was never to think again, of another woman, for though even Fanny's dearest friends can never have called her beautiful, her vivacious little face and attractive figure, her level brow and restful wide-apart eyes, her ready wit and subtle understanding, her captivating manner and complete lack of self-consciousness were utterly irresistible. The engagement of the young couple quickly followed, and they were married on 11th December 1742.

CHAPTER II

EARLY MARRIED LIFE
1742–1747

FANNY BOSCAWEN's marriage was fated to be a marriage of continual separations. Within a few weeks of their wedding Edward was again at sea, and for the next two years he and his ship, the *Dreadnought*, as part of the Channel Fleet, were almost continuously employed in the English Channel and the Bay. The various ships of the Fleet at this period, sometimes alone, sometimes two or three in company, spent much of their time in escorting convoys of merchantmen. Some of these vessels were more important than others; and here let us look for a moment at the small ship *Winchester*, 500 tons, sailing from London to Plymouth in March 1743, bound for the East Indies. Amongst her passengers is a seventeen-year-old clerk, called Robert Clive, going out to Madras to join the Company's service. Five years later, as an ensign, he served under Edward Boscawen at the siege of Pondicherry. Twelve years later he won the Battle of Plassey, and shaped the destiny of India.

Fanny's first home after her marriage was a small house in George Street, Hanover Square. Actually, she much preferred a country to a town life, for although her husband's family were closely connected with the Court, she herself had been brought up in quieter and less sophisticated surroundings. Few of her own friends lived in London; and she imagined, moreover, that she would never be able to sleep in London air. But she wanted, while the war lasted, to be close to the seat of news; and London was a direct journey for her husband, whenever his ship came back for a spell in port.

As her mother's heiress, Fanny, as soon as she married, was entitled to a fortune of £3,000 a year. But at first she only succeeded to a small part of her income. Her father, apparently, with many commitments at home, and a growing second family, did not conform to his first wife's wishes as quickly or willingly as he might have done, and Fanny was far too kind to bring any pressure to bear. Edward, as a younger son in a family of eighteen, had naturally only a very small allowance. No chance of important prize-money had as yet come his way; and his own contribution to the family exchequer was probably limited at first to what he could save from his pay. But money was the last thing that Fanny coveted. She was happily married; she had a home of her own; her tastes were simple; and better times were ahead. And that was all that mattered.

Household expenses in 1742 were not an inordinate burden, even for Fanny's income—and the thought of their relative cheapness excites one's envy to-day. Meat, for instance, was only fourpence a pound, and other home-grown food in the same proportion. An experienced London cook—provided she had had the small-pox, an essential qualification—got £15 a year; a nurse or housemaid got £5 to £6; and though a footman would demand £6 to £7, with one new livery a year, he always had to pay for his own washing. The well-to-do would keep a coach and four, or even a coach and six, which sounds the height of extravagance in 1939. But the keep of a horse was only sixpence a day, so a coach and four would have cost little more to maintain than a man of limited income will happily spend to-day on a Baby Ford.

Up to the end of 1743, despite the Paris–Madrid axis, France had done nothing to assist the Spaniards at sea, for the war of the Austrian Succession was raging on the Continent, and France's energies had for some time been expended in an effort to gain the military predominance in Europe. In England, too, so far as the Government was concerned, the Continental struggle was distracting attention from the maritime war with Spain. George II was espousing the cause of Maria Theresa; and in June 1743, though England and France were still officially at peace, he was personally present, and nominally in chief command, when a mixed force of Hanoverians, Hessians, Austrians and Dutch gained a lucky victory over the French at the Battle of Dettingen.

Meanwhile, England's Navy was too small for its task. To the disgust of English traders the loss of English merchant ships was almost as heavy as the losses inflicted on the enemy, and the work thrown upon England's available warships in home waters was arduous and never-ending.

In December 1743—twelve months after her wedding— Fanny's husband at last returned to London on short leave; and while he was still there, London and the south coast were thrown into alarm by rumours of an impending French invasion. These rumours were only too well founded. Trusting in the belief that England's naval forces were so widely dispersed abroad that she could not fight a major action at home, France had decided to send a large fleet into the Channel, sweep the English shipping from the sea, and make it impossible for any further help to be sent to Maria Theresa. England was then to be invaded by a force of 20,000 Frenchmen already assembled at Dunkirk, with the Pretender's son, Charles Edward, at their head; and it was then hoped to cause a revolution in England and bring about a Roman Catholic succession.

By good luck, far more than by good management, these amiable intentions were frustrated. A large English fleet, including Edward Boscawen in the *Dreadnought*, was gradually assembled under Admiral Norris, and, rounding the South Foreland on 24th February, they found the French at anchor off Dungeness. But, when they were within six miles of them, the tide suddenly turned, and Admiral Norris, since the cumbrous ships of those days could make no headway against a strong tide, was obliged to come to anchor. The French Admiral, utterly surprised at the unexpected sight of so large an English fleet, promptly decided to abandon all idea of battle, and to run for home as soon as the tide would permit. Orders were consequently issued that every ship should get its anchor apeak, and as soon as the tide turned should weigh and make for home.

Most of the French captains did not even wait to obey this order literally. Directly the tide turned, they cut or slipped their cables, and with a strong north-westerly breeze springing up at that moment, they started at a great speed. The breeze freshened to a gale; and the French ships eventually reached Brest in a more or less battered condition. Realizing that he could never overtake them, Admiral Norris made no attempt to pursue, and Captain Boscawen, with the other three-deckers, was ordered to Spithead. Meanwhile, a number of the French transports waiting at Dunkirk suffered heavy damage in the storm; and thus, very ingloriously, the plan of a French invasion came to nothing.

A week later, Edward Boscawen was cruising in the Bay of Biscay; and there, on 27th March, after a chase that lasted sixty hours, he captured the French cruiser *Médée* (Captain Hocquart), the first French warship to be taken in the war. His return to Portsmouth with his prize was the occasion of much public rejoicing, and added a lot to his rising reputation.

Two months after her husband's triumphal return, Fanny made him a present of a son and heir (Edward Hugh, born

13th September 1744), and in the following December, to her
great delight, Edward was posted to the *Royal Sovereign* and
placed in command at the Nore—his first shore appointment.
His period in command of the *Dreadnought* had given proof of
exceptional powers of leadership and had won him golden
opinions not only in the Admiralty but also on the lower deck.
Though a stern disciplinarian, his kindliness, sense of justice
and daring personal courage had won the respect and affection
of his ship's company, and throughout the rest of his service
he was familiarly known to the lower deck by the nickname
"Old Dreadnought." As an instance of his fighting qualities
a story may here be told, which was firmly believed and freely
repeated at the time. One night in the Channel, after he had
turned in, the officer on watch rushed down to his cabin with
a "Sir, two large men-of-war, look like Frenchmen, are
bearing down on us. What am I to do?" "Do, damn 'em,"
said Boscawen, "why, fight 'em!" and he rushed on deck in
his night-shirt to take command.

In the spring of 1745, while the Boscawens were living at
Sheerness, the Young Pretender landed in Scotland—this time
with only seven supporters in place of the 20,000 who were to
have accompanied him twelve months earlier—and entered
Edinburgh in June at the head of an army of Highlanders.
Two thousand English troops melted away before him at
Preston Pans, and by 4th December he had penetrated as far
south as Derby. In London panic prevailed. There was a
run on the Bank of England, where money was paid out in
sixpences to gain time; the Guards marched out to Finchley
to protect the capital; the King made ready for flight. In the
Midlands, however, there was no enthusiasm for a Jacobite
revolution; and though people flocked to watch the Pretender
pass, it was only the English love for a travelling circus that
brought them away from their homes. Prince Charlie's own

followers began to disappear; he retreated the way he had come, and after his defeat at Culloden and the bloody massacre of his men, his only safety was flight. Fanny gives us some idea of the relief felt in London at the English victory of Culloden, when she refers to that battle, a year later, as "the event of greatest benefit and consequence to the nation since the time of the Duke of Marlborough."

The panic caused by the Young Pretender's successes had not been confined to the capital. On the south coast there were renewed fears of a French invasion. There were no troops available for home defence; the civilian population were unarmed; and all classes were frightened out of their wits. All along the coast of Kent householders were packing their valuables into carts and preparing to evacuate their homes at a moment's notice. At this juncture Edward Boscawen, at the beginning of January 1746, was uprooted from his shore appointment at the Nore and posted to the Channel Fleet in command of the *Namur*, seventy-six guns. Fanny returned disconsolate to George Street, Hanover Square, and there, on 7th March, her first daughter was born, and christened by her mother's name of Frances.[1]

By the summer of that year Fanny had obtained a little more of her money, and in addition to her London house she rented a small furnished house at Beddington some twelve miles south of the river, in order to give the children "a little country airing." In August her husband's sister, Lucy Boscawen, a Maid of Honour to the Princess of Wales, was married in London to Sir Charles Frederick, a Member of Parliament, with a house in Berkeley Square. Fanny was at that moment expecting her husband's return on leave; and from the first existing batch of her married letters it is easy to see that her

[1] She subsequently married Admiral the Hon. John Leveson-Gower, of Bill Hill.

husband and her babies are filling her whole life, and that, for the moment, at least, there is very little room for other interests. The reference to being invited "to accompany '*les mariés*' to Burwood" is a reminder that in the eighteenth century it was hardly respectable for a bride to set out on her honeymoon without a chaperone.

BEDDINGTON,
13*th August*, 1746.

I sent you a large packet yesterday, dearest husband, and have therefore little to add to-day. Only having received a letter from your sister, to summon me to her wedding next Monday morning, I acquaint you that I shall go to London next Sunday evening, the 17th; for I believe I need not say 'twould be a great disappointment to miss you, and be absent when you come to Beddington.

I shall return as soon as possible, Monday evening if I can, for I don't sleep well in London, and will avoid lodging there more than one night. There is to be a dinner (I believe) either at Lady Falmouth's[1] or Lady Frederick's, and I reckon I can be present at it and yet get out of Town time enough. They invite me to go with them to Burwood (Mr. John Frederick's house, which is lent to them) but I don't choose to be so long absent from home when I expect so welcome a guest.

And now, my dear Ned, I can only advise you once more to make haste to us. Your little son has this moment been talking of you, and hopes you will bring him grist to his mill, if not a mill itself.

Adieu; I can't write you a long letter; my spirits are in too great an agitation, for I figure to myself you are already arrived at Portsmouth, the news of which will greatly rejoice
Your ever affectionate,

F. B.

---

[1] Edward Boscawen's mother, Charlotte Godfrey, daughter of Arabella Churchill. She died in March 1754.

I should like to meet you at Guildford, 'though I think 'tis most likely I shall see you before I hear you are coming, and I begin now to start at every noise I hear, and fly to the door at every knock. In short my spirits are in such agitation that 'tis quite an uneasiness. Today I wakened crying so heartily that my face was bathed in tears, and I had a headache for some hours.

Pray remember that I am ready and willing to come to Portsmouth at a moment's warning.

BEDDINGTON,
Sunday noon,
17th August, 1746.

MY DEAR LOVE,

As I have already sent you letters by Wednesday's and Thursday's posts, I have little more to add. Your three weeks are expired, and yet you don't come, my dear Ned; 'tis therefore with a heavy heart I go to London. I had rather give five pounds than go: nothing could be so great a punishment this heavenly weather.

I know not what is to become of me when I get there, for I doubt I must carry the *mariés* to Burwood, but I don't intend to stay there longer than is necessary to rest the horses; which I suppose will be Tuesday morning.

Your brother Jack dined here today and goes with me to London. I leave the children with the utmost regret. Sweet lambs, they are vastly well. I will write to you again before I go to rest. Dearest husband, God Bless You.

George Street. 10 night. I'd give the world you were here, and half of it to know where you are. I *am* to go to Burwood tomorrow, it is just by Weybridge, 6 miles from Kingston; so I shall set out Tuesday morning for Beddington cross the country, for I cannot be cosy anywhere else now I expect you. God bless you, and give us, after all these troubles, an agreeable meeting. You may depend on a kind one from

Your faithful

F. B.

Fanny's return home was only just in time, for her husband, too, arrived at Beddington on 19th August, his birthday. He stayed there for nearly a fortnight, and Fanny's next letters, speaking only of how much she missed him, were addressed to his ship at Plymouth. But a letter dated 23rd September, remarking on the constant leak in the wine-cellar roof in George Street, and complaining of her mother-in-law's thoughtlessness in not saying whether or not she wanted a box which Fanny had sent her for the play, might well have been written yesterday:

GEORGE STREET,
Tuesday night,
23rd September, 1746.

MY DEAR NED,

I shall write you two words, no more, and you'll not lose anything, for I am incapable of saying anything worth hearing.

The cider and vinegar were safely conducted into the vault, where it seems the water comes in plentifully, but it is to be visited tomorrow (he would not come today) by the Governor of the pipes, who will 'tis to be hoped, find a remedy for this evil.

Mrs. Glanville having sent back the ticket for the play, I have sent to your mother to know if she will have it tomorrow, but she has sent no answer, and 'tis now 10 o'clock; so she will at least take care nobody else shall be the better for it.

I have two solicitations to go tomorrow, Ripley's box, or the Prince of Wales's, but I shall have the virtue to stay at home.

God bless you,

F. B.

On 26th September, and once again on 7th October, there is a record of Captain Boscawen putting into Plymouth with two other seventy-gun ships, for he was now in acting command of a small squadron; and in the middle of October he collected fresh laurels by the capture of two prizes. One of these was the *Intrépide*, a troublesome French privateer, the other a dispatch-boat, sent to Europe from North America with news of the total failure of the Duc d'Anville's expedition to recapture Louisburg.

A few words here on French policy in North America in the middle of the eighteenth century will probably increase the general reader's interest in Fanny's letters to her husband at this juncture. The thirteen English colonies in North America held little more than the eastern fringe of the continent. To the north, in Canada, and to the south, in Louisiana, were the French; and the French Government's aim was to claim the hinterland for France, to deny the English colonists all access to it, and eventually to squeeze them out of America altogether. Realizing that the great rivers, the mouths of which they held, were ready-made roads to the interior, they aimed at extending their territory southwards from the St. Lawrence river and northwards up the Mississippi to the valley of the Ohio; and by establishing a line of posts in the Ohio basin to prohibit the English settlers from crossing the Alleghany mountains. French privateers, meanwhile, operating from Louisburg in the north, were to prey upon and destroy English trade with the colonies, and to ruin the growing fishing industry off the Newfoundland Banks.

This policy, which, if carried to fulfilment, would have made the French the predominant power in North America, will be referred to again later, and it need only be noticed here that in 1745 Louisburg and the whole of Nova Scotia had been captured from the French by the gallantry of New England troops, assisted by a small squadron of the English Navy, and that the Duc d'Anville's expedition was an attempt to win it back again. This expedition had met with every misfortune. Many of the French ships and transports were destroyed by gales in their voyage across the Atlantic. The surviving personnel, on arrival in American waters, were in a very sickly state; d'Anville died of apoplexy; his successor committed suicide; an epidemic of small-pox carried away the greater part of the already attenuated force; and finally, in blank despair, the officer left in command returned with his troops to France. On his return voyage he encountered an English squadron, and several of his ships were captured.

Early in the following March the *Namur* returned to Portsmouth, and Edward contrived a few days' leave to London, where Fanny was six months gone with her third baby. But on 14th March he again set out on his four days' journey to Portsmouth, travelling in his own coach and four.

The next batch of Fanny's letters includes some interesting accounts of the trial of the aged Lord Lovat on a charge of actively supporting the Young Pretender. These accounts, given to Fanny by an eye-witness, and jotted down by her on the actual days of the trial, agree so well with the official version of the case, that they inspire confidence in Fanny's credibility. The letters also contain a reference to Handel's Oratorio, and to a benefit for Mrs. Cibber, who in addition to her fame as an actress, was Handel's favourite English vocalist. Fanny's father and his second wife were now living in Bond Street; but the visits Fanny paid to her stepmother were apparently more of a duty than a pleasure.

GEORGE STREET,
Wednesday 4 *p.m.*,
18*th March*, 1747.

I give you many thanks my dear Ned, for your kind letter, a pleasure I did not expect to have had today. I was glad to hear your journey had been prosperous and pleasant; I think they seldom are at this season, especially when they remove us from all that is most dear;—and you left behind three people that claim that rank of you. Two of them laugh and play just as much as if you had not left them. I cannot say so much for the third, whose spirits are very low.

I have not yet seen Dr. Sandys; but before you pish at me, consider I have given audience to Mrs. Chapman, and one of that sort in a day is enough to show you I obey your commands. I have ordered Mrs. Chapman to come with her baggage in the second week of May; the 10th was the day I appointed.

The Lords have condemned Lord Lovat, in whose defence no witnesses were examined, but he spoke long and well. The particulars, I must give you in my next, as your mother and Mrs. Gore have succeeded each other in troubling me and spending my afternoon. Tomorrow I'll write you everything I can learn, and at present only assure you

I am most faithfully yours,

F. B.

GEORGE STREET,
Thursday noon,
19th March.

MY DEAR NED,

Your brother sent me a ticket for today, and your Sister invited me to go with her, to hear the Lord High Steward's speech (at the Lovat trial). I did deliberate, I own to you; but at length virtue got the better, and here I have been all the morning, playing with my boy and entertaining Captain Geary,[1] who is much your humble servant. We have been talking of you—*cela est naturel.* I find his opinion agrees with mine about the West Indies, and he gave me many reasons (good ones I thought) why it would be probably less advantageous to you than staying at home. He says any man will risk his reputation extremely that goes there; and yours is so high I don't think it worth while to hazard the loss or diminu-

[1] Later Admiral Sir Francis Geary; was at this time the *beau* of Hester Grenville, who subsequently married William Pitt. Francis Geary married, on 20th September 1748, Miss Bartholomew of Malling, heiress of Oxon Hoath, Kent.

tion of it for any profit whatever. A rich Sea-Officer is not now an uncommon thing, but one approved of by all his countrymen is extremely so. This you are, and this I hope you'll continue. Besides that, by staying in England you are by no means out of the way of probable gain.

To all this, methinks, I hear you answer:—"Well, this you have told me before. Why repeat it now, when there is no prospect or thought of my going to the West Indies?" For that very reason I say it now, to show you 'tis the result of my sober reflection and not of the passions of fear and grief under the influence of which I probably was when first I declared these sentiments to you!

I can by no means give you so good an account as you used to give me of the proceedings at Westminster. Yesterday I told you Lord Lovat spoke long and well: but after I had wrote to you I went to Berkeley Square, where Charles Frederick told me he talked impudently and foolishly. He found fault with all the evidence in the order they were examined. I think he said Chevis was not worth a shilling and had a character of the same value. As to the herd of Secretaries, who had been so busy in his condemnation, "they had all a private interest." Sir E. Falkner had the least, and "even he was liable to an action from Lord Lovat for meddling with his estate and playing the landlord unwarrantably." John Murray, Esq., of Broughton "was by much the most infamous rascal alive."

You see there was at least freedom in his speech; there was likewise Scripture. He talked of Susanna and the Elders; of Samson and the Foxes, and some other story which I've forgot. He said he could not expect to live long in the course of Nature, and he thanked God he had no indecent fear of death: some say his countenance changed excessively; others, that he was not in the least moved or affected with his condemnation.

The solicitor-general spoke finely. *Au reste*, I must refer you to the printed account when it comes out. Meantime Mrs. Cibber's Benefit, which was to have been to-night, is put off on account of her illness, and I am not sorry for it, being in no spirits for a public place.

I am going to dine at Sir Frederick's where I shall probably stay the afternoon and where I shall finish this letter.

10 *p.m.* Company being at Mrs. Frederick's, I could not call for pen and ink there, and now I am every moment in fear of the last bell.[1]

Lord Lovat's sentence was pronounced. He made a long harangue, more incoherent than ever, and concluded with saying, "Well, God bless you my Lords, I bid you an eternal adieu, for we shall never meet again in this place."

There were several loud laughs to-day, which I should think never happened before at the time of passing so dreadful a sentence, but they tell me 'twas unavoidable, so ridiculous was his speech.

Goodnight. The boy is a most beautiful sleeping Cupid, and the girl is pure well. I am tolerably so, and ever faithfully yours,

F. B.

Saturday,
21st March.

MY DEAR NED,

Just as I received your kind letter to-day I was pledging Mr. Eddowes's toast, "Success to the *Namur*." I entertained him and his son very handsomely to dinner to-day; some thanks are due to you for a part of the fare, which would not have been easily had without your honour's bounty.

First Course.	*Second Course.*
Soup à la Reine with fowl.	Woodcocks.
Pidgeon Pye.	Asparagus Sallet.
Broccoli & Tongue.	Fillet Veal stuffed.

I don't give you this as a dinner worthy writing about, but perhaps 'twas a pretence to fill so much paper, and give this the air of a letter. More, I doubt, 'twill not have, since 'twas 10 o'clock e'er I began it. You may be sure there can be no good reason for using you so ill, and truly I'm at a loss for any at all.

Eddowes stayed till past six, and then I purposed to have

[1] A postman used to walk down the streets of London at night ringing a bell, to collect the last letters.

27

wrote you, but Mrs. Frederick tempted me by a saving scheme (for I did not intend to use my horses) that she would carry me first to your brother George's[1] and then bring me back to Mrs. Clayton[2] where I was engaged to drink tea. This proposal suited my affairs extremely well, and if I have stayed at Mrs. Clayton's longer than I intended, they have paid me for my time, and I have brought off a guinea and eighteen pence tax paid. Our party was Miss Grenville,[3] Miss Spede, Mr. Warde, Mr. and Mrs. Clayton and I.

Upon the whole I perceive I am writing you a long letter to tell you you must expect a short one.

I must have one observation in it that savours of vanity, but upon so true a foundation that it ought to excite your gratitude. The comparison of our children with your brother George's. I went directly from our boy to his girl. What a difference! In every circumstance, and in nothing more than behaviour. She would not come near me, and is as far from an agreeable child as she is from a pretty one. Ours is both, in the highest degree, and so everybody thinks. I wish you had seen him at his grandfather's yesterday, and riding in the chair with mama. He stood, you may imagine, and was so delighted 'twould have entertained you.

William[4] arrived safely yesterday about six. I gave him an audience at night to enquire after poor Gig,[5] who he assured me is much better than when he left you, and will come right again with a little rest, which he gave me to understand would be welcome to all; but the labour which I shall require of them will be little other than rest. I have paid William his expenses back, which amounted to £2. 9s. 10d.,[6] including the hire of the one horse, for which he produced the receipt, as well as all the bills at the Inns.

[1] Colonel (later General) George Boscawen.

[2] Wife of Robert (later Sir Robert) Clayton, M.P., of Harleyford, near Marlow. Harleyford is still in possession of the Clayton family.

[3] Later, as Lady Hester Grenville, she married William Pitt.

[4] The Boscawens' coachman. [5] One of the Boscawens' coach-horses.

[6] This included board and lodging for two men, and stabling and forage for five horses, and hire of one horse, for the four days' journey from Portsmouth to London.

CHAPTER III

THE BATTLE OFF FINISTERRE
3rd May 1747

IN the winter of 1746-47 the French began to prepare another fleet for the recapture of Louisburg, as well as a small squadron for service in the East Indies, where M. Dupleix, at Pondicherry, was in high hopes of gaining possession of all the English Settlements. Both these expeditions were to sail in the month of April, and for greater safety, in case they should meet an English fleet, they were to sail in company for the first part of their voyage.

The East Indian squadron, under M. de St. George, left Groix, in the northern part of the Bay, towards the end of March, to join the larger squadron, under the Marquis de la Jonquière, at Brest. It met, however, with two mishaps. First it encountered a small British squadron, from which it turned away; and then it was struck by a heavy gale and had to run for shelter to the Ile d'Aix. Here it was eventually joined by the North American Squadron and, as will be shown later, the whole force set out on their voyage on 2nd May.

In England the intensive work in the French harbours had not passed unnoticed, but nothing definite was yet known of the French plans. This was the situation when the next batch of Fanny's letters were written.

Amongst Captain Boscawen's friends was a Captain Savage Mostyn. His name is often mentioned in Fanny's letters, and, as a report, which he made in March, had a bearing on

Boscawen's fortunes, it will be necessary to refer to this matter in detail.

As in the Great War of 1914, London in 1747 was always full of rumours and gossip from the Fleet, and as the eighteenth-century navy was very small, and the names of its senior captains known to everyone, rumours of their doings at sea would normally conform to the popular estimate of their characters. A popular captain, for instance, could rarely do anything wrong. An unpopular one, or one who had ever been (even unjustly) criticized, could seldom do anything right.

Two years before the events now to be recorded, this Captain Mostyn's behaviour in a certain action had been stigmatized. He had demanded a court-martial, and the court had acquitted him with honour; but it was a case of giving a dog a bad name. Now, in March 1747, after capturing a French privateer, near Brest, he had found himself in the presence of a superior force, and deeming himself too weak to attack it, had sailed home to report. This much, apparently, he confided to Boscawen in a letter which Fanny opened on 24th March, and sent at once to her husband. Immediately afterwards, however, another clamour arose about Mostyn's conduct. Some of the old mud was still sticking. He was again accused of running away, and Fanny, eager to champion her husband's friend, makes frequent indignant reference in subsequent letters to these ill-natured reports.

GEORGE STREET,
Tuesday,
24*th March,* 1747.

MY DEAR NED,

I enclose Mostyn's letter, I won't make you any apology for opening it, because it did not proceed from an impertinent curiosity, but knowing he was at sea 'twas a friendly desire to hear that he had met with success. I wish it had been still greater, 'though the taking so large a Privateer must be of great service. I am not terrified with the list of the French ships, I wish you may meet with one or two.

Mrs. Frederick dined here, and carried me in the afternoon on a most formidable expedition, nothing less than waiting on Mrs. Walton in Throgmorton Street. Gig continues mending, his comrades won't be at all angry with me for preferring another equipage on this occasion. I thank you for the wine; 'tis the sort I like mightily and shall be very glad of a month hence.

Eddowes tells me that he thinks Admiral Warren will certainly agree with Mrs. Cavendish about the villa. I envy her, and expect and require of you, dear Sir, to provide me with some such agreeable villa. For this I empower you to draw on the French for such sums as you shall want.

The chariot is arrived, and Madame Frederick you know will not wait for me with great patience. I must therefore conclude my dull epistle. There would perhaps have been more of it (for I was up soon after nine) but Lady Bisshopp[1] visited me in the morning, inviting me to go with her to the Ridotto. I had the grace to refuse, for I don't know one creature that stays at home—the whole town goes—therefore I conclude there'll be no room for me.

Preserve me room, always, in your heart and memory, and believe me your faithful affectionate wife,

F. B.

GEORGE STREET,
Wednesday night,
25th March, 1747.

MY DEAR NED,

I begin (or rather end) the day with asking your pardon for not sending you the Lord Steward's speech, but I really did not see your order for that purpose till just now, when I

---

[1] The Hon. Anne Boscawen, the Admiral's sister, had married Sir Cecil Bisshopp, Bart. of Parham, Sussex.

31

returned from Mrs. Frere's,[1] tired worse than the dog, and by the way of regale was reading over your letter again: from whence you may infer you stand in no great need of being acquitted for writing what you're pleased to call a dull epistle. I know not whether they are so or not, but this I know, that I always expect the post with vast impatience, and that when it comes and I have read your letter over and over again, I am vexed to think I shall not have so much pleasure again in four and twenty hours. Thus, you see, they are vastly welcome, and that answers all other purposes.

I am sorry you are uneasy at your situation, for tho' I would not have you perfectly happy without me, yet I lament your being otherwise than easy; and I hope a release from your convoy will soon make you so, for sure it cannot be right to detain ships of that force merely to conduct one merchant-man, for whom a smaller convoy might be shortly provided.

I hope your cruise will be more fortunate than mine has been to-night. I will give you the detail of it; but first, suppose me completely rigged *en Madamoiselle—Sac-Gauze agremens*, and striped ribbons; *à la Jolie Catharina*! Thus equipped, I obtained a passage on board Mrs. Frederick's chariot, and Lady Boteler's visiting room was the first harbour I put into. There Lady Bouverie, Mrs. Hales, Mrs. Scott, and Mrs. Best inquired after you, and above all her Ladyship of Boteler, who desired me to make her compliments to you, and I make them accordingly. Our cousin of Wotton was not at home, so I was re-conducted as far as Leicester House,[2] where Mrs. Frederick alighted; but I went into my own coach which I had appointed to meet me there, and this conducted me to Mrs. H. Norris's, where Mr. Norris[3] and I discoursed on naval affairs, and agreed we would not bring our sons up as seamen, because in future wars with France or Spain the captures will not be (wholly) allotted to the captors.

[1] Mrs. Frere, a niece of Fanny's stepmother. Walpole tells a story of "Lord Abergavenny and [this lady] a pretty Mrs. Frere, who love one another a little," visiting Cornbury to see the pictures in 1750.

[2] The Prince of Wales's house.

[3] Captain H. Norris, commanding H.M.S. *Prince Frederick* in the Channel Fleet.

From hence I went to Lady Winchilsea's,[1] where Mr. Edward Finch[2] asked me what was become of his namesake. I gave him an account of you, and having heard a conversation between two countesses that was worthy a place in Joseph Andrews, I made my curtesie and repaired to Madame Frere's. There was all the world, old and young, foolish and wise, as your Harry Legge's[3] and Harry Fox's.[4] Chairs not being plenty, I thought proper to play one rubber at whist which cost me three half crowns. My father (much diverted with my dress) brought me home, and so I bid you a good night.

Thursday morning, 26th. I long to be extravagant, that is I long to hire Henley Park, which in me would not be extravagance were I now free, because I would certainly go there next month for the whole Summer; but as I cannot get out of town till towards the end of June, to be sure it would be unwarrantable extravagance. It belongs to Mr. Perry (*celui qui fouetta sa femme, vous ne l'en aimez que mieux*); it is completely furnished from garret to cellar, is a beautifully pleasant place, has a fine view of the Thames, and stands in a park of two hundred acres. My father met with the Mr. Byrom you went after, and he asks one hundred and sixty a year for it: but 'tis more than probable something of that may be abated and that the park will go part of the way towards paying the remainder. In short, were it not for my present state, I believe I should set out for Henley to-morrow morning. As it is I cannot guess what will become of me by way of country house, for all those which are to be let are unfurnished; and I don't see a possibility of my furnishing one, as I think that would require three or four journeys at least; but let's have your thoughts on this matter.

[1] Daniel, 7th Lord Winchilsea's second wife, Mary, daughter of Sir Thomas Palmer.
[2] Edward Finch, Lord Winchilsea's brother, and husband of Lady Winchilsea's sister, Elizabeth Palmer. He took the surname Hatton, in addition to Finch, and his grandson, George William Finch-Hatton became 9th Earl of Winchilsea in 1826.
[3] Henry Bilson Legge, third son of 1st Lord Dartmouth.
[4] Henry Fox, 1st Lord Holland.

33   D

I am much discontented with Philip, I think he intends to be drunk for the rest of his life. Mrs. Frederick's Philip would I fancy do much better for me than where he is, on board the *Salisbury*, a servant of Captain Edgcumbe's.[1]

Friday morning. I might as well have gone to the Ridotto as lain awake all night disturbed, anxious, and miserable about you. The wind was excessive high. You had assured me you would sail in the morning, so that my fears suggested that you would not be able to recover the harbour with safety. Perhaps these fears appear so ridiculous to you that you cannot help laughing at them, but I assure you to me they were no laughing matter, and that I do not find myself at all the better for them this morning. I am going to see if the air of the Park, and the company of my children, will not recover me again.

God bless and prosper you.

Saturday morning. My rest was broke again last night, and if not for you, for your friend. Mostyn, they say, has met the French fleet and could not engage them. *Quel mal-rencontre!* I don't mean that 'twas possible for him to do anything, but I lament that *he* met them. If it had been you, it had been conduct, prudence. As it is him, I assure you, people give it other names. People ignorant of sea affairs, I grant you; but what signifies that, if it be the generality of people. For my own part, so far from thinking him worthy of blame, I think he deserves the highest praise for resisting a temptation which I should have yielded to,—I mean sacrificed my duty to my reputation, than which there could have been nothing more unwarrantable, or to say the truth, more wicked, as so many brave men must have perished in order to restore me to the good opinion of the ignorant and partial. These only are the sort of people that can have a thought to his disadvantage, and these I hope he will have the sense to despise.

---

[1] Hon. George Edgcumbe, afterwards 3rd Baron Edgcumbe and 1st Earl of Mount-Edgcumbe, was an old friend of the Boscawens.

GEORGE STREET,
Tuesday,
3 1*st March.*

MY DEAREST HUSBAND,

Lady Frances[1] and Mr. Medows are to drink tea with me to-day. Ramsay[2] dined and is now sent out on a cruise to Mrs. Clayton's etc. to see if he can bring in any prizes by way of addition to the fireside. Lady Bisshopp and Mrs. Frederick have been tried without success, so difficult it is to find anybody that is master of his own time, and can on demand bestow an hour quietly. However, as Lady Frances and Mr. Medows are returned, I shall never be at a loss for a sober party. Mine last night were by no means so; they began at Lady Bouverie's where I met Sir John Norris,[3] and learnt that Mostyn was come into Plymouth. There was all the Norris's, Romneys and Hales's, amongst whom I picked up a shilling, sufficient to defray the charge of a sixpenny chair which had conveyed me from Gaffer Gore's where I dine, and not only me but your son.

You do well to be sensible of his merit and charms, truly, I believe there is not his fellow in the world. He was as free of Gore's house as if he had passed his life there. In a moment (Anne says) he caught the servants' names, 'twas Mrs. Jenny, Mr. Edward and Mr. Thomas; and he never mistook. The servants were ready to eat him, and neglected their victuals to admire him. It puts me in mind of Orpheus charming the brutes.

I suppose you did not get my letter of Saturday, neither is it very certain you will have this; I hope at least nobody else will read it, for 'tis filled with such trifling anecdotes as will make the author pass for a very senseless woman, in the eyes of all but my husband. To him I may naturally give an account of my insignificant actions, thoughts, or even dreams.

Yesterday the coach came at eight and conducted me to Mrs. Spence's Drum Major, so much Drum Major that half

[1] Lady Frances Pierrepont, sister and heiress of 2nd and last Duke of Kingston, married Philip, third son of Sir Philip Medows.

[2] Allan Ramsay, the portrait painter, was a great friend of the Boscawens.

[3] The Admiral, *vide* p. 17.

35

an hour's survey of it satisfied my curiosity; and thence I proceeded to Leicester House and there I saw the man that saw the *Namur*, or at least the Commander of it—this was Mr. Scott, of whom, having asked some questions and conversed a little with Mrs. Anne Evelyn, I took myself home to bed: not without perusing your letters for the third time.

By the list you send me of your squadron, it appears indeed you will not be ashamed to look your enemy in the face, but as *I* cannot bear to turn my thoughts that way, I must not enter into a discourse on the subject. Yet one thing it leads me to observe, that as the fate of the nation, at least that of the war, may depend upon *you*, sure it had been fitting to give you some distinction, pendant or flag. They will not ask me which is most proper, but in their conscience surely they must allow that one was extremely so. You will wrest it from them sooner or later, and then we shall be the less obliged to them.

9 p.m. Ramsay returned from his cruise without bringing in one prize, so that Lady Frances, Mr. Medows and himself have been all my company and are now all gone. If I could have laid hold on Charles Frederick to-night, I would have made him write to you, for I must refer you entirely to him for news and public transactions. My knowledge extends no farther than my own household. Within this the article of stable is properly comprehended, and under this head I am to tell you that William advises me to swap away Gig, for tho' he has by choice used him once in Hyde Park since he returned from Portsmouth, yet he is of opinion he will never be thoroughly serviceable any more. This I take for granted is the case, else he would not have ventured to have told me so while you were within reach of hearing it. Must not I therefore apply to Colonel George[1] to assist in this exchange?

My father has not done anything about the money, but has said it will be ready in a few days. I spent Sunday there, and if penance and mortification had been any part of the duty of

---

[1] George and John Boscawen, Edward's brothers, both had the great knowledge and love of horses which was inherited by the famous racehorse owner, John Evelyn, 6th Viscount Falmouth, the Admiral's great-grandson.

the Lord's day, I had spent mine well. There were no Smythes (he being ill). Madame Glanville had been at Court with Madame Frederick, which supplied them with nonsense for the day, the longest I ever passed. My daughter wisely went to sleep, and I had nothing to do but regret that I was awake.

The weather was charming on Sunday, and Lady Dalrymple sent her son to carry yours airing, which was performed accordingly. The latter observed that the former was a stupid boy, and it seems he let our son have all the talk to himself, greatly to the amazement of the Scotch maid, whose young master is turned of three years.

I think 'tis most likely the Roman history is very dry, at least the beginning: but Pliny I believe is entertaining, at least I know I was hungry to read him, but spared him to you because I thought he would amuse you. I wish you had a sensible companion, that is best of all. I am sorry to find you meet with so little to make you amends for the loss of those who are too near to you not to be dear, were that all their merit. I ascribe to myself some merit of a domestic sort, that sort which can alone give peace and satisfaction to your mind when you are absent, and turn your thoughts homeward. To that comfort, may every other be added to you. This is the sincerest wish of your most affectionate, faithful and obedient wife.

When Boscawen reached Plymouth, and heard the news of the sighting of a French squadron, he was at once on fire to be after it, and he asked permission, as senior captain present, to proceed to sea with all the ships in port and try to bring it to battle. For a moment, apparently, he hoped his request would be granted. But the Admiralty had now learnt that the size of the French squadron was very considerable, and Vice-Admiral Anson, at that time First Sea Lord, himself decided to put to sea, with Rear-Admiral Warren and all the ships available. Leaving London at short notice on 1st April, the two Admirals sailed from Portsmouth on the 7th; and Boscawen was told to await their arrival at Plymouth.

Fanny wrote on 2nd April:

> GEORGE STREET,
> *Thursday night,*
> *2nd April,* 1747.
> 10 *o'clock.*

I can only tell you my dear Ned, that I and your children are well, for I have had a Drum tonight, which has left me so little spirits or time that I cannot otherways entertain you. I have had the Fredericks, Spences, Bests, Champneys, Gearys, Lockwoods, Smythes, Hales's, Westons, Ramsdens, Bisshopps, Evelyns and Harcourts. In short my two rooms have overflowed, and I have been sufficiently tired, tho' by no means the worse.

I am in tolerable good health, but in extreme bad humour, Anson's and Warren's journey to Portsmouth makes me quite peevish; I don't understand it, but I venture to dislike it.

I miss your letters sadly, the want of them makes me cross and low-spirited. I have some (tho' little) hopes of hearing from you tomorrow. I repine at this westerly wind; I want you to sail before these admirals reach you. I am sure you can perform the service, whatever it be, as well as they or any.

The clock strikes 11.

> God bless you,
> Yours ever,
>
> F. B.

I wrote you so long a letter last post that it must atone for this short one. Mrs. Frederick carried me a long airing this morning. Your mother and Nick[1] came and dined.

> *Saturday,*
> *4th April.*

If my last letter was but short, dear Ned, 'twas not for want of matter, as I had a long story to tell you of our ride on Wednes-

---

[1] The Rev. Nicholas Boscawen, Fanny's parson brother-in-law, was Dean of St. Buryan. He married Jane, widow of Hon. E. Finch-Hatton, and had one son.

day. Meanwhile I wish you joy of the *frappe*: 'tis a good omen. *Frappez toujours, Monsieur, frappez; c'est un métier que vous connaissez si bien que je suis au désespoir de ce que Messrs. les amiraux songent* à *l'exercer.* You have a fine easterly wind; 'tis vast pity if you are not suffered to make use of it: I shall be vastly pleased to hear you are sailed with your squadron, and they (the Admirals) returned.

The stage was now setting for the Battle of Finisterre. Admiral Anson, with thirteen or fourteen ships of the line, including Edward Boscawen's *Namur*, had sailed from Plymouth on 9th April, to bring the enemy to battle; and for the next five weeks, till 16th May, their friends at home waited, waited for news. Fanny, within a few weeks of her confinement, wrote a letter in journal form, battling in vain to cloak her grim anxiety.

GEORGE STREET,
14*th April*, 1747.

MY DEAREST HUSBAND,

Since I find you are gone out of the reach of my letters I shall not write to you any more regularly, as I hope you do to me, but set down my thoughts occasionally as they arise, and as time (a scarce commodity in this place) permits. First I shall take notice of any parts of your kind letters which have not yet been answered: and among these the chapter of Mostyn might take a long discussion.

I know not what fresh intelligence, or new light the people here have reached, but one and all now condemn him, even of those who at first would not admit a possibility of his doing otherwise than he did; that is, they allowed seven men-of-war of the enemy, but his enemies have found means to sink at least five of these seven, and at the same time to urge that he never ventured near enough to know what they were. For my part I only know this, he has been so unlucky as to do a very material injury to his friend.

You had certainly sailed had it not been for this chimera of a fleet, of which perhaps there was enough reality to have fixed

39

your honour and fortune for the rest of your life. It was the 31st of March you proposed, and could have sailed from Plymouth at the head of a squadron; 'twas the 9th of April e'er you did sail, a private captain under two admirals. The difference is great, to the nation perhaps!—For in ten days (most, easterly wind) you might have gone far and done much. But to you, certainly, the difference is inestimable, for, though you should do great things now (which God grant!) will it be Mr. Boscawen? Not at all! Mr. Anson will have the great crack; a little echo for Mr. Warren, and you will have no more share in the applause and thanks of the public than Captain Mostyn, whom they hate. He, I repeat, has been the (innocent) cause of all this injury to you, and it hurts me to think of it. I don't doubt but it vexes him sufficiently. I pity him upon that and every other account, but I must leave the subject, for I cannot talk of it with temper: these admirals disturb my rest.

18*th April.* Proceed we to consider another point. We have a very agreeable one in the dear children, who are, I thank God, in perfect health. I wish you could see your son in Kensington Gardens—the admiration of all there!

28*th April.* Having now apparently neglected you, my dear Ned, for some time, I have a great deal to say to you, and to complain that Mrs. Norris[1] has heard from her husband and I have not heard from mine. But no, I will not complain, much less chide, but will rather take for granted that you have not let slip any opportunity of writing to me, but that, by some means or other, you missed of that which Mr. H. Norris made use of. I wish he had mentioned you in his letter, but he did not. I carry his wife out airing and we talk of our husbands. She seems excessively fond of hers, and therefore cannot be very happy, poor young woman!

Forgive me if I own to you I am far otherwise. The near approach of my labour terrifies me and sinks my spirits to a degree that you would be sorry to be witness of. Indeed, were you here, it would not be thus. I frequently get no sleep of

[1] Wife of Captain H. Norris, Captain of the *Prince Frederick* in Anson's Squadron.

nights, and not through indulging in a morning, for I do not breakfast in bed, nor continue there longer than nine—seldom so long. I was obliged to send for Sandys, and he ordered me to be blooded, which I was, and on sight of the blood he said I had very great occasion for it.

I wish to God you was at home, for I don't believe you are doing yourself any good abroad, and I want you more than Mr. Anson does, so long as he has the seas to himself, which I daresay is the case.

30*th*. The air revives me most of anything, and at Easter I enjoyed more of it than I believe I have yet told you. Charles Frederick and wife, with the addition of Madame Smythe[1] (whose husband, being in Kent, left her a widow at large) persuaded me to pass three days at Burwood. I was entirely of that mind—all but leaving the dear babes. That made me tardy in my resolution and exposed me greatly to their mirth. (But till they have such a lovely boy as mine, they cannot tell how they would dote on it.) However, I did at length abandon the boy, charming as he is, to Mrs. Ann's protection, and regaled myself from Tuesday till Friday with country air, nightingales, flowers, milk and contemplation. The rest of the company walked. I sat out of doors all day long, twenty chairs (at least) being dispersed all over the gardens for that purpose, and during the course of the day perhaps they were all visited. We had lovely weather, and perfect freedom. Nothing could make amends for leaving it, but the sight of my children in perfect health, and the satisfaction I had at my return.

I thank you, dear Ned, for your letters from the 9th to the 17th, which I have received. That you are in health rejoices me—other good news I did not expect, so was not disappointed. I want to know what command of mine you have disobeyed that you want to ask pardon for. And as to your wavering in your resolution about writing to the Great Ones, I am sure I

[1] The Smythes often appear in these letters. Sidney, son of Robert Smythe and Lady Dorothy Sidney, widow of Earl of Sunderland (*vide* Evelyn's Diary, Vol. l, 275), became Lord Chief Baron. His wife, Kate Evelyn, was a cousin of Fanny Boscawen. Their country house was Bounds, near Tunbridge Wells.

am the last body in the world that should blame you, never having had anything material in my choice, but I have balanced from side to side a long time and perhaps fixed on the worst at last. I am incapable of resolving at once and there fixing; so I am very unfit to condemn you for changing your opinion. Mine is, that in case of a peace we are undone, for my honoured father has not yet paid the money, and 3 per cents are $86\frac{1}{2}$. If you'll believe him, 'tis not his fault. I'm sure 'tis mine, to have been too passive, though, if to dun him perpetually would signify, I have not spared him; but that he can bear *à merveille*.

Julia is at Chelsea, where your son and I visit her at least every other day, for I have entirely left off dining, visiting, etc. and spend one part of the day airing somewhere, the other at home. I have not good spirits, and you will own my prospect is rather melancholy, but I must not launch out on this subject. I stop myself short and send my letter to Mr. Brett.[1] 'Tis possible he may have an opportunity of conveying it to you.

I shall be out of all patience if you are not either Admiral, or Lord of Admiralty. Yet, I do by no means think myself able to advise concerning the letters in question. I should think one to Pelham (at least) not improper and, since the Peer, your brother, gets nothing for himself, I should write him a letter in very strong terms requiring his whole strength on this occasion—the only one, perhaps, in which you'll ever want him. And if he does not regard you, I would certainly remember it, and return it in the many points wherein he wants your service and assistance. Indolence and *mauvaise honte* are not excuses fit to be alleged on such occasions as this.

God bless and prosper you!

Remember with tenderest affection your faithful,

F. B.

On the 16th May, the tension of those at home was at last broken, and the news arrived of Anson's great victory. The battle had taken place off Finisterre on the 3rd May and was a victory beyond all hopes. All ten of the French ships of war

[1] Timothy Brett, Esq., of the Navy Office, then at Plymouth Dock.

had been captured. Edward Boscawen, in the thick of the fighting, had particularly distinguished himself, for the *Namur* had been one of the first ships to become engaged and at one period of the action was fighting single-handed against four or five of the enemy's largest ships. The booty on the French ships exceeded the highest expectations. And finally, by a strange coincidence, one of the three French Captains who had surrendered to Boscawen personally was M. Hocquart of the *Diamant*, the same man who had been in command of the *Médée* when captured by Boscawen two years before. Only on the following Monday (in her delicate condition) was Fanny allowed to know the disturbing side of the story. Her Edward had been wounded by a musket ball in the shoulder—but the Admiral said the wound was not dangerous.

Fanny's letter of exaltation and fear is a very human document:

GEORGE STREET,
Monday,
18*th May,* 1747.

10 *a.m.*

I ask your forgiveness, my hero—for that is your justest appellation—that I did not write to you on Saturday. But unless you had seen how I was besieged and beleaguered that whole day, you can hardly excuse me.

My father and Mrs. Glanville never lost sight of me, lest I should hear of your wound, which, being ignorant of, I was almost out of my wits for joy. But Captain Geary, after having consulted all my friends, decided 'twas best to tell it me, since I had ordered a Gazette. So he told it me with as little ceremony as might be, and everybody present made very light of it and referred me to my letters from you, for which I can never sufficiently thank you. To be sure they were a great and solid comfort to me. Yet I own your being hurt at all changed the whole face of affairs in my eyes;—entirely sunk my spirits, which before were raised to a pitch too high (as I myself observed) to last long, and kept me waking the whole night, for till past five in the morning I never closed my eyes. I revolved all the arguments there were to compose my mind, but ineffectually, for my heart told me that though your wound was slight, a fever might ensue or some other bad consequence. In short, my hero, I was miserable till I saw Captain Denis, and he quieted me extremely.

To-day, I have seen two letters, beside a third from Hursfield from on board the *Namur*, and as they all say their noble Captain (whom they seem ready to worship) is well, I trust in God I shall likewise see him so. I long for that pleasure beyond all expression. I do not intend (and may Providence favour me!) to be brought to bed before you come. The presence of so great a man may spread a happy influence, and inspire the child with some of his heroic virtue. Indeed, my love, I can't express how much I reverence your virtues. 'Tis not your courage alone—that, perhaps, is common to most of your men—but the magnanimity, the serene presence of mind, the coolness and calmness in the midst of so horrid a conflict— in fact all the various excellencies and perfections of conduct, with which you—YOUR INDIVIDUAL SELF—have achieved for this Nation an event of more consequence, more solid benefit and advantage, than any (the Victory of Culloden only ex- cepted) that have been performed since the time of the Duke of Marlborough, your uncle, whose bravery and conduct you have equalled rather than imitated. I must not wish you his honours, since I should share them, but I wish you his length of days, his prosperous children and every blessing which he enjoyed. You have not so handsome a wife, but I think you have an honester woman and one more sincerely attached to you and more likely to be a comfort and friend to your children.

I thought to have increased the number of them as long ago as this day se'enight. I was taken ill in the afternoon and continued in pain all night, so that at 5 a.m. I sent for Mrs. Chapman (who had appointed to come the evening of that day) and, at noon, I informed the doctor how I was—but without desiring any of his assistance, for I did not think it was time for that. And I judged right, for I have continued much in the same way ever since; sometimes in pain so that I think execution is at hand; sometimes quite easy, much as I was with the boy, when (if you recollect) I sent for both nurses in a vast hurry and went three weeks. But I don't believe this will be so long. I have appointed it as next Wednesday, which completes the 39th week. I have been miserably terrified with the thoughts of it—such horrors and tremblings as were indeed dreadful. But now, since Saturday, I think nothing of it— I think of you and you only.

I want to send you your coach, but as you mention nothing of it, I don't venture to do it. The 4 horses are in fine order. Two were to have gone to grass on Saturday (but I stopped them on this news) to a place I've hired for £25. a year— neatly and completely furnished at the top of Hendon Hill. 'Tis a fine air for a nursery, and there's a charming meadow with sheds and a fine pond for the horses—and 'twas entirely out of regard to these two sets of animals that I hired it, for, as to myself, as there is no garden (beside a large orchard), no flowering shrubs, open groves, or serpentine walks, I see no charms in it. Only, little thinking how happy I should be in your return, and growing too heavy to run out of town every day after houses, I took this that I might be sure of being able to breathe in the air as soon as I recovered, and of not confining the children in London longer than was absolutely necessary. With these views only, the cheapest place was the best, and I thought this was extreme cheap.

But I wonder I can talk so much about it: I have so many millions of other things to say. I have just turned James Lockwood, my Father and Madame out of doors—all which desire me to mention their joy to you. But, indeed, I am too full of my own, though to say the truth, 'tis now mixed with other emotions, such as fear, anxiety, hope, expectation, impatience. Your mother was not so easily got rid of, so her I have drove into the next room with Lucy. Your children are perfectly well, the boy vastly grown—at least, I flatter myself you will tell us so. He is so well informed of events that, if you ask him who beat the French, he will immediately bawl out "PAPA."

His Majesty is vastly delighted with this glorious event: talks much of you and says your wound is exactly such a one as he should wish for. (God send it be no more, says your careful wife!). What a secret *mon vainqueur* has made of it.

I beseech you take care of yourself and, though I firmly believe my labour will be infinitely better for your being by, yet I conjure you do not hurry in your journey so as to fatigue yourself. You have had fatigue enough. 'Tis high time you had some rest and reposed yourself on the faithful breast of your tender and affectionate wife.

F. B.

The action off Finisterre had indeed been a great victory. Horace Walpole wrote on the 19th May: "It is a very big event, and by far one of the most considerable that has happened during this war. By it Anson has defeated two expeditions at once; for the fleet that he has demolished was to have split, part for the recovery of Cape Breton, part for the East Indies. He has always been remarkably fortunate!"

The treasure captured in the action amounted to £300,000, besides stores of all kinds of great value. The money on arrival at Portsmouth was put into twenty waggons, and taken in great military procession through the streets of London to the Bank, amidst the wild enthusiasm of the populace. "The King," said the Duke of Bedford, then First Lord of the Admiralty, "told me this morning that I had given him the best breakfast he had had this long time; and I think that I never saw him more pleased in my life."

Actually, only eight of Anson's sixteen ships had been engaged, and the credit for such a complete victory was principally due to the magnificent behaviour of three captains —Boscawen in the *Namur*, Denis in the *Centurion*, and Thomas

Grenville (brother of Lord Temple) in the *Defiance*—who were the first to overtake the enemy and bore the brunt of the action. But Fanny had been right in her fears that in the event of victory "the Admiral" would get the "great crack." Anson, as Walpole truly said, had again been "most remarkably fortunate," and was at once raised to the Peerage. No one, to be sure, would grudge to a commander the glory and honour due to the man who has borne the responsibility. The feeling was to remain, however, that the Admiral had been less than generous in his acknowledgment of what he owed to the men who had won the victory. The gallant Grenville, killed in the hour of battle, was beyond the need of any lesser distinction. But Denis, who commanded the *Centurion*, and brought the dispatches home, got nothing but the usual £500 from the King "to buy himself a sword," and Edward Boscawen had to remain content with the promotion to Rear-Admiral of the Blue, which had been decided upon before the battle was fought. This promotion made him the youngest flag-officer in the service—he was still only 36 years old; but rightly or wrongly he apparently felt that Anson had done him less than justice, and this, as the next letter shows, was obviously his wife's opinion.

18*th May*,

10 *p.m.*

Are you satisfied with the Gazette? I am not, but Lord Winchilsea, who has made me two kind visits on this occasion, says that, in a long conversation with the King, he found him well informed how much he owed the success of his arms to your conduct, and you are accordingly in high favour with His Majesty. I think there's nothing you may not pretend to. As to your flag, 'twill have a pretty air on this occasion. But I do assure you—and assure you upon good grounds—that it was done (that is, settled) ten days ago. A promotion of 6 was

47

agreed to, of which you was the youngest. I don't know whether 'twould have been declared before the return of Anson, as they would have complimented him with signing the Commissions, but indeed, 'twas fixed. Therefore, 'tis not properly the reward of this Action, though 'twill appear so to the world, so, if that's all they give you, they'll come off cheap. My Father says they talk of a Knight of the Bath and, in *the same breath*, adds you won't accept such a "kiss mine A——" thing. Indeed, I'm of his mind. Children will be taught to point at you, as you walk along, without a bit of red ribbon to know you by, which were it the reward of war-like deeds only, would be worth having. But the coward C——e and the scoundrel W .... ms wear it; therefore 'tis not for you.[1]

Most people think there have been omissions in the reception of Denis, who has only been told that the King has ordered him £500, whereas people say he should have gone immediately to Court, where his Majesty should have drawn his sword and presented him with a thousand guineas to pay his Knighthood fees. This would have been at least as proper as for the Duke of Bedford to go out of town yesterday to dine with Lord Vere, instead of carrying Denis to Kensington and presenting him to the King, which I would have persuaded the latter was absolutely necessary. I know if such a thing had happened in Lord Winchilsea's reign, he would not only have carried him to Court, but when he got there, he would have asked people, "what will you give me and I will show you Captain Denis, Commander of the *Centurion*?" Would not Winchilsea have been in vast spirits about it?

As I think of nothing but your coming, I prepare for it. I have this day made you (alas!) 3 pairs of cuffs. I have likewise examined your wardrobe and find you have a coat for deep mourning, but no frock, so I've sent for Regnier, and as I could not venture to fancy a grey, I ordered the same superfine blue you used to have, with black buttons and black cape, and it will be ready to-morrow. This I thought necessary, as you

---

[1] Throughout his brilliant service, despite his many promotions, Boscawen was never made a K.B., so perhaps he always refused it.

would not like to go abroad in colours[1] and you won't be able to stay at home.

9 *p.m.* Mason appears, so can only add God bless you and send you a good journey! I long to embrace you and am with inexpressible affection,

Yours
F. B.

---

[1] Edward Boscawen's favourite sister, Lady Bisshopp, had died three weeks before his return to England.

CHAPTER IV

THE ADMIRAL SAILS FOR INDIA

FANNY held successfully to her resolve. Her victorious husband, his wound already healing, returned to London on 27th May; and her third baby, Elizabeth, the future wife of the 5th Duke of Beaufort, was born the following morning.

The happiness of the young couple was not, however, to remain unclouded for long. Within a few days of his promotion on 15th July, Boscawen was ordered to hold himself in readiness for service in the East Indies; and he and Fanny were now faced with the prospect of a separation, the completeness of which is almost incomprehensible in the days of Empire air-mails, wireless telegraphy and the B.B.C.

In June 1747, news had at last reached England that the French had captured Madras in the previous September, and that the Governor of Fort St. David, the last remaining English settlement on the Coromandel Coast, was threatened by the victorious Dupleix. The English Government thereupon decided to support the East India Company by the dispatch of a strong armament, and Edward Boscawen, though still under 37 years of age, was appointed to command it. Nor was this all; he was given the unusual appointment of Commander-in-Chief of the English land and sea forces in the East Indies, and for this purpose was promoted to the rank of Rear-Admiral of the White and given in addition a special commission of Major-General in the Army. It was a real case of "soldier and sailor too." Six ships of the line (including his old friend the *Namur*, which was to be his flagship), two frigates and a hospital ship, a number of transports and store-ships, and 1,500 troops were to accompany him from England; and on arrival in India, including the ships and troops already there, his force would consist of a squadron of thirteen ships of the line and an army of about 3,000 European and 4,000 native troops—the largest armament that any European Power had ever yet sent to the East Indies. Much though Fanny might dread the separation, it was at least a proof of the high esteem in which her husband was held.

The objects of the expedition were twofold. After leaving the Cape of Good Hope, the Admiral was to proceed to the French island of Mauritius, and "if he considered the operation feasible," was to capture it. The decision, however, was to rest with him; and he was in no circumstances to jeopardize the main object of his voyage, which was definitely stated to be the capture of Pondicherry.

The expedition was to leave England as soon as it could be made ready, and Edward Boscawen eventually started from London for Portsmouth on 14th October, to superintend the final preparations.

To Fanny, who said good-bye to him at their new home at 14 South Audley Street, into which they had only recently moved, the parting was almost the agony of death, so great and so manifold were the dangers and uncertainties of the whole undertaking. Even in time of peace, a voyage to India was likely to take from six to nine months, and it sometimes took a year; so in all probability eighteen months would pass before she could even hear of his arrival at Fort St. David. Adding to this the risks of war and climate, Fanny was sunk in misery. It was arranged that immediately after his departure she and her children and her cousin, Julia Evelyn, her ever-faithful friend, should go to her aunt at Boxley; and it was from that house, on 16th October, that her first heartbroken letter was sent. Happily for Edward, it was followed by a braver one two days later.

Then, to the agonies of his going, were added the mortifications of long-drawn-out delays in the date of sailing—first through the ships not being ready for sea, and then through contrary winds; and as day followed day, and found him still in port, his anxious wife, already well versed in things appertaining to the sea, begins to dread the dangers of November gales in the Bay of Biscay.

BOXLEY,
Friday,
16th October, 1747.

MY DEAREST LOVE,

I imagine it will give you satisfaction to hear that we are got safe and well to our journey's end, and therefore I sit down to write you thus much. More you must excuse me from as yet, for I cannot so soon recover my spirits or a headache that has kept me company since I left you, but which I hope a good night's rest will remove, for last night my sleep was very unquiet.

I hope you are well; I long to hear from you. I will write you more on Sunday and I am more than I can express, your affectionate, faithful

F. B.

The children and little Betty are well.

Sunday,
18th October, 1747.

I hope you was not angry with me, dearest husband, for sending you so short a letter, for, in the state I was in, I could have said nothing that would have given you satisfaction, which you will never find in perceiving me to be uneasy and unhappy. I am rather better now, and can talk to you with more freedom. I can give you an account of our journey, though I can never forget what I felt on that day.

It seemed as if the children had taken pity on me, for neither of them were in the least troublesome. Little Fanny went to

52

St. Clere, Kent

Farny Boscawen's Birthplace

sleep, and the poor boy kept saying, "why do you cry, my dear Mama? Don't cry, and I'll give you some plums." But this, without teasing me at all. So we continued our sorrowful journey till we arrived at Foots Cray, where we found my father's coachman, and where we refreshed our children and horses. We arrived at St. Clere not much before 5 and yet found a very gracious reception.

My father read me a sort of lecture concerning your absence —which I was to rejoice, not grieve at. That if he had an only son and was to give him 10,000 a year, he should be proud to see him in such a station. He spoke much in your praise, exhorting me to be easy, and proving that I ought to be gay. We are to lie here on our return, which must be before the 8th November, when they go to town.

My aunt received us very graciously here. She is amazingly well, and neither her health nor understanding seems at all impaired since you saw her.

I have had messages from the gallant Geary,[1] whose affairs go on well at Malling. He seems to have a very good opinion of the girl. I wish she may answer it.

I long to hear from you. Be pleased to remember the 20 yds of red stuff for Audley Street. Also, please tell me how accounts stand between you and the coachman; whether you have paid him to the 14th or whether there be any wages, or helpers' wages, or bills at Croydon[2] due to him.

Your boy sends his duty to you and says (these are his own words) that you must not cry, because he loves you and wishes you would come here.

I am ever tenderly yours,

BOXLEY,
19th October, 1747.

I return you many thanks, dearest husband, for both your kind letters. You judge very well that they give me the utmost satisfaction.

I pity you heartily in the hurry you live. But, for my sake I beg of you, endeavour to get rest and take care of your health.

[1] See p. 25 *n.* [2] Croydon was then a stage on the road to Portsmouth.

53

I am frighted to think you get no sleep; 'tis so unnatural to you that I'm sure it must be very prejudicial, and I beg therefore, you will banish all uneasy thoughts when you lay down on your pillow. 'Tis hard if they must follow you there. Have no anxious thoughts for the children. Assure yourself they shall be my sole care and study and that my chief purpose and the business of my life shall be to take care of them and to procure for them a sound mind in a healthful body. God give me success! I do not ask you for any directions, as whether, if one has the Smallpox, I should put away the others, etc., for I reckon that in all these cases one's conduct must chiefly depend *sur la conjuncture*, and therefore 'tis impossible to take any resolutions beforehand. Let it suffice that all my faculties and studies will have for aim the benefit of these dear children. And, generally speaking, where one applies one's whole strength, one brings the end to pass, and success crowns such hearty endeavours.

Adieu, mon très cher. Aimez-moi toujours dans quelque pays que vous soyez.

21st October, 1747.

I am very sensible, my dear Ned, what an expression of your kindness it is to write to me every day, and how few moments you can command for that employ. I am the more obliged to you and wish I could send you in return such letters as would be worthy to take up your precious time. But at this place, where the matter is wanting, and at this time, when my own wits are more than ordinary clouded, I believe the shortest letters I write will be the best.

I thank you for remembering to feast me on Saturday, since on Mondays you know I fast. I wish you may sail so soon as this week. I want to get you safe out of the Channel before November winds begin to blow. 'Tis a great distress to me here that I have no weathercock, but I believe the wind is fair just now. The black, cold air denotes it East.

I forgot to desire that you would send up to London such books as you have done with, especially Horace and Pliny. Pray remember to get the *Fable of the Bees*, if it is to be had at Portsmouth.

22nd October, 1747.

How shocking is the account of the *Lyme's* fate,[1] and that terrible storm the West India fleet met with. I could not read it without trembling.

Why do you talk of sending me the tea the East India Company has given you? Can good tea be better bestowed than upon you? Certainly no. And therefore, I forbid your sending me more than two or three pounds, that I may think of you as I sit and sip my melancholy tea.

Adieu, my love. There's a sound of coaches and the hour of cats[2] approaches. 'Tis with regret I leave so much blank paper.

I am ever your most affectionate

F. B.

BOXLEY,
Saturday morning,
31*st October,* 1747.

I was a great beast for not writing to you yesterday. I ask your pardon, my dear Ned, and I don't intend to serve you so any more. But indeed, I had nothing agreeable to tell you, for the high wind at S.W. on Thursday night made me so excessively uneasy that I got no sleep (for I fancied you sailed on Tuesday). I thought you in danger, and I was so thoroughly disturbed that I jumped up in the morning before anybody came near me, "tired of my restless couch." Could I have persuaded myself that you had not sailed, I might have escaped a very sad night. But you know the situation of this chamber, and how a South West wind howls against our crazy bow-window.

Yesterday we feasted on a carp, the weight whereof was $10\frac{1}{2}$ lbs, the girth 2 foot and the length 22 inches. After dinner came in Mrs. Knipe and Mr. Calder, with whom I lamented the S. West wind. I attempted several times to escape and write to you, but a "niece, where are you going?" gave me to

[1] H.M.S. *Lyme*, twenty guns, foundered on her return from the West Indies in 1747.

[2] Presumably country neighbours were coming to call.

understand 'twas expected I should entertain the company. Part of our entertainment was the letting off a brass cannon which Lord Romney[1] has given your son, who stood fire extremely well.

The two Marsham boys[2] have been to see him. They are fine children and the best behaved I ever saw, doing everything at a word—and, indeed, a look—of their father's. Charles makes a much better figure in breeches than I could have imagined, for he is considerably shorter than our boy, and my Lord scolds me vastly keeping him in petticoats. He desired me to give his kind service and best wishes to you. The boys were delighted with our humming top, so I put it into Bob's pocket and made him excessively happy. But his father made him pull it out again, and the boy complied without saying a word. However, I contrived they should carry it home.

I long to talk to you a little more about Hawke's business.[3] Have you seen the Gazette? 'Tis his letter transcribed and, by his phrase, "seeing some of our ships at that time not so closely engaged as I could wish," I suppose it was a little like the 3rd of May, when one ship did almost all the business and several engaged at a safe distance. Pray write me your sentiments of this affair[4] and the behaviour of Hawke, whose character I'm not at all acquainted with. If he had not said the enemies' ships took a great deal of DRUBBING,[5] I should have liked his narration very well, but that word sure is much too low for the subject and should never be applied to so important

[1] Robert, 2nd Lord Romney, married, 1742, Priscilla, daughter of Charles Pynor.

[2] Lord Romney's eldest son, Robert Marsham, was born 1743, his second son, Charles (1st Earl), 1744, so they were 4 and 3 years old.

[3] A dispatch from Admiral Hawke had just been published, saying that on 14th October, at a point quite close to where the action of 3rd May was fought, he had defeated a French squadron escorting a fleet of ships for the West Indies, and had taken six of the eight French men-of-war engaged. Hawke and his prizes reached Portsmouth on 31st October.

[4] The conduct of one officer—Captain Fox, of Kent—was the subject of a court-martial, at which he was acquitted of cowardice, but dismissed his ship.

[5] See Fanny's later letter on this subject, p. 81.

an action in which so many Englishmen fell. Where is Mostyn—that unlucky dog?

Make my compliments to Mr. Brett[1] upon his marriage if you think proper, though I am as angry with him as you are. He will certainly find himself mistaken, and that a low bred woman capable of brawling and scolding till she's out of breath (which most low women are), is very unlikely to secure the peace of his life.

BOXLEY,

1st November, 1747.

Sunday evening,

If I intend to have a letter ready to-morrow, I must write to-night, for, be it known to my dear Ned, that hitherto I have never once been abroad since I came here, so that to-morrow we begin to return our long list of visits, much to the discomfort of the cousin, who had rather stay at home and play with the babes and amuse the old lady. But, since we must now live in our coach, 'twill be necessary for me to seize every favourable moment to write to my dear friend at Portsmouth.

I am much disturbed at your being still there—I remember you said it would do if you sailed on the 1st November, but I don't remember that you admitted any time after that, so that I begin very anxiously to wish you gone.

The arrival of the French prizes[2] must be some amusement, as well as a great satisfaction, to you. I join in wishing you may not try Captain Fox, both because I would have you otherwise employed, and because such a sentence as (I fear) he deserves, will be irksome to pronounce.

I pity Mr. Harland[3] and I hope Saumarez[4] had no wife.

---

[1] Charles Brett, the Admiral's flag-lieutenant. He was apparently dissuaded from this disastrous marriage, for he subsequently married a charming lady (Miss Hooker, of Croome Hill, Greenwich) who became a great friend of Mrs. Boscawen.

[2] See note 3, page 56.

[3] The *Tilbury* (Captain Harland), a third-rater, gallantly tackled and stood between a big French ship and Hawke's temporarily disabled flagship.

[4] Capt. Saumarez was killed.

There is an unparalleled fatality in Mostyn's fortune.[1] He was the first person I thought of when I heard the news, which was known here on Tuesday noon. That is, that 6 men of war were taken. But I could not learn by whom till night; then I heard 'twas Hawke and then I was quite happy, concluding Mostyn had been among them and not in the least doubting that next day I should see the *Hampton Court* approved by the *London-Evening* itself. But alas, it seems determined that he shall never wipe off those unjust aspersions, which is a great pity and troubles me whenever I think of it. I love him for loving you.

I shall take very particular care of the *piedro d'India*;[2] insomuch, that no mortal shall ever behold it or know I have such a thing, except her Royal Highness,[3] to whom I will present the large stone and five others, if you approve it. Perhaps I may give my father a ring ready set, to supply the place of the diamond one he has resigned to me.

I can conceive how mincing and fine Mrs. Marshall must be when the Admiral dined with her. You must return her my compliments.

God preserve our dear lambs to bless your return, and in the long, long interval, to comfort your faithful and affectionate,

F. B.

BOXLEY,
Tuesday,
3rd November, 1747.

MY DEAR NED,

We have begun to return our visits and now *nous roulons sans cesse*—much to the disquiet of your poor wife, who set out yesterday morn to breakfast with Mrs. Champneys. We met Miss Mann on horseback, coming to see us. And indeed, she appeared to be a very pretty man.

Just as we were going to sit down to dinner yesterday,

---

[1] The *Hampton Court* (Captain Mostyn) temporarily detached from Hawke's squadron, took no part in this action.

[2] This refers to a box of some precious stones which Edward had taken with one of his prizes and given to Fanny.

[3] The Princess of Wales.

arrives the gay Geary and puts my aunt in a little sort of fuss. However, the best foot was put foremost; some syllabubs were whipped in a minute, and she received the Captain very graciously and cordially; drank the Admiral's health—"Long may he live!"

Geary imparted to me a little sort of perplexity he is in. He offers to settle £12,000 upon Miss B. She has put but £5,000 down and they want him to settle £14,000. I told him that was unreasonable, and that he was not to mind all they say to him; that what he offered was very handsome and I advised him steadily to adhere to it. I don't find the girl meddles in this, but has left it entirely to her friends. That is to say, her mother, Sir R. Twysden and Mr. Brooke.

I am fatigued to death just now and am dying with the headache, having been to Lady Boteler's this morning to breakfast and tore myself up for that purpose much earlier than I choose to rise. I carried your boy to return Master Philip's visit and he behaved vastly well and came home *chargé de bon-bons.* He is not, I find, half so much tired with his journey as I am, for I hear him making a great riot in the next room.

I can't imagine that you could receive a letter unsealed. What! had it *never* been sealed? I can hardly think I was so boonish, or that the servants would be so senseless as not to tell me.

I believe it is pretty certain that I am not with child, but I can't imagine why you should be desirous to be so certain about it, for, when I thought I was, I longed to refrain from telling you, both because 'twould have saved you a good deal of anxiety and because 'twould have been a very agreeable surprise to you to have found a little Willy-boy sucking at the breast, with blue eyes and a fair face—in short such as you would have no scruple to own.

Adieu, très cher.

5th November, 1747.
Thursday evening.

MY DEAREST HUSBAND,

You guessed but too right for, having no letter from you yesterday, and having beside heard by the papers that you was fallen down to St. Helen's, I thought it to no purpose to write to you, everybody assuring me the wind was full north, so that it seemed to be very near a certainty that you was sailed.

To tell you the truth, my spirits were so sunk with the thoughts of your sailing (though 'twas the most desirable thing in the world) that, when Tom brought me the letters without one from you, I was perfectly struck and never recovered it the whole day. In the afternoon, I went to Lord Romney's, who began by telling me 'twas a charming wind, but soon found 'twas too tender a subject just then, and changed the discourse. However, it never left my thoughts, not even in my sleep, which was interrupted with the sad remembrance that you was really gone for so long a time! I own I was surprised at my excessive weakness on this occasion, for 'tis certain I wished for your sailing of all things in the world; and yet, when I found you was gone, I coloured and fell into such an agitation and, afterwards, depression of spirits, that I could hardly have been worse if I had not expected any such news. To-day, I am sorry it is not true, for the bitterness of death was past and I was again in a great measure composed. But, however, I hope at least you go to-day.

This is Assembly Night, and I shall have all my Kentish friends upon my back for not going, but indeed, my spirits are by no means equal to cards and fiddles and company.

I have not time to-night to answer my dear love's letters— for, not expecting one from you, I did not sent to the post-house as usual—and shall only tell you at this time that we return to London by way of St. Clere, where we propose to arrive next Saturday at 4 p.m. and set out the next morning for London; my father and family going at the same time; cousin Julia repairing on her side to Rooksnest, thence to Felbridge.

Adieu, très cher et très aimé. Croyez que je suis tout ce que vous pourrez souhaiter.

Actually, the fleet had sailed from St. Helen's on the 4th November, and though the fair wind had only served for twenty-four hours, the Admiral, anxious to get out of the

Channel, had decided to turn to windward rather than to put back. Meeting with hard gales, he was obliged to put in to Torbay on the morning of the 10th, but he again proceeded to sea the following day, only to meet a continuous succession of storms.

Meanwhile, Fanny had returned to Audley Street, and her return home was naturally making her miss him more than ever.

AUDLEY STREET,
14th November, 1747.

MY DEAREST NED,

I am safely arrived at this place and brought my pretty ones in perfect health.

I have been here 6 days, but have never yet parted with my short hoop—that is, I have neither seen, nor been seen. An extraordinary melancholy seized me on my arrival at this house, which is not yet worn off. I believe you would be surprised to see the change that your absence has wrought in me. Instead of being lazy, I am active, industrious, diligent. I rise every morning at 8; I am settled at my writing table by 9; and I have done more business in one day than I used to think of for a week, without doing.

I have been here six days, in which time I have caused an appraisement to be made of my goods in George Street, which I have sold to Lord Carpenter, and have finally settled with him, paying him only £30 for this last year's rent. I have had all my bells hung and have moved myself into my dressing room. I have been at Bromwich's and have chosen the paper for my 3rd room, which is now actually putting up. I have bought me some clothes; short-coated my daughter; got my boy a maid, and, in short, am worthy to be related to you, so active and industrious have I been.

We left Boxley on Saturday, the 7th, and were very kindly received at St. Clere, from whence we set out pretty early on Sunday. My father rode. Madame and I, my boy and Betty Wingate went in the coach and six. My two maids, little Frances and they were in my coach. They were going a very moderate pace (for my father kept before) when the coachman was, by a jolt, thrown off his box and must have been killed if the horses had not stopped the very instant he called to them, which, however, was not time enough to prevent the fore-wheel's running over his leg. As the hind wheel would infallibly have gone over his head if the horses had not stopped in the manner I describe, he made shift to drive us home. I sent for one of Bromfield's men as I passed by, and he met him there and let him blood immediately and still attends him. He has no bones broke, only his leg is much bruised and swelled, but I hope he will be well soon. Meantime, the helper drives me very well and all the cavalry are in good order.

16th November. I have your letters from Torbay, where I imagined the high wind of Monday would oblige you to have recourse, but I see by the papers that you sailed again the next day.

I have carried your son to wait on his Grandmother. She is a great deal younger than I am, witness her last Sunday business, for she went to St. James's; thence to Carlton House; dined abroad; visited all over the town—amongst the rest, to Newcastle House; and, instead of wanting to go home after all this, she came in at 11 o'clock to sup with Mrs. Boscawen.

29th November, 1747. Having spent the night with my dear Admiral, I think I can't do better than dedicate a part of the day to him; the rather, as I have not done myself that pleasure since Mr. Vanbrugh sent back my letters with his opinion that you was gone, which I think is now confirmed by two different ships. You have surely on this occasion shown yourself worthy of the good opinion your country has entertained of you as an officer.

I have found out a newspaper that loves you mightily. I saw it at Aunt Hussey's and immediately bid Beuvregny[1] take it in. The first night he did so, there was Admiral Boscawen's name in 4 different places, one of which was that he believed "THAT DILIGENT COMMANDER" had carried his fleet out

---

[1] Mrs. Boscawen's butler.

in spite of all the storms of wind to the contrary. And, since this, he has often treated me with a flattering paragraph.

Such are the amusements of your poor wife, to whom even a dream is entertaining. Last night I dreamed I had letters from you, with a particular account of your meeting with Monsieur de la Bourdonnais.[1]

'Tis very odd, though, to entertain you with dreams, and you may well expect events, I think, after so long a silence. The case is, I believe, that I feel I have so much to say to you that I know not where to begin. I can't do it better than by informing you that your daughter, Elizabeth, produced a tooth the day she was half a year old and was, and is, perfectly well— the finest child in the world. His honour continues charming, and Frances continues to improve. The former often discourses with me about dear Papa, whose name helps me to keep him in order.

I do little else but stay at home and attend to it, and I find full employment changing so many servants, for the maid I took in the room of Bab does by no means please me and I'm seeking another. I am also seeking one in the room of Leonard; and have agreed with one to succeed poor Mrs. Moreton;[2] and, before she goes, I intend to get a new cook. Yet I won't complain of domestic distresses, since my dear babes are well.

I must give you the history of my presenting the *Piedro d'India*, which was performed last Wednesday at Leicester House. I wiped every stone, wrapped them up in several sheets of gilt paper and sealed them with my seal. Thus equipped, I went to Leicester House and had a private audience of her Royal Highness[3] in her dressing room, before the drawing room began. She was very gracious; thanked me extremely, and bid me thank you when I wrote. I gave her a great many more than you ordered, but, when I came to empty the box in order to pick out the brightest for her, I found so large a quantity, and so little imagined how I could use them myself, that I thought I could not present them to anybody so worthy as her Royal Highness. I told her these

---

[1] The French commander at Mauritius.   [2] Her lady's maid.
[3] The Princess of Wales, mother of George III.

were all that were bright (and, indeed it was the greatest part) and I wore one of my buttons, which she liked. So I told her there were enough of a size to make buttons for the young Prince's coats and waistcoats. This appears odd on paper, but the conversation was made so easy by her affable behaviour, that I believe you would not have thought there was any impropriety in it. I have not been at Court since, but I intend to go again on Wednesday.

I have heard nothing of Mr. Clevland, but that he's turned a fool, which I believe you'll own when I tell you he saw a girl at the play in a puckered satin, with whom he became so enamoured, that he took the utmost pains to know who she was, but without success. So, after pining in vain a considerable time, at last she appeared to him—puckered satin and all—at Richmond Assembly. There he told her all his suffering. She gave him a gracious hearing, and they quickly married, he graciously presenting her with wedding clothes, for she had no money to buy them. How long it is since this event happened, I cannot tell, but 'twas but yesterday that I heard it.

11th December, 1747. I must write to my dearest husband to-day, as I hope he has thought of me and of this day five years and has not, upon the strictest scrutiny, found cause to regret the event of that day. Were it now undone, and your passion remaining for Lady Augustus,[1] 'twould not avail, for she is engaged and just going to be married to Mr. Jeffreys *aux cheveux gris*.

And this is, I believe, all the news I shall write you, for I know none: I live little in the *beau monde*. I have been to one play, tempted by the Mostyns, and one Opera, which I heartily repented of. Mrs. Holman's drum I have slighted, nor have I been anywhere, but to sit with some infirms of my acquaintance.

Ramsay is still in Scotland, without having fixed any time to come away. I have at length an answer to my letter of September, and I will transcribe a paragraph:—"The papers

[1] Widow of Lord Augustus FitzRoy, who had died in 1741. She married James Jeffreys, Esq., as his second wife.

inform me Mr. Boscawen has put to sea. I most heartily wish his safe return, stored with health, fortune, contentment. I would have added 'honour,' but that I think is so much a part of himself that he has no chance of being separated from it." So much for Mr. Dandy, who is, I fancy, far gone in love and has sent me an Ode to Miss Mary Scot, whom I take to be the dear object, etc. I am sure we want him excessively at our commerce parties, which are as dull as funeral sermons.

I am often with Miss Grenville.[1] I like her more and more. Her family are much pleased with my Parson Evelyn's[2] verses, that he has dedicated to you. They are published in the newspapers, and—Miss Grenville told me—by Lord Hillsborough,[3] who is going to be married to Lord Kildare's sister.

I spoke to Miss Grenville about putting up her brother's picture, which she very obligingly said was the greatest compliment you could pay her and it would give her great satisfaction to see such a mark of your regard for him. This being the case, my outward room only waits for that sad dog Ramsay to paint your sister Lucy, who has promised me her picture, which will make the 6th. I think Ramsay is more likely to hit her face for being used to it, else Hudson[4] should do it, for my room is quite ready; has been three times painted; the ceiling made white; the floor planed; the chimney-piece back and hearth finished—as well as the tables and glasses. My second room is not yet hung, not having been able to get any paper to my mind under an exorbitant price. At length, however, I have agreed for one, and Bromwich comes to put it up to-morrow. So that, upon the whole, my house is much nearer completed than you expect, I believe. I have tried at china ornaments for my chimney-pieces, which demand them in great quantities, but I have not been able yet to raise myself

[1] Hester Grenville, daughter of Lady Cobham (later Countess Temple), married 16th November, 1754, William Pitt, 1st Earl of Chatham. Her brother was killed in action off Finisterre 3rd May, 1747, see p. 47.

[2] Rev. Wm. Evelyn; became Dean of Elmley.

[3] Wills, First Earl of Hillsborough, married Margaretta, daughter of nineteenth Earl of Kildare and sister of first Duke of Leinster, 1st March, 1748.

[4] Thomas Hudson was for a time Sir Joshua Reynolds's master.

F

to the price of anything good and I don't care for a parcel of trumpery—like some chimney-pieces we know of.

But, methinks, this is a strange letter to send so many thousand miles, yet what can I say to my dearest? I could certainly talk to him on serious subjects (for generally I am but too seriously disposed) but I think, when my dearest opens a letter of mine, he don't expect to find a solemn discourse.

I write in a morning, when I have generally one of my 3 babes with me, and insensibly they spoil my letter and divert my thoughts. If it be only the fat Bess, she *will* be heard and spoke to.

And now, my dearest, as I have laid hold of such charming apologists, I don't think you can find in your heart to criticize my epistle, were it worse than it is. You know I live little in the *beau monde*, and now less than ever.

CHAPTER V

FANNY'S JOURNAL. JANUARY 1748

THE beginning of 1748 found all the belligerents on the Continent heartily tired of fighting. The war had brought to each in turn a chain of disappointment, and Louis XV in particular was ardently longing for peace. England's naval successes had confirmed him in this wish, for his coffers were nearly empty, and the overseas trade of France was faced with ruin.

In England, too, especially on the Opposition side, there was a strong desire for peace; but the English Government, while agreeing in principle to the opening of negotiations, were convinced that the best way to secure good terms was to prosecute the war with vigour. With this object large sums had been voted for naval and military expenditure in 1748.

Sailing from Torbay on 11th November, Admiral Boscawen had encountered so many gales that his voyage across the Bay had taken him three weeks. Arriving off Lisbon on 2nd December, his letters for England were landed there, but it was the 8th January before they reached London. By this time Fanny had begun to keep a journal for her husband, jotting down in it the daily life of her family, and purposing to send him a section of it whenever a chance occurred. Of this journal, which was continued till the Admiral's return in April 1750, at least a half has survived the voyage to India and back again, the wreck of the Admiral's flagship in a hurricane, and all the other risks of a hundred and ninety years. This surviving portion, all of it written in 1748, gives a vivid and complete picture of Fanny's life in that year, for very appropriately it begins on 1st January and ends on 31st December.

So here we can let our heroine continue her own story, beginning with her best wishes for the New Year:

AUDLEY STREET,
1st January, 1748.

It is very fit I should assure my dearest husband that I wish him a happy new year and many of them, crowned with all the glory, honour and plenty that his services have so greatly deserved. I am preparing, to the best of my powers, a part of your reward, which will not be the least valuable—the comfort of seeing three healthful, beautiful, tractable children. They are now, I praise God, perfectly well; and have been today to wish their Grandfather a happy new year, who has endowed them with a piece of gold each.

Mrs. Glanville and Mrs. Frere went to Court, but, for my part, I was better employed in attending to my babes. I carried my boy to Mr. Gore's, where I met Mr. Winter, who covered me with compliments about the Admiral, believing he was the only man in England that would have carried the Fleet out through all those storms. I entirely agreed with him, as I do from my heart believe the King has not such another sea-officer. That, you'll say, is very natural, but I believe there is as much truth in it as love or partiality.

This afternoon I saw company in my dressing-room for the first time since its being furnished, and had Mrs. Evelyn, Mrs. Boone, her sister, two Mr. Evelyns (St. James's Palace), Mrs. Porter, Miss Cotterell and Lady Sandwich; and everyone admired my apartment, which is indeed a very pretty one and wants nothing but the approbation of its Lord.

2nd January. I am very busy to-day, my dear love, in discharging Mrs. Moreton and installing Mrs. Marshfield, who is neither old nor ugly, and that is all I know of her at present.

4th January. I long to write volumes to you. I know every-thing would be acceptable—but I have nothing to say. The minute I sit down to write to you, the minute I have wrote "my dear husband," I remember how far he is off, how long he will be absent, and how many dangers he runs, and these thoughts are more than sufficient to destroy any bright ones I might otherwise have, and damp my imagination to such a degree that it is with difficulty I can write at all.

6th January. I don't carry the children into Hyde Park as usual, for I don't find time to go out in the morning, and I imagine 'tis not necessary in this airy Audley Street—at least, I'm sure they can't be better than they are. I wish you could see us all supping together, for you must know I always regale with your fine tea before I go abroad. And with it enters two immense pieces of bread, which, being sopped in very weak tea, are put into two different plates for Ned and Fanny. The former feeds himself with great seriousness and solemnity; the latter jumps and skips and sings, still minding the main chance all the time. After they are satisfied, *c'est l'étiquette* to have a great game of romps, in the height of which I escape and gain my coach.

To-night I was carried directly to Lady Folkestone[1] and stayed till 10. Last night I sat with Miss Grenville; and the evening before Lady Frances Medows carried me to the play and I brought her back. I assure you we had gallants with us—viz, school boys!

8th January. At night. I have spent this afternoon with Mary Evelyn, who told me there were two mails come in from Lisbon. 'Tis impossible to express my impatience to get home, or how long I fancied William lingered on the way. At length I am arrived, my dearest love, and have got your kind letters. But alas, I feel you have suffered vastly; I feel your sleepless nights, your anxious mind, and the many dis-appointments and distresses which I hope you will have forgot e'er this reaches you.

[1] Elizabeth Marsham, sister of Lord Romney, and Lord Folkestone's second wife.

I shall not sleep well to-night, and little thought that hearing from my dearest husband could thus have lowered my spirits. But I am sure you was very uneasy when you wrote me these letters, for this same Lisbon mail brings advice that your ships *Vigilant* and *Pembroke* are at Lisbon to refit. Oh, that cruel Bay of Biscay. And oh, that my dearest Admiral had sailed ten days' sooner and got before and beyond all these storms. What would I not give to know you safe at the Madeiras, with all your squadron! But three days' fair wind out of thirty —'tis too much. I cannot talk to you upon any other subject and, as it will be (I trust) very unseasonable when this reaches you, I had better not talk at all. Therefore, *adieu, très cher.*

11*th January.* I spent yesterday (Sunday) at my father's *à l'ordinaire,* where I was much upbraided with my low spirits. Indeed, I have not been able to get out of them since I had your letter, for I cannot think of the uneasiness you have endured without suffering a great deal myself.

I have been at Court to-day and I am indebted to you for five minutes' conversation I have had with His Majesty, whom I had the honour to inform that you was well on the 2nd December. He asked me, "Where?" I said, "in sight of the rock of Lisbon," and added that you had had contrary winds almost ever since you parted from England. He asked me if any of the squadron were parted from you. I answered, "Not that you mentioned to me." I thought that was best to say, not only because 'twas true, but because I would not seem to have any other information than that you was well and had had a fair, or a contrary, wind.

I do assure you, my love, that you have just honour by your countrymen, who say you have got as far with a foul wind as any other Commander was used to do with a fair one.

Lord Anson is going to be married, and I am glad of it, for I approve his choice. He has escaped all the trammels and snares that were laid for him and, flying the traps of the Levesons, he has voluntarily surrendered to Miss Yorke.[1] You know her person: it deserves no commendations, but I've long

[1] Elizabeth, daughter of Philip, 1st Earl of Hardwicke, Lord Chancellor.

since heard that she is extremely sensible and good-natured, and that sort of stuff (to borrow my father's expression) that will make a good wife. Her father and mother are remarkably happy together and have bred her up with all the care imaginable, so I believe you'll approve your friend's choice.

I am told that Lord Chancellor and Lord Anson are already closely united in friendship and politics, being both strenuous advisers of the war, together with the Duke of Newcastle, etc. On the other hand, the Duke of Bedford is for peace. What becomes of our witty minister[1] in this struggle, or whether he is so much consulted as he ought to be, my author does not say; but whatever his counsel be, his wit is always ready, *dont je m'en vais vous raconter un trait.*

I've told you already that Lady Augustus Fitzroy and Mr. Jeffreys, the gamester, were married, at which some one was expressing his surprise in the presence of Lord Chesterfield, and saying they did not imagine it ever would have been a match. "No," said his Lordship, "what more likely to make a *match* than *card* and *brimstone?*" Don't you like this?

Lady Coke is not with child nor likely to be, since she is going to be parted from her worthless Lord, who games and drinks and stays out till 8 in the morning.[2] I hear that Lady Suffolk is married to Jack Pitt, *aux gros yeux.*

As to your brother Jack, *entre nous (bons amis)* I despair of him. He told me that at Christmas his affair with Miss Surman was to come to a crisis. He was to be admitted to visit her and had great reason to hope the rest, the father having desired him to say what he expected with her. But truly, after all these fair prospects, when Christmas comes, my gentleman goes down to the Duke of Richmond's for a fortnight or 3 weeks. *Qu'en dites-vous, Monsieur—n'en voilà-t-il pas assez pour rebuter la petite femme, au moins si elle est aussi délicate sur le chapitre de tiédeur qu'une autre petite femme de votre connoissance.*

I wish you could see the frame I have got made (from a

---

[1] Lord Chesterfield. He had just resigned.

[2] Edward, Viscount Coke, married 1747 Lady Mary Campbell, daughter of the Duke of Argyll, and died without issue. This story about him, written down by Fanny on 11th January, was repeated in almost identical words by Horace Walpole on the 12th January, in a letter to Horace Mann.

design of my own) for one of your prints, which I am going to send as a present from me to the Corporation of Truro. It is the finest carving I ever saw, of heaps of trophies joined together by cables. There is every ensign of Admiral or General, and the best piece of workmanship that I ever saw. The price is 5 guineas. I told Lord Falmouth[1] to-day at Court that I thought I ought to send another of them to Saltash, since you had the same, or greater, obligations there.

My father and Uncle Edward[2] are reconciled, which I am glad of. The former having obtained leave for the latter to sell his half-pay, my uncle will, I believe, pay my father the money in dispute. Meanwhile, I have half a year's interest on 24 thousand odd hundred pounds due to me from my father, who has paid me £50 these last two Sundays, but you know he is not fond of parting with LUMPS of money, and I am so good an economist that I am never distressed, till Child's shop[3] breaks! But jesting apart, I do reckon that I am a very house-wifely young woman, and that you yourself would allow that I am extremely reformed. As one instance of it, I am arrived at keeping my account book with perfect exactness, so that I know my expenses to a shilling, and I own the sum total of each month frightens me, though I hope it won't hurt me.

My house is an hourly expense to me, as you may imagine. The job of repairing the sluices in the back houses, making the pump, etc., was £9, and now I am paving the street with broad stones, the vault underneath having threatened 'twould fall in, if we did not repair gutters worn between the pavement where the rain settled. Then, my furniture, which is now pretty complete, costs many a penny. So elegant am I, that my fender is a Chinese rail. *Je connois des gens qui portent tellement envie à ma maison et à mes meubles qu'ils en sont presque malades*, and worry their husbands night and day to go out of that odious, beastly house.

I want abundance of chintz for my bow-window room.

---

[1] The Admiral's eldest brother, 2nd Viscount Falmouth.
[2] Edward Evelyn of Felbridge, Julia's father.
[3] Messrs. Child's bank.

Not but I have got an extreme pretty linen for half a crown a yard; the same pattern as the hangings, only they are coloured, and this is only blue and white. I consulted nobody about either—not one single person having seen either the paper or the linen till both were made up. Everybody commends each separate, but dislike them together and maintain I must have coloured linen to my coloured paper. I agree so far with them that I shall bestow my old chintz gowns as fast as they wear out, but till then I shall not give up my taste and opinion that 'tis now extremely pretty.

I have bespoke Wilton carpetting of a very uncommon and very pretty sort. All manner of carpets and mattings will be at all times vastly acceptable to me. You will also remember me as to muslins, both clear and thick, which are so immoderately dear that 'twould ruin one to stock one's self at present.

Your son maintains his superiority over Neddy Medows, than whom he is taller by 2 inches, though the latter is turned 5 years old, and our jewel is three and a quarter. Bess, too, is a jewel that has not its fellow—there never was such a girl. I am obliged to suppress many of her perfections for want of probability. Frances is a charming little, plump, blue-eyed maid that would pass for a beauty in any house but this. God bless them all! I am sure you say AMEN.

'Tis impossible for me to do the many people justice as to their expressions of regard for you. If I were to begin a list of your well-wishers, I have the Dukes of Dorset, Newcastle and Montagu at the head—or, rather, I ought to have mentioned his Royal Highness the Prince. In short, all your relations and mine insist that I should give their kindest service to you and make mention of their good wishes, which you must thus take in the lump.

The day after I received your letters, I sent Beuvregny with a card to Lord Winchilsea,[1] to say I had had the satisfaction to hear you was well on the 2nd December off the Rock of Lisbon. He would see Beuvregny himself, by whom he sent

[1] Daniel, 7th Earl. First Lord of the Admiralty, 1741. His daughter Charlotte, died unmarried.

me his compliments, and said he would have come to thank me in person if he was not just stepping into his coach to go into the country, where his family (except Lady Charlotte, whom I have visited) still are. I have also visited Lady Warren, Sir Peter's lady, on her arrival, being desirous to pay all due respect to your profession.

Lady Folkestone sent to me to go to the play with her to-night, but I thought it much more my business and, indeed, more my inclination, to stay at home and scribble this sheet of paper to my dearest husband.

And now, my love, adieu. May the Almighty bless and prosper you and all your undertakings.

Remember always with affection your faithful wife.

20th January. I have not wrote you for above a week, my dear love, and yet I don't fear your suspecting that I have forgot you. Alas! I have had but too many reasons to think of you and wish for you, too. I have been in distress, and when that is the case, I never trust myself with pen and paper, for I should naturally pour out all my griefs to you and use expressions that would make my letter a pain to you instead of a pleasure: to avoid which, I have required of myself to refrain from writing to you when my mind is out of tune. I am now easy again and, therefore, can relate (after this long preamble) what has been the matter.

All three children have been ill at once. The two girls had coughs and fevers occasioned by teeth, which were lanced immediately. The boy had a violent and never-ceasing cough, which I am inclined to believe he caught from his sisters' breath. It totally deprived him of rest, so that, by the 3rd night, he too was in a fever. By this time, you may imagine, we had decreed them for the measles; all three coughs, all three fevers, resembled it too much. You can imagine the state I was in. For poor Fanny I trembled, her breath and lungs being already so oppressed that 'twas pain to hear her, and the slut would not drink anything, though she was dying with thirst. There was no sort of liquor I did not try her with. Tea I made in her sight; water with a roast apple; mingled a drop of wine in warm water; milk; jelly. No, nothing would do, and she still persisted to cry, "No, no, no, can't." This she had occasion to repeat twenty times a day, sometimes when nobody asked. As to the medicines, the few we gave her we threw down by force, but you know it must be a trifle that could be obtained that way of drink.

As to the dear boy, he would at all times take anything I brought him; but then I dreaded a bleeding, which would have been necessary in the measles. I did not doubt my being able to persuade him to it. I had even got his promise. But I distrusted myself. I doubted my being able to stay in the room, and the least signs of fear in me would have inspired and justified his.

In short, my dearest husband, I have endured a great deal, and can never be enough thankful to the gracious providence that has comforted me and cured them. The boy and the little one now come downstairs. Frances keeps chamber still; but they have been purged, and to-morrow the two eldest begin asses' milk. Bess, as you know, has provision of that sort nearer at hand![1]

Mr. Burgess has done vastly well for us on this occasion (I have had no doctor), for his powders soon abated and removed their fever, and a white mixture he sent did much good to the cough. So Mr. Burgess is my first favourite. Yet he is not now admitted to come to the house, for he attends a daughter of Mrs. Ennys's, who is lately seized with the smallpox. Her sister had it about a month ago, and she would stay in the house. Sir Edward Hulse did not let her purge or bleed, as a person inoculated, or rather condemned for it. Neither did she refrain from going out, for she was taken ill at a concert! I hear she is in great danger.

27th January. I have been at Leicester House to-day, where I met Mr. Legge,[2] to my great satisfaction, being the first time I had seen this great little personage, except once at my father's.

---

[1] Bess was still only 9 months old.
[2] The Hon. Henry Bilsan Legge, son of 1st Lord Dartmouth. Afterwards became Chancellor of the Exchequer.

Know ye that he is *Monsieur l'Ambassadeur Extraordinaire auprès de sa Majesté le Roi de Prusse!* I told him, if my son were but 15 years older, I would list him in his train, and he assured me he should be welcome. Don't you approve of my thought, dear love? 'Twould be a safe, an improving, as well as a cheap, way of travelling, and Mr. Legge would, methinks, treat a son of yours with great friendship and distinction. He besought me to imagine how he, in whose house no victual had ever entered, except bread and cheese, could with any grace *faire le personnage d'Ambassadeur*; and I besought him not to drown himself in old hock. I likewise advised him to get a book which set forth the ceremonials of Ambassadors, else I was sure he would never guess whom he should conduct to the stair head and whom to the door only. In short, his Excellency was just as pleasant and good humoured as when he appeared to me an honest tar at Beddington.

It was not until the end of 1747 that any regulation uniform had been prescribed for naval officers, though a few years before, at Admiral Anson's instigation, two or three patterns for a standard uniform had been prepared. One day towards the end of 1747, however, when King George II saw the Duchess of Bedford (wife of the First Lord) riding in the Park, he was so attracted by her habit of dark blue cloth with white facings that he at once gave orders that all naval officers should in future wear a uniform of blue and white. The Prince of Wales's second son, Prince Edward Augustus, then only ten years old, must have been one of the first to be dressed in this new uniform in London, for Fanny's journal continues: "I forgot to tell you that their Royal Highness's second son, Prince Edward, is now always dressed in the uniform of a captain of a man-of-war."

Her letter continues:

I was not at the birthday; my children not being quite recovered. But imagine to yourself the sensation made by my step-mother in her new sedan with yellow tassels, and her three servants which, with the two chairmen, made five men all in new liveries!

29th January. I was at the play last Tuesday, and you little guess that you are the cause of my getting good places whenever I want, for Mr. Berrisford is a sort of box-keeper, and having a son on board the Admiral's ship, he is my most devoted creature. I think I have not troubled him above three times this winter, for 'tis really a good day's work from hence. To send for places, to send to keep them, to go, and to return, is so much trouble that, did not Mr. Garrick provide very well for our entertainment, I should never take it.

Last night I was well content with such entertainment as *Roderick Random*[1] affords. He shall wait on you—and undressed—for I foresee that all your officers will be desirous of a visit from him. I am already indebted to him for many a horse laugh, so that I am greatly prejudiced in his favour.

There is a thing much read, called *Clarissa*, but as I hear 'tis by the author of *Pamela*, I have neither seen it myself nor send it you, though I would be very sorry to omit sending you anything that had the least chance to amuse you for half an hour. With this view, I have ordered Brindley to send me every pamphlet that comes out, and Mme. Dunoyez brings me all the *petits livres*. I send you some which, if one may judge by their frontispiece, are not in the most chaste style, but she assured me they were well wrote and cost but a shilling, which last circumstance decided me in their favour.

A lady's maid in the eighteenth century was always called "the servant." Fanny had just engaged a new one, who stayed with her some years; and her name now appears for the first time. Her household apparently consisted of lady's maid, butler (a Frenchman called Beuvregny), footman, cook and kitchenmaid, two housemaids, nurse and nurserymaid.

I like my servant very well. The Mrs. Marshfield I told you

[1] First published 1748.

of. She is very intelligent and a sensible person; quick, both in her understanding and actions, so that I think she will do very well. But I am afflicted with bad cooks, and just now have a drunken one, who departs to-morrow. I have likewise had 3 nursery maids since Bab went, but the present—which is the 3rd—seems to be very good. Leonard is departed and to him succeeded a John, who presently made way for a Daniel, who occupies at present and seems likely to continue. The housemaid I took from the lady in Hill Street proves very good, so she remains with the rest that you left. And this is the state of my family, than which there are few more orderly and sober.

But you will see by the papers that *notre quartier* is come into great disgrace, there having been a robbery over against our chapel,[1] by highwaymen on horseback. There have been two since in Grosvenor Square, but they have not been half so much talked about as ours, which, being the first, surprised the more, and the loss was much the greatest, a West Indian woman and her daughter losing jewels to the value of £400. They had been visiting in Park Street and, returning into our street, met these new-fashioned gentry before 10 o'clock. Lady Gertrude Hotham's coach was one of the two that were robbed in Grosvenor Square, Sir Charles, some other children, and a governess being in it.

Tuesday, 2nd February. I would talk more to you, though I sat up all night for it, but I have been at your brother George's, where instead of cards, we had such another hop as last year, which was very agreeable, and without any sort of ceremony, as you will imagine when I tell you I had 4 different partners— *Monsieur l'Ambassadeur* Trevor; Charles Frederick; Charles and George Montagu.

Adieu, cher, cher ami! Conservez-moi toujours votre cœur et croyez que je le mérite par ma tendresse et par ma fidélité!

5th February. I dispatched a bundle of newspapers with a letter of mine to my dearest husband last Wednesday morn. I sent you, at the same time, a few French stories, but omitted

---

[1] Grosvenor Chapel, South Audley Street.

Roderick Random, which I purposed to have sent, but Mr. Killigrew had got the first volume and I had not enough notice from Mr. Hume to get it away again, but it shall go in this packet. I am told 'tis not Fielding's, but the produce of a Scotch sea surgeon called Smollett, and that the ground of the story is his own, allowing for embellishments. I laughed at first, but I grew tired before I had done.

I now send you a few more lines for I understand that this may yet go by the *Lapwing,* provided I send it to Mr. Hume to-day.

My cousin, Eliza Evelyn, and all gay ladies have feasted these two or three days, for last night there was a masquerade and the fullest (it seems) that ever was seen. The day before, her Grace of Bedford had a very grand Ball. His Royal Highness the Duke of Cumberland was her partner, though the ball was given to Lady Louisa Egerton, who danced with Lord Trentham,[1] to whom 'tis said she is going to be married. The Duke of Bridgewater (in consequence of this ball) people have married to Lady Essex's eldest daughter.

His Majesty invited himself to this ball, so he came in a mask with 30 other women masks, who assembled at Lady Tankerville's[2] house and, when his Majesty came by, they all got into coaches and followed him. The masks were Duchess of Dorset, Lady Pembroke, Lady Lincoln, Lady Holderness, Lady Cardigan, Lady Yarmouth, Lady Car. Pierrepoint, Lady Rockford, Lady Car. Petersham, Lady Tankerville, Lady Camillo, and 20 more whom I don't recollect. Amongst these, three masks appeared who stayed together and did not go to the top of the room with the rest. They were fine but dirty, and soon discovered to be Miss Fanny Murray, Mrs. Kitty Hamilton and another lady. The Duke of Bedford assured them he would be glad to see them there any other night, but just then

[1] Granville, Lord Trentham, eldest surviving son of 1st Earl Gower, and subsequently 1st Marquis of Stafford, married as his second wife Lady Louisa Egerton, daughter of Duke of Bridgewater, 28th March, 1748. His half-brother, John Leveson-Gower, subsequently married Fanny Boscawen's eldest daughter Frances.

[2] Alicia, daughter of Sir John Astley, married Charles, 3rd Earl of Tankerville, 1742.

must desire they would excuse him, but took care they should be safely escorted to their chairs without any insult. So much for this festive where the King supped.

Mr. Horace Walpole has for these two Saturdays given most elegant entertainments at breakfast to the ladies, and has introduced a morning hop, which saves the expense of *bougies* and is not, I think, a bad scheme. As to the company, 'twill be sufficient to tell you that they were the *élite de la jeunesse.* Mr. Walpole himself danced with Lady Caroline Petersham.

Next Wednesday *La Venitienne* gives a ball. 'Tis but a few weeks since she lost a son and daughter, so that, being much scandalised at this unseasonable mirth, I said she danced over the ashes of her dead children, but Mrs. Smythe assured me I was mistaken, for they were not yet reduced to ashes!

Mais que dites-vous de la belle Fanny, qui est présentement MADAME GREVILLE? She went out of town yesterday (the 7th) in Mr. Greville's coach and six and left letters for Lady Caroline Fox, Mrs. Ellis (late Mrs. Stanhope) and Mrs. Frere, to acquaint them with her marriage, which I am extremely glad of, as I admire her, and think her well bestowed on Mr. Greville, though not upon Lord Northesk.[1]

I am extremely well satisfied with my house and grow more and more settled in it every day.

In the list I gave you of the affairs I have transacted, I omitted to tell you that my garden is in the best order imaginable, and planted with 100 shrubs and flowers. With all this, I am in a very dull, melancholy sort of way, and have no pleasure in anything but my children. As to books—I never look into one.

Your brother Jack, as I said before, is regularly admitted to Mr. Surman's and will, I think, soon become his son-in-law. I think it was he told me for news that your friend, Lord Winchilsea, is going to part with his wife.[2]

---

[1] George, 6th Earl of Northesk, a captain in the Navy, 1741, married, April 1748, Ann Leslie, daughter of 3rd Earl of Leven and Melville.

[2] This story was apparently ill-founded. Lord Winchilsea's 2nd wife (Mary, daughter of Sir Thomas Palmer), whom he married in 1738, presented him with a fourth child in 1751 and died 1757.

I have seen Mrs. George (but not Mr. George) Boscawen,[1] who enquires much after the rum, which is not yet come, nor anything else of what you sent me, except 3 dozen Claret in one hamper, and 2 boxes of tea, which is so delightfully good that I can drink no other.

I believe I have already mentioned that Julia and I parted at St. Clere with a mutual promise to meet at Highwood Hill for ten days next April (Easter), when I propose to wean Elizabeth, and think the country air and the cows will facilitate that great work, which, beside, I shall have more leisure to attend myself as well as Julia, who is excellent with children—romps, dances, sings, and is vastly acceptable to them.

I suppose you have met with Lord Chesterfield's *bon mot*? It was spoilt in the newspapers, and I don't think I shall do it justice, but, in short, His Majesty was taking notice of the word "drubbing" in Hawke's account, and jestingly asked Lord Chesterfield if that was a sea term, to which his Lordship answered very gravely that if it was, without doubt the Duke of Bedford could explain it to His Majesty.[2]

Your mother appears, and I must finish.

Adieu once more. I chat with you, my dear love, as if you could answer me, and I will not allow myself to reflect that is not the case.

You are already persuaded of my utmost regard for you, and all the care possible of your children. Upon this account, I will depend upon the continuance of your esteeming me always as your most faithful, affectionate and obedient wife.

[1] Ann, daughter of John Marley Trevor, of Trevallyn, married Hon. Geo. Boscawen, 1743.

[2] According to Beatson's Memoirs, published in 1804, which confirm Fanny's story, the Duke of Bedford (then First Lord of the Admiralty) had only recently, when at Lichfield Races, received a drubbing in some political *fracas* in which he became involved. (See *ante* p. 56.)

CHAPTER VI

ENGLEFIELD GREEN AND ASCOT RACES, 1748

FOR the summer of 1748 Fanny Boscawen rented a furnished house at Englefield Green, on the borders of Windsor Great Park, where a succession of friends came down from London to stay with her, and her cousin Julia was an almost permanent guest.

She was by now a great deal happier. Actually, she had had no word from the Admiral since he sailed from Madeira in December 1747, but on 13th May the King had informed both Houses that the preliminaries for a general peace had been signed at Aix-la-Chapelle, the basis of which was to be the restitution of the conquests which each Power had made during the war; and though there could be no possibility of this news reaching her husband till November at the earliest, and the risks of active service must still surround him till then, Fanny could at least begin to put a limit to his absence, and look forward with some hope to his return in the summer of 1749.

Meanwhile, under summer skies, Boscawen and his squadron had anchored in Table Bay on 29th March, having sailed from Madeira on 23rd December.

One of the unexpected problems with which the Admiral had to deal during his short stay at Madeira was the stormy behaviour of the captain of an English man-of-war which was cruising in the neighbourhood of the island and had come into port on the same day as Boscawen. This officer, Captain the Hon. William Montagu, a distant cousin by marriage of

82

Fanny's future great friend, Elizabeth Montagu, had apparently celebrated his arrival in port by having a violent quarrel with the skipper of one of the Company's ships accompanying Boscawen's squadron. But the story, which gives an insight into the Admiral's character, had best be told in Boscawen's own words. His letter, addressed to the Admiralty, is now in the British Museum.

Namur,
MADEIRA,
21 *Dec.*, 1747.

MY LORD,

Captain Montagu in the *Bristol* joined me the day before I anchored here. I have been much troubled with him and have been obliged to confine him at the desire of the Governor of the place, having put up a paper at the Custom House that he would beat one of the captains of the Indiamen wherever he met him, and at the same time telling everybody he would put him to death. Upon enquiry, I found the captain on the Indiaman to blame in nothing but want of spirit for suffering himself to be insulted without having in the least offended.

Arriving at the Cape on 29th March, an advance party was landed next day "to clear a camping ground for the troops," for it had been decided to put the whole expedition ashore while the ships were refitting, in order to give the men some rest and exercise after their five months' voyage from England.

From a contemporary report we read:

The men made a good appearance, and no pains were spared, as to discipline and refreshment, in order to fit them for their better performance in action. The admiral by his genteel behaviour entirely gained the love of the land officers; and never was greater harmony among all degrees of men than in this expedition, everyone thinking they were happy in being under his command. The time they spent at the Cape was of great service to the land and sea forces, who had fresh meat all the time.

By the beginning of May, the ships and the troops were again ready for sea; and on 6th May, the squadron weighed anchor and headed out to sea on the second stage of their voyage. The Admiral had no knowledge or suspicion that an armistice had already been signed, and his immediate task, if he found the place not too strong for him, was to capture the French island of Mauritius.

The next section of Fanny's journal begins on 3rd June:

ENGLEFIELD GREEN,
3rd June, 1748.

MY DEAREST HUSBAND,

Your children are all charming, in health as well as beauty. There are many children upon the green whom we meet in our walks, and I enquire their age, not only because I am *la belle questionneuse,* but because I have always the pleasure to find that my boy and Bess are taller by the head than anything of their age—and stout in proportion.

I think I have nothing new to tell you just now. Yes, you'll reckon it extremely new if I inform you that Julia and I were on Coopers Hill at 7 this morning. 'Tis within a little walk of this place (as I suppose you know). We had strolled there one evening and admired the view excessively, but fancied 'twould look still more beautiful of a morning. So, to-day we tried, but I like the evening best, unless perhaps soon after the sun rises.

8th June. Sunday we were at Church and dirtied our gowns extremely, though we had the precaution to send to the clerk to say we desired to have the pew cleaned.

There was 7 or 8 coaches, which produced a world of Misses, none of which I knew by sight except a Miss Foster, who was robbed in London and is Mrs. Barham's daughter.

As we went out of Church, the bells struck up in honour of my ladyship, which I could well have excused.

I believe I've never told you that Harry Norris has taken a house at Thorpe. They came down here on Saturday, so

84

Sunday evening we resolved to dispatch all our visits, that we might be at liberty to go to the Norris's. Accordingly, we proceeded to Windsor and rapped at Mrs. Rice's door, and Mrs. Trevor's, with equal success. Thence we proceeded to Miss Montagu's, whom we found, and stayed in great form about an hour. Thence we returned home, where we found that in spite of all laws to the contrary, Mr. and Mrs. Norris and Miss Vansittart[1] had been to visit us, and had left word they begged we would dine with them the next day; which we did, and I returned in raptures with my habitation by comparing it with theirs, which is so shut up and surrounded with pales and rails and iron gates that it looks like Mr. Carey's at Hampstead. In short, I would rather give ninety pounds a year for this, than fifty pounds the *half* year for that, which is the price they pay. And they will not get their pennyworths out of it, for they are going to Mr. Jenning's in Hertfordshire, and to St. John Norris's in Kent, and to Tunbridge, and I know not whither, so that 'tis wonderful they took a country house at all. However, 'tis lucky for us since, while they stay, we have a very agreeable neighbour whom we live with in all ease and familiarity.

I am pretty positive that you would approve my resolution of hiring this place, since the situation is so charming, notwithstanding it almost ruins me, for the gardens will cost me near £50. But then, I have such a lawn for my babes to skip on when 'tis shady, and such a wood to hide 'em in when 'tis sunny, that 'tis worth all the money.

15th June. I have for some days desisted from writing to you, which I deem advisable whenever I am in a gloomy humour, for there are such thoughts as that 'tis six months since one has had any account of a husband's health, and may be twice six more before one sees him. I say such thoughts there are, and such reflections may follow as would not be most apt to form an agreeable epistle. Nevertheless, I have

---

[1] Susannah Vansittart, Maid of Honour to Princess of Wales, was daughter of Arthur Vansittart Esq., of Shottesbrook, Berks. Three of her brothers were members of the Hell-Fire Club at Medmenham.

twice sat down to continue mine to my dearest husband and have been both times disturbed, first by Lord and Lady Folkestone (who are at Sunninghill Wells) and secondly by Mr. Norris, whom, as I have told you, we often see.

21st June. Yesterday, we went with Mr. and Mrs. Norris to see Mr. Southcote's[1] near Chertsey, which is a charming *ferme ornée*. We narrowly missed of Lord Anson, who had been there with his lady and Lord and Lady Duncannon, from London, to see the place, but had been gone about half an hour when we came. I hear Lord Anson is excessive fond of his wife and, moreover, that she is pregnant. This news is Mrs. Norris's, who gathered it, I guess, of Miss Cleveland.

23rd June. The agreeable Vansittart has gone, which is a great loss for us, for the Norris's are so taken up with one another that they employ more time in kissing and toying than in entertaining us. I don't mean, however, that they are not very agreeable neighbours, for we live with one another upon the easiest footing imaginable, and exchange a family dinner without any manner of ceremony.

Lord and Lady Folkestone talk of carrying us to see Ditton and the Duke of Marlboro's island.[2] If they do—well. If not, Julia and I can amuse ourselves with the children for months together, without desiring to see a soul.

The fact is, however, that we do see a great many souls. Among the rest, who but the Miss Bisshopps have been to dine with us, and who but Mrs. Frere brought 'em. I sent for Van to meet 'em, so we had rather a jolly day of it, only the weather was cross and sour. However, we drank tea at the lodge, but Lord Bateman,[3] who came to my house *au sortir de table*, would drive Mrs. Frere and the Bisshopps in his chariot to see Dicky Bateman's, while the Buck Bisshopp, Frere, Van, Julia

---

[1] Woburn Farm, near Chertsey, the property of Philip Southcote, Esq., and described by Lord Bath as "a dainty whim."

[2] The 2nd Duke owned Monkey Island, near Bray.

[3] Lord Bateman married Miss Elizabeth Sambrooke, 10th July 1748.

and I walked about the Duke's gardens at the utmost peril to our shoes, for it had rained excessively. The Bisshopps seemed vastly delighted with the day's expedition which, contrary to their fears, had been approved by Sir Cecil. They go out of town in about ten days. Meantime they live with the *élite de la jeunesse*, and are at the frequent balls at Ranelagh with Lady Tufton, Lady Falkener, Mrs. Pitt, Lady Charlotte Johnston, Miss Chudleigh,[1] Miss Nevill, Miss Howe, Lord Eglinton, Lord Lauderdale, Lord Bute, Mr. Pitt, Lord Barrington, Horace Townshend, Mr. Maitland, Mr. Stanley, etc.

Lord Bateman will be married in a week to Miss Betty Sambrooke, on whom Sir Jeremy has settled his estate.

Frere is gone to Tunbridge, where my father and Mrs. Glanville have earnestly invited me to spend a fortnight, but I shall not quit my peaceful groves, much less my pretty babes for that tumult. I shan't easily forget how ill my boy looked when I returned last year, nor shan't be easily persuaded to deprive him again of his mother's eye. Beside, Bess is toothing and requires care. We have one of Mr. Burgess's men, of whose skill and prudence he gives me the strongest assurances, just come to settle at Egham. I thank God we have had no occasion for him, but if we should, 'tis a satisfaction to think one may confide in him.

Mr. and Mrs. Smythe, who were to arrive to-day, are not come, so I have the more time to talk with my dearest husband and tell him our important employments (for I don't love to think of his).

Yesterday, we were to wait on Mrs. la Roche, where we met the Duchess of St. Albans[2] and Lady Diana Beauclerc. Also a Mrs. and Miss Shackerly,[3] who said they intended to wait on me. They

[1] The notorious Elizabeth Chudleigh, who in 1744 was married secretly to Hon. Augustus John Hervey, later Earl of Bristol, when he was 20, and, subsequently, in the lifetime of her husband, was publicly married in 1769 to the last Duke of Kingston.

[2] Lucy, wife of Charles, 2nd Duke, was daughter of Sir John Werden, of Holyport, Berkshire. Her daughter, Diana, then 22, subsequently married Shute Barrington, Bishop of Durham.

[3] Miss Shackerly subsequently married Sir Watkin Williams-Wynn, see p. 94.

are a Welsh family, who have been burnt out of their house in Wales, and have taken one as you come up the hill from Egham hither. They hire it of Lord Dalkeith.

Amongst all my visitors, Madame Peggy Trevor has not yet done me the honour, though I have both sent and been to her. I don't see why she need espouse her brother-in-law's quarrel, for I hear the Colonel George[1] is immensely angry with me for telling him he should change or wash his coat after nursing his boy with the Smallpox. Now 'tis certain that, if my fears are ridiculous (and I don't pretend to defend 'em), the folly is mine and reflects upon me—not on him.

Midsummer Day. I have a letter from Ramsay, lamenting that he can never come here, being immersed in business, which he describes by a parody on Milton's *Lamentation on his Blindness.* I forget the words of that, but Master Ramsay's parody is as follows:

> . . . While with the year
> Seasons return, but not to me returns
> Strawb'rys, or sweet approach of curds and cream,
> Or sight of vernal bloom, or summer's rose,
> Or flocks, or herds, or cousin's face divine:
> But smoke instead, and ever during work
> Surrounds me, from the cheerful ways of fun
> Cut off . . .

25th June. Norris, who has been here this morning, tells us a piece of news, dire and horrid. Lady Charlotte Johnston,[2] Lady Dorothy Hobart[3] and Mrs. Pitt being late at Vauxhall this day se'ennight, walked into the dark walks when their gentlemen were not with them and stumbled upon 6 or 7 men who, not content with kissing them—which they were

---

[1] George Boscawen, brother-in-law to Peggy Trevor.
[2] Born Lady Charlotte Montagu, sister of Earl of Halifax, married Col. James Johnston; died Twickenham, April 1762.
[3] Sister of John, 2nd Earl of Buckinghamshire. Married, 1752, Sir Charles Hotham-Thompson, Bt.

obliged tamely to suffer—whipped them. Lady Charlotte Johnston has since miscarried. Pitt too, had like to have had a quarrel with some gentleman who knew nothing of the matter, but was mistaken by the women for one of the persons who had abused them. In short, 'twas a most horrible affair that one would not have had a part in for a thousand guineas. I never was whipped at school, and a whipping now would certainly kill me. I pity the poor young women and blame 'em too, for all three of 'em go often enough to Vauxhall to know that the dark walks at 12 at night are for other purposes than for three women of fashion to wander in.

I believe I am fancying you are lying on the couch yonder, and I am talking any nonsense to lull you asleep.

But I must continue with my soporiferous narrative, and tell you that young Peter Burrell[1] was here a few days ago. He was visiting Lord Londonderry, who has a house somewhere in this neighbourhood.

28th June. I have a letter from Charlotte Bisshopp. She says there's no truth in the ladies being kissed, much less whipped. That Lady Charlotte Johnston and Lady D. Hobart fell a running at the sight of some drunken 'prentices, which made these imagine they were women of the town and run after them. That Mrs. Pitt was never taken any notice of, because she walked quietly, and that the gentlemen came up in a minute and beat the 'prentices, so there was an end of it. As to Mr. Pitt, he was not there that night. So upon the whole I never will attempt to relate any such idle reports to you, for I can't endure to write lies.

3rd July. There has been a duel at Marylebone Fields, which has made great noise. The best account I can give you of it is what Lady Lambard told Mr. Smythe the day she dined with Mr. Bellenden, who is one of the duellists.

The scene of this duel—that is, the beginning of it—was in this neighbourhood, at Sunninghill, where Lord Coke and

---

[1] Of Langley Park, Kent.

89

Lady Mary have been this month. Mr. Bellenden[1] and Mr. Mackenzie[1] were in the house with them. One night at supper, Lord Coke told Lady Mary he would invent ways to torment her more than ever he had done, and that for all his life, for all the world should not part them. She said she might defy him to use her worse than he had done, and, after some more unpleasant discourse of this kind, the ladies (for Lady Betty[1] was there) retired in tears. When they were gone, Mr. Bellenden expostulated a little with my Lord and asked him if he was not afraid of provoking her family to such a degree that they might unite in getting a separation. He seemed not to mind Bellenden, but affected to turn the discourse and said, "I've bought the prettiest pair of pistols that ever were seen. I must show 'em you." Immediately rang and bid his servant fetch his new pistols. He shewed the gentlemen all the beauties of 'em and, when they had done admiring 'em, he bid the servant put 'em in their place again.

By the next post, Lord Coke wrote Lord Gower[2] word that Bellenden had insulted him and that he had challenged him to fight, and the other had refused. As soon as Bellenden got to London, the Duke of Argyll sent to him and told him what Lord Coke had wrote to Lord Gower, the latter having shewn him the letter. Upon this, B. takes horse immediately and comes down to Sunninghill last Sunday or Saturday se'ennight. Asks Lord Coke if it was true that he had told Lord Gower he had refused to fight him, who answered, "yes." "Then," said Bellenden, "you have told a damned lie." Upon this, Lord Coke bid him observe that the house was so small and thin that they must be overheard there, but that, if he lived till the Monday morning, he would meet him in Marylebone Fields and bring a second.

[1] James Stuart Mackenzie was Lady Mary's brother-in-law, having married her sister, Lady Betty Campbell. Harry Bellenden was also connected with her family, his sister Mary having married John Campbell, Lady Mary's cousin, who afterwards became 4th Duke of Argyll.

[2] Lord Gower's third wife, Lady Mary Tufton, and Lord Coke's mother Lady Margaret Tufton (Baroness de Clifford) were sisters and co-heiresses of their father, 6th Earl of Thanet. Lord Gower was therefore Lord Coke's uncle by marriage.

This was agreed on and they met accordingly, Mackenzie with B., and a Mr. Hamilton (an officer, I think) with Lord Coke. He insisted upon fighting with pistols only, so B. had his servant's, which were very bad. Lord Coke fired first and missed. B's shot went through the brim of his hat. Then C. fired again, which narrowly missed B. Then the latter fired his second pistol, which flashed in the pan; enraged at which, he threw it with such force at Lord Coke's head that, missing him, it stuck in the ground. Upon this, the seconds interposed and parted them.

5th July. The whole story has made a great noise, as you may suppose, and was told me first by Lord Folkestone, afterwards by Mr. Smythe who, with his wife and Ramsay, came here last Saturday and went away again Sunday evening, Julia and I escorting them as far as the Duke of Argyll's at Hounslow, where we were much entertained with the gardens, which we saw in the pleasantest manner imaginable.

No gardener at our heels, driving us with his hat off; but Ramsay, not being a proper Cicerone for trees, plants, etc., which are there most uncommon, fetched us a certain Master Fletcher of Saltoun, who stays with the Duke now, in the room of Johnny Maul. This Mr. Fletcher told us the names of all the trees, from the Cedar of Lebanon (which are there in great abundance) to whatever crept upon the wall or ground. Then entertained us with fruit, and we drank coffee in the Tower, which is a mighty pretty building.

About 7 o'clock we parted; the Smythe's for London, Ramsay stayed with the Duke, and we returned home, where we arrived at 9—supper upon the table.

9th July. This morning, Mr. Mason has been here to tell me that there is soon to be a division of the (3rd May) Prizes; that your share would be about £1,200 and that he wanted my orders how to dispose of it. I told him he was a perverse man not to bring it a few weeks ago, when Stocks were 14 per cent lower than they are now (or even a fortnight ago, before Spain had acceded), but that I would consult and resolve how to lay it out before the time he prescribed to me.

Lord Anson's secretary, Mr. Stephens, was with Mason, and he told me that Lord Anson and Sir P. Warren had determined to receive all their share in Navy bills, which were at 2 per cent discount, and bore 5 per cent interest. Mr. Mason added that he was sure I could put it to more advantage in the Stocks, so that I resolved he should pay a thousand-pound-Navy-bill into Child's hands, that with the rest (which he said would be short of £200) he should buy an India Bond, and pay the remainder in cash to me here. I can well dispose of it, for meat is 4 pence a pound and everything else in proportion.

12th July. I asked Mason to bring his wife and dine with me. You know he lives at Datchet. I have never been at that village since we lived here.

If my husband were here, I should like to explore the country "all in my chaise and pair," but as it is, I seldom sally forth without some company to induce me, for, my gardens being large, nothing can be pleasanter than to sit and walk in them and see all my olive branches flourishing round me. If you would know our way of life, I can tell it you very exactly. As soon as I am up (which is not so early as if my lord were at home) I sally forth into the garden, the boy in my hand, and by the time his shoes are wet through with dew (which never gives us any cold) we come in to breakfast. The instant breakfast is over, we retire into another room to say our lesson—a ceremony never omitted nor broke into, whether I have company or not—by which means he has made a considerable progress since we came into the country, and, if he had but half as much application as he has genius and capacity, he would read soon. But this same application is an ingredient seldom found in the composition of such a sprightly cub.

But, to return to my journal: after I have instructed my son, we usually take a little walk together, either on the Green or in the garden—the weather determines. Then come in and sit close to business for an hour and a half. Mine lies chiefly at my desk, where a number of correspondents, *et mon cher mari par-dessus tout*, find me continual employment. Then half a quarter of an hour's dressing, then dine exactly at 2. After dinner, sit awhile (whatever you may think to the contrary); then walk in the garden, where we have a charming green parlour, stored with chairs. Here we fix before 4, the table, workbasket, and book. The latter is my province, as the former is Julia's.

Hard by, there is a grove. Here my son and his sister make hay beside us, Mrs. Smythe having presented the former with a rake, fork and spade, and I treated him with a large wheelbarrow. We likewise stole a haycock from our neighbour, Sir John Elwell, which has amused the young ones for these three weeks past, and the rule is—and is very strictly kept to—that the hay never peeps out into our green parlour, but stays in the grove, which is full of dead leaves and twigs, so that it could not be kept neat, which the rest of the garden is in an eminent degree.

The haymakers have interrupted the thread of my narration, which goes on to tell you that, still in the same green retreat (if the weather permits), we drink tea at 6. And here I should be very ungrateful if I did not thank my dearest for the charming Dutch kettle he gave me, which is quite the comfort of one's life.

After tea, we see the young ones safe settled with their maids on the lawn, and then we sally forth to take our long walk, either on foot or *en carosse*. If the latter, the babes are of the party, but the former is much the most frequent.

Sometimes, we get in by 8 to see the young ones put to bed: (Bess, in that situation, is a sight) and sometimes not till 9, which is the hour of supper, after which I read and Julia knots till 11, when we retire, she to dream of her parents and I of my husband.

19th July. I could not even sleep last night, so much elated was I, for yesterday I received a letter from Mr. Stephens to say the *Syren* Man of War would sail express to you and carry you orders to return. I assure you, my dear, you have deprived me of a night's rest, for I employed it in thinking when and where (not how) I should receive you!

20th July. I have the same complaint to make to-day, for I have laid awake above half the night thinking of your coming home; when it will happen. Sure, in March or April. God grant my children may look as they do now. Just such rosy countenances, and my boy just as orderly and well behaved as he is now.

You can't imagine what a triumph I had on that subject yesterday. I must relate it to you. Mr. Mason has told me he had a boy a little older than mine. I asked if he was bigger; he said, not stouter, but a great deal taller. Yesterday, we were there and this tall boy proved to be half a head shorter than mine, to the great astonishment of his father. But here my triumph did not stop, for the Mason boy did nothing he was bid to do, nor minded father nor mother: would not speak to your son, nor play with him: whereas mine obeyed my very looks, was very talkative and civil, only asked Mrs. Mason if she was that boy's mother and, upon being answered yes, he said, "why does not he mind what you say to him?" In short, there could not be a greater contrast than between these two children—as well in figure as behaviour—so much so, that I thought Mason and his wife seemed mortified (for theirs, too, is a darling) and the former cried out, "What joy it must be to the Admiral to see such a lovely, such an extraordinary, child!"

21st July. This whole day I dedicate to my dearest husband without any one interruption, except teaching my boy. I shan't allow myself a book or anything that may hinder me, for this packet must be sealed to-night, and to-morrow I carry it up to Mr. Cleveland, to go by the *Syren* or *Charmer*.

Now to tell you some news of this place, which consists of a burying and a wedding. The former is of that poor wretch, Lord Forester, long since buried to everything that he ought to have lived for. He died at Egham, where it seems he had taken up his dwelling above a year.

The wedding is no less than the great Sir. W. W. Wynn,[1] who was married last Saturday to Miss Frances Shackerly,

---

[1] See *ante*, p. 87.

youngest daughter of Mr. Shackerly, who lives in the road from hence to Egham. The bridegroom arrived only on the Friday; threw himself at Mistress Shackerly's feet and said he would not rise till she consented he should be married the next day. She begged him to stay a fortnight only, till preparations were made, clothes bought, etc., but he was inflexible and all she could obtain was for him to put off his weepers (his wife not having been dead above 6 weeks). For my part, I commend his impatience, for 'tis certain he has no time to lose. The lady he has married is about 26; is his Goddaughter, for there has always been a great friendship between him and her father, to whom he declared his intentions about 3 weeks ago; but they did not imagine he proposed to have executed them till his deep mourning was expired. He says his late lady[1] enjoined him to marry immediately and, with that view, left him her whole estate.

On Sunday Fred Evelyn[2] dined with me. We carried him back to Eton, and your son was vastly delighted with seeing the place where he is to go to school. As I was leading him along King Henry's Square, he said to me, "Mama, I'll make haste and read my book, that I may come and play with all these little parsons," meaning the scholars, who were just then crossing the Square in their gowns. My boy was vastly pleased too with seeing his Grandfather's name engraved on the stone in the Cloisters, and he spelt it, I assure you, as well as I could do and without the least hesitation.

The Fredericks are at Maisonette, Tunbridge Wells, where Lucy writes me word she proposes to produce a boy in about 2 or 3 months, but I hope he (Charles) will write to you by this opportunity, as he may tell you of many things which I omit; for my letters are full of nothing but childish talk, that "to-day we did this and yesterday, that." But, as I am neither informed nor qualified to talk of great events, I think tittle tattle may be acceptable, and when it concerns those who have the greatest

[1] The official announcement of the wedding, which was solemnized on 16th July, 1748, stated baldly that it had taken place "at the request of his late lady, under her hand." His late lady had died in March.

[2] Son of Sir John Evelyn and Mary Boscawen, and then a schoolboy at Eton. Subsequently became 3rd Baronet of Wotton.

share of your affection, it even grows important. You know P.P.'s Memoirs are entitled "The importance of a man to himself." Mine might properly enough be called, "The importance of a wife to her husband, and of children to their father."

Indeed, my dearest, these tender names draw tears from my eyes, and I do not believe you will read them with greater indifference. God grant you the joy of seeing them! Seeing them answer your utmost desires! Seeing them everything you could wish, and conformable to the highest picture your fancy could paint. Hitherto, my prayer is heard, and the children improve daily in beauty.

With me, 'tis not so. Beauty and I were never acquainted. But may I not hope, dear husband, that you will find charms in my heart, the charms of duty and affection, that will endear me as much to you as if I were in the bloom of youth and beauty. But I must return to my trifles, for talking thus from my heart kills me, and my tears blot my writing! I will go into the garden and take a turn or two. When I have composed myself, I will come to you again.

Mr. and Mrs. Smythe have been with me these two last Saturdays and Sundays: and I have had a very fine promenade with them *sur l'eau* as far as Laleham. 'Twas a charming, soft, serene day and Mr. Smythe treated us with a punt, which we found at the Bells of Ouseley, where we embarked and continued our navigation as far as Laleham, where our coach met us. Julia and I (who had never been used to anything but "oars, your honour") did not at first much like this punt, and had some thoughts of our chairs going overboard, but half an hour convinced us of the safety of our navigation.

Another day when the Smythes were with us (for we never have the genius to go anywhere by ourselves) we went to Cranborne Lodge, the terrace of which is charming.

And I believe it is since I wrote to you that I have been at Shottesbrook,[1] the seat of Mr. Vansittart on the other side of the forest. I went to carry home their agreeable daughter,

[1] Now the property of Miss Oswald Smith, great-granddaughter of Arthur Vansittart of Shottesbrook and Foots Cray.

THE HON'BLE MRS. EDWARD BOSCAWEN
The bracelet on her wrist is the Admiral's miniature
(*From the painting at Bill Hill*)

whom Mrs. Vansittart dropped here in her way home from Sunbury, where they had been to see Lady Hudson, Mr. Van's sister. Van stayed with us a few days and I wished I had been allowed to keep her longer, for she is very good-humoured, very cheerful and sensible.

Lady Folkestone is still at Sunninghill, where she has been ill of a miscarriage. We went to see her when we thought her well again, but she was gone out airing, and yesterday she sent to desire we would come and dine with her and afterwards to see Mr. Hart's, near Maidenhead, and named to-day or to-morrow or next day, but neither suited me on account of my journey to London.

To-morrow I propose to dine with Mrs. Smythe, who is to fetch me from Audley Street.

And now I think, you have all my peregrinations. I have had another letter from my father, who is at Tunbridge, about coming there, but I am immovable.

I am beyond all expression impatient for a packet from my dearest husband. Oh, that we had a bird that would carry our thoughts to each other, then I might know whether you shall like to be here next summer; for, as to buying anything before you come—that is out of the question since Hatchlands[1] is not to be had. Perhaps you won't be able to live much in the country the first summer; even then, we shall want some place for the children, and this, I believe, you will like better than any place that is to be hired that I know of.

Here's your son:—

DEAR, DEAR PAPA,

Pray come home. I have made you a great many ships to come in and Mama says you will bring me something pretty, and pray do, Papa, for I am very good. Your dutiful son,

E. H. B.

This sign is his own, without my touching his hand—the rest was of my guiding, his dictating—by which you may

[1] Hatchlands Park, near Guildford, which they subsequently bought and built a new house there, decorated by Robert Adam.

perceive my son is not quite disinterested; but, if he takes after his father, he will become so in time.

Come then, happy father! Listen to the voice of this charmer, this syren. Come, and bring joy and happiness to a faithful wife, and the delight of a father's presence to the most lovely babes in the world!

23rd July. I sent you an immense letter yesterday. It consisted of 32 folio pages and was consigned to the care of Mr. Cleveland. I sent likewise, by Mr. Brett,[1] some newspapers, etc. and the fine edition of Lord Anson's voyage with cuts and charts.

My journey to London was vastly disagreeable, occasioned by the extreme heat, which never fails to accompany me whenever I go to London. I think I have not been in spirits since. I must needs be enquiring of Mr. Brett when he expected to hear from the *Namur*, whose answer was in December or January. This so ill suited my wishes or expectations, that I was resolved to enquire of another Oracle, and accordingly applied to Mr. Henshaw. He, you'll say, is always a dismal one. Neither did he, upon this occasion mend the matter, for he answered, January at the farthest. So, this has put me in the dumps, for I DEPENDED to have heard from you this month of August.

4th August. You'll say I have skipped finely, since my last date was 23rd July. Yet so it is, for I have had good folks in the house with me, in which case it is impossible to write with that undisturbed attention which I would have when I address my husband.

Mr. and Mrs. Smythe and Mrs. Clayton came last Thursday. Next morning, before dinner, we walked to Cooper's Hill, where we all sat on haycocks and listened to Mr. Smythe, who read us Sir John Denham's poem on that subject.[2] After dinner, as Mrs. Clayton had never seen the Duchess of Kent's, we carried her there and, having walked over the gardens and

---

[1] Timothy Brett, of the Navy Office.
[2] His best-known poem, published 1642.

ferme ornée, a maid treated us with tea which was very acceptable.

Have I told you that the Duke of Roxburgh[1] and family are to be my neighbours at that house?

6th August. On the Saturday, the third day of the Smythes' reign, I carried them about 8 miles to a Mrs. Hart's, who lives on t'other side Ascot Heath, who has a fine garden and *ferme ornée à la Southcote* (but not equal to his, in my opinion). Mrs. Clayton preferred it greatly. But a fine cascade, which falls and roars only when company stays, disgusted me, who should be apt to form my villa for myself, not strangers.

I do not enter into a particular description of these places, because I cannot help flattering myself that you will one day see these things with me. Next May, I flatter myself, you will return, and the little leisure you will have for the country will, I suppose, be spent here. You cannot imagine how many schemes I form to receive and entertain you. It has kept me awake many an hour. I adorn myself, I dress my children, I decorate my house. You arrive! I figure to myself your looks, your words. As for mine, they will be few—I shall be past speaking. Sometimes I cannot determine whether I shall be dressed in blue, or white, or yellow, or red, or green. My last resolves were white, I think, for sure 'twill be another marriage and I once more a bride, happier than the first time by as much as I am enriched with 3 beautiful infants, as well as the means of maintaining and endowing them. Thus have we gained great riches since our marriage, and hope we shall not be less rich in love and affection, esteem and friendship for each other.

10th August. But I wander from my history and do not tell you the half what I have seen.

Lord and Lady Folkestone make it a rule to go see everything within their reach, and would have my company. That cannot

[1] Robert, 2nd Duke. He was a grandson of Daniel, Earl of Winchilsea. He married Essex, daughter of Sir Roger Mostyn, and his two daughters, at this time 4 and 2 years old, were afterwards bridesmaids to Queen Charlotte.

always be, but to-morrow I meet 'em at the lodge in order to go with 'em to Beaconsfield. And Saturday last they treated us, as well as Norris's, with a fine tour. All met here to breakfast and set out first for Ditton, where we saw house and gardens—in both, many traits of the master. An hospital for dogs, quotations from Rabelais and many such things said, "We belong to His Grace of Montagu."

From this cousin of yours, we proceeded to another cousin, the Duke of Marlborough's Island.[1] The road *entre deux* the most agreeable in the world. This, I thought very pretty, and being what the country folks would call the Duke of Marlborough's folly, I must say I think it the most excusable of all his expensive ones. 'Twould have been worth as much again if it had been nearer his house (Langley) which, by the way, I hear is to be sold, but not knowing whether you would like it or the country about it, I have made no enquiries, my heart still fixed at Hatchlands.

12*th August*, 1748. I think I carried the Smythes to the 3rd day of their stay, which was the last, and then wandered away to something of a later date, whereas I should have made you accompany them as far as Uxbridge in their way to Hertfordshire, for so far did your wife, your son and cousin Julia attend them. Mr. Smythe treated us at the Crown at Uxbridge with a very good dinner and 'tis not easy to describe how much your son felt himself a man of consequence, to dine at an Inn, to sit up at the table with all that company and see the whole town of Uxbridge go to and from Church (for 'twas Sunday). After tea drinking, we parted with these agreeable companions; they proceeded on to Hertfordshire and we got home a little before sunset.

Now to return to Lord Folkestone's expedition, which I left in the island. I must, therefore, re-embark it and land safe at Windsor, where his Lordship had provided a most magnificent entertainment—champagne and what not.

As our Inn was the White Hart, I could not help looking for the chamber where we spent a night—the first I had ever spent

[1] See *ante*, p. 86.

at an Inn. Does my love remember it? I likewise called you to mind at the Duke of Marlborough's island (as indeed, I do at most places). I knew you had been there, for one evening, long since, when you and I loved one another and told it only by our eyes, I remember being greatly disappointed with not finding you at Lucy's; but soon you entered and I revived. You told us you had been at the island aforesaid and gave us such a description of it that, when I saw it, I recollected the painter and found his picture was just. Particularly I remember your description of the grotesque figures of monkeys fishing, etc.

I should say something to you of our famous races. I was at those of Datchet 2 of the days, once in my own equipage and once with Mr. Norris, whose Blossoms (for so he calls his sorrel nags) made a gallant appearance, as well as his 3 men on horseback.

Since this, there has been races at Ascot Heath, where was little sport but much company. The first day we, as well as the Norris's, dined at Lady Folkestone's and went to the race after dinner. The second day, I went on purpose to delight my boy, who has a very great passion for chaises, wheels and carriages of all sorts, down to a wheelbarrow, so I fancied he would be vastly happy in the midst of so many, and indeed he was. I, too, had my share of diversion, both in seeing the raptures of that sweet child, and in being spectator of as good a heat as ever was run—between a horse of Mr. Greenwood's and one of Mr. Panton's. The latter won, but when I saw them, 'twas impossible to say which was foremost.

At these races, Mr. Withers of Carshalton had a grey horse ran and fell lame. Mr. Bowles of Windsor ran one with better success, and there is a match for next Thursday between it and one of Mr. Jennison's. One of Lord Portmore's was entered, but he drew it because he would not sell it for 80 guineas in case it won, which was an article at starting.

19th August, 1748—Happy days! The third day of the race, which was last Wednesday, I went to fetch Miss Vansittart, who appointed me to meet her there. We had no sport, so got home soon and the Norris's drank tea with us.

All yesterday we stayed at home quietly, regardless of the race. And this morning Mrs. Vansittart has been here to breakfast and to carry away her daughter, whom I thought I should have regretted extremely, as she is a most agreeable companion; but this good day has brought me such good news that I care for nobody nor nothing. I have had a letter from Mr. Cleveland to tell me YOU ARE WELL!

I praise the Almighty providence, who has preserved you through so many dangers to such distant climes, and pray for a continuance of His blessing on all you undertake. These sentiments become the birthday of my dearest Admiral, which has been celebrated here by everyone of us. Cousin Julia, Brother Will, and myself, adorned with new ribands, drank bumpers of Malmsey. The children, too, had each their proper bumper of Malmsey, and the two eldest repeated the toast, which was health and success and many happy days to Papa. The servants had a flowing bowl of punch, and the evening concluded with songs and dances and all demonstrations of joy.

21st August, 1748. Thus was the 19th of August remembered by us and, as I hinted before, the morning was ushered in by a most welcome letter from Mr. Cleveland to inform me that Mr. Mostyn had fallen in with the Dutch East India Fleet, by which he had learnt that you arrived the Cape on the 29th of March, was in perfect health the 13th of April, and your fleet and troops most remarkably healthy. Cleveland adds that all your dispatches were in the Dutch East India Company's packet, which could not be opened till it came into Holland, so that I must expect my letters from thence, which I do with a great deal of impatience, mingled with joy. Mr. Cleveland has promised me as soon as they come he will send an express hither with them, which is very agreeable, else I should not be quiet here.[1]

But, as no pleasures are unmixed, so this welcome intelligence of Mr. Cleveland is accompanied by another by no means so acceptable, viz.: that the *Syren* (which carries your orders to come home) is not yet sailed. What can she be detained

[1] These letters did not reach her for another four weeks, see Chapter VIII.

for? 'Tis well I have had something to put me in my sweetest humour, else I should be vastly peevish at this delay.

Ramsay comes here to-night to take his leave of us, for he sets out for Scotland the day after to-morrow. The wretch has neither been here nor wrote since we were at the Duke of Argyll's some two months ago, so that he hardly deserves a welcome.

Meanwhile, I ought to give you some account of our journey to Beaconsfield, which was very agreeable, both because we had good weather and I was in high spirits with my late happy news. Mr. Waller's is a fine place;[1] fine water, charming beech woods, pretty buildings, a prospect rather *riante* than extensive. And, above all, one of the finest rooms I ever saw and in the prettiest place, for 'tis situate at the head of a large piece of water, on each side of which the verdant banks ascend and are crowned at the top with beech. The room is 45 foot long, 30 wide and 30 high; the ceiling coved and the whole room more ornate than I ever saw one. I named it the Temple of Apollo, for many of the ornaments dictate that title. It is joined to the house by a corridor, and the family always dine there in summer.

22nd August, 1748. Ramsay arrived here last night after we had supped, and goes back again to-night. We have been entertaining him with Windsor Castle this morning, where I should have yawned vastly if it had not been for my pretty son, whom I carried to divert him. And he asked, "Who painted that?" as smartly as any connoisseur.

Ramsay takes this supplement to town with him to-night, which makes me end it abruptly.

Adieu. I long to hear from you. Oh, dear mail from Holland, make haste.

---

[1] Hall Barn, now the property of Brigadier the Hon. Frederick Lawson, D.S.O.; but the room on the lake was unhappily destroyed by fire at the end of the eighteenth century.

CHAPTER VII

A FOOTMAN GETS THE SMALLPOX

ENGLEFIELD GREEN,
26th August, 1748.

MY DEAREST HUSBAND,

Your children are well!

I sent you yesterday an additional packet to go by the *Syren* Man of War. Ramsay took charge of it to deliver it to Mr. Cleveland.[1] I thought her a long time setting out and grow very impatient to hear she is sailed. Not being so exact and clever as you, I have neglected to number the letters I have sent you. All I know is that I have always one on the anvil and am, therefore, always ready on the shortest summons. Mr. Hume and Cleveland have promised me too that no ship shall go without my knowledge, and indeed, 'twould be monstrous if there did.

I wish I knew of anything else would be acceptable to my dearest husband beside letters. *Les petits presens entretiennent l'amitié*, but I can't guess what sort of presents would be useful or pleasing to my love, so all I can do is to study to make him a handsome present when he comes home of the most beautiful, most healthful children that ever were seen, with the most tractable tempers and the most engaging behaviour. To preserve these is my delight and my study.

'Twill be some time before my letters are tolerably cheerful for I have had a great distress, and my spirits are much oppressed by it. I would not mention it in my last letter to you, because you might have feared bad consequences from it, and must have been three or four months in cruel uncertainty and without knowing whether all was safe or not. For the misfortune is no less than one of my servants dead of the smallpox. Not in the

---

[1] Secretary to the Admiralty.

house, you may imagine, but you will wonder how any one got into my house without having had it. Why, the poor fellow was assured by his parents that he had had it, and these people were so persuaded of it themselves, that 'twas hardly possible to convince them their son died of that distemper.

He was an excellent servant—succeeded Leonard, whom you know I always disliked and turned away as soon as I was enough settled in town to look out for a new one. This, named Daniel, I took from my Father's, where he officiated while one of theirs was sick, and came down with me hither, where last month he was ill of a cold and fever, and blooded. The next day, my servant took me in private and told me she was sure Daniel would have the smallpox and that it was actually come out.

I shall never forget that hour, nor the terror it threw me into. My three children and my cousin! I recollected how solemnly Daniel had told me he had had it. Mrs. Marshfield, my servant, said he persisted in that, so far as that his parents had told him so; but that 'twas in his cradle and he did not remember it. Marshfield assured me she had seen many, and that it actually was the smallpox.

Upon this occasion, my fears lent me judgment, for I directed and conducted the whole without the assistance of anybody. I find everybody around me as stupid as horses, and rather marring than advancing my designs. The difficulty was where to lodge him, the lord of the manor having (very humanely) pronounced destruction upon anyone that should harbour a person sick with that disease. Another difficulty was concealing it from poor Julia. Both these difficulties I got over —the first by the sole force of God, the last by great ingenuity and contrivance.

I affected to suppose that Daniel was well and would wait at table, he actually having been down that morning. Meanwhile, I sent ample instructions to the apothecary to come with a message from one of my neighbours (by way of showing 'twas a chance visit). Then I told him that if the man was within, whom he blooded yesterday, I would have him see whether he was quite well, for the poor fellow had had no sleep all night for a cough. Accordingly, the apothecary goes out and makes report that he had got a cough and sore eyes, in short, a violent cold. But, at these words of cough and sore eyes, I pretended to take the alarm and said, "sure, it won't be the measles? For God's sake, go and ask if he has had 'em."

This farce was all carried out before my cousin, as you may believe, and nothing less than such strong prepossessions would have signified.

Mr. Dancer comes back and reports the man had never had the measles.

"Then," cries I, "he goes out of the house this very night."

"Oh no, madam, there is no occasion for that. If it be the measles, 'twon't come out yet."

"Very well," answered I, "and, if it be not the measles, I'll fetch him home again and there's no harm done."

In short, contrary to all Mr. Dancer's reasons, I affirmed he should be moved that night, when alas! both of us knew we could get no place to send him to.

In the evening, however, by great industry and greater promises, we found a woman who had been used to nurse people with the smallpox, and who took him in for the sake of the money. So I got a close post-chaise, which drove up to the door, and he was safely put into it with the apothecary's man— and the smallpox out upon him.

When I heard the chaise roll away, I began to breathe, but from ten in the morning to 7 at night I was in an agony not to be described.

You won't wonder, I dare say, that I have told you such a long and tedious tale of it, as it made so deep an impression on me, for, since I parted from you, I have never suffered so much.

6th September, 1748. I must say one word more of poor Daniel, lest it should occur to you (as is natural) that there was a method more prudent than that which I took, viz: removing to London. This I thought of, but the weather was sultry hot and dog days, so I feared lest, if I should remove my children to a place where they must of necessity be confined, after having been in the air all day (which a grove behind the house and another before enabled them to be), I might make 'em sick that way. Indeed, I might have carried them to Boxley. That I thought of, too; but then the objection was—supposing they had already taken the infection (for now this poor wretch said he had been ill for some time), the journey would then be extremely dangerous in hot weather, besides the removing them from the assistance of everybody on whom I could depend.

In short, I was to a great degree miserable, and for some days could neither eat nor sleep, nor hardly speak. All I could have done was to write my distress to my dearest husband. This would have relieved me, but have been death to him, so I refrained and, what was more difficult, wrote to you about this and that and t'other in a seeming cheerful strain. Indeed, when he had been gone about a week, I was pretty easy, because I saw my children well and because he had manifestly got no harm by being removed; an apprehension which had given me great uneasiness.

At length, upon the fourteenth day, he died, poor creature and I was most extremely concerned for him. He had the confluent sort, and in so violent and terrible a manner that Mr. Dancer had great fears of him from the beginning. However, they abated about the tenth day and he began to think him in a safe way. So much the greater was my disappointment when he failed.

And now, my dearest, do not let my concealing this event from you in my last make you distrust the veracity of my letters—a thing I have always held sacred, and without which letters cease to be any information, and consequently any satisfaction. No, my love, I will never conceal anything from you, who have the right to know all that happens to me, and therefore, if it should please God to send me any affliction, instead of the blessings He has hitherto continued to me, you should certainly know it. Your fortitude and strength of mind would enable you to struggle with it much better than I, poor wretch, could do. But, thank God, no such trials are sent to us, and when I wrote you that your wife and children were perfectly well, I told you the literal truth and should have as plainly told you the state of the poor servant if it had been determined either way, either by death or recovery. But uncertain as it was, 'twould have been madness to have mentioned it, as it must have filled your mind with fears which have happily proved entirely groundless. And, as to Julia, I so well deceived her, that now if anyone was to tell her Daniel died of the smallpox, she would not believe them.

CHAPTER VIII

A VISIT TO OXFORD

9th September, 1748.

AND now, my dearest husband, I have done with distresses and have nothing but pleasing stories to tell you, at least I shall have (I trust) in another week, for the Smythes are returned from Bounds, and they have a mind—and so have I—to go and see the world. 'Twas some time debated where. Stowe was talked of, but at length 'twas decided for Oxford, and decided chiefly by Captain Butler, who, coming to see Julia one morning, told her that if we went to Oxford he would give us a letter of recommendation to Dr. King, Principal of St. Mary's Hall.[1]

Accordingly, having sworn all my maids that they will never once go out of the place till I return, and that 3 of 'em, viz. the two nursery maids and Marshfield, will watch and attend the children night and day; also, having desired Mr. Dancer, the apothecary, to call every evening to know whether they are well, and ordered Beuvregny to write to me every evening; all these human precautions taken, and prayers being offered to THE GREAT PRESERVER for them, I set out next Monday, the 12th.

Till I return, adieu.

19th September, 1748. Returned safe from Oxford, and have found all my children in perfect health and spirits, God be praised. Boy looking like a full blown rose; Fanny blithe as

[1] William King, at this time 63 years old, had been Principal of St. Mary's Hall since 1719, and was one of the last adherents of the Stuarts in Oxford. He built the east side of his Hall, and his monument in the chapel quaintly records that "though he had faults he had also merits." He was a friend of Swift, who highly praised some of his writings.

a bird; Bessy vastly improved, talking almost everything and having gained a vast deal of language since I have been gone. In short, they are all improved and I can hardly believe 'tis but a week since I saw them. The pleasure is exquisite to see 'em thus, after having been a week deprived of 'em. For, to tell you the truth, I have pined after 'em a little and have often wished myself at home and wondered how I could have come out, though at the same time I had all the satisfaction in my journey that I could dream of.

The history of it I must reserve for the leisure of Boxley, being to set out for London next Thursday in our way to that place, so that the few days between this and then will be fully employed in settling affairs and paying debts, for I come here no more *en famille*, and we leave it with heavy hearts, for the weather is fine and the place is delightful. But duties must be performed both at Boxley and St. Clere, where I promised I would visit my father to get off going to Tunbridge. And he is in such good humour with me that he has laid out ten guineas (the Smythes say) in a fairing of Dresden china for me.

BOXLEY. *26th September*, 1748. Safe arrived here this day with all your children in perfect health. But before I begin the history of my travels, I must tell my dearest husband that I have had the satisfaction to receive his sixth, seventh and eighth letters, for which I return him a thousand thanks.[1] I won't pretend to describe what joy these letters give me. Mrs. and Mr. Smythe were by when I read them and, if they had consulted my eyes, they might have supposed they were full of bad news. As to Julia, she is too much used to cry over letters to wonder what was the matter. And as soon as I was able, I imparted all the good news—the first and chiefest, your good health, which God long preserve! I rejoiced afterwards in the health and good state of all under you; in the respect and regard paid to you by everybody; in your grandeur, and in every circumstance of content and satisfaction you have enjoyed

[1] These letters, posted from the Cape, the first she had received from her Admiral for eight months, were the letters she had expected since 21st August (see Chapter VI). The special messenger from the Admiralty delivered them to her at Henley on her way back from Oxford.

during your residence at the Cape—for repose I cannot call it. However, I have long thought that business and even fatigue agrees with you and therefore I am easy on that head.

The only secret I have for remaining easy is not to attend you any further than the Cape. In the East Indies, I see you marching with all your train of magnificence through aromatic groves; my imagination refreshes you with spicy gales, cools your thirst with delicious drinks and fruits of exquisite taste. I see your sumptuous tent; I hear the martial sounds, and behold all the pompous circumstance of glorious war. But further than this—I durst not go. I never suffer myself to think of it, but give one great leap from thence home—to our meeting, to our joy, to our happiness!

And now I must give you an account of our Oxford journey. I begin with telling you we set out from Englefield Green on Monday, 12th September, at 3 o'clock in the afternoon; Mr. and Mrs. Smythe, Julia and I in the landau, drawn by Punch and Nob, Silver and Ball, and conducted by Wm. Fletcher. Other attendants we had—2 servants on horseback of Mr. Smythe's, and one of mine, viz: Tom (Shorehamite) upon old Rockwood. We proceeded then, with the finest weather in the world, to Henley, where we had both time and opportunity to have seen Park Place, but I would not believe we were near it till we got below the hill.

Alighted at the Inn, which was on the banks of the Thames, we ordered tea and chose our beds and sallied forth to walk; pursued the course of the river, which conducted us first to the house of Squire Cooper, and afterwards to the seat of Squire Freeman.[1] After this, we compassed the town and regained our Inn at close of day. I began to be more chatty at tea-time and supper, soon after which we retired, and poor Julia and I discovered we had made a very injudicious choice of a room with two beds and (as we thought) with every other good quality—and if every, then sweetness, to be sure, among the first. But alas, when we came to shut down our sashes at 10 o'clock, and to go to bed, so barbarous a stink assaulted our noses that, after having accused each other for some time, we

[1] Fawley Court.

joined in resolving not to lie there. But alas, the maid told us the house was full. The Smythe's generously offered to change with us, but, after some deliberation, we decided to bear the stink rather than lie together. And this stink was no other than a place to refresh nature, happily situated just at our bed's head. So—after making a libation of lavender water to the Goddess Cloacina and muttering many words—we retired to rest.

I should not omit to tell you that, not willing to part with the title you gave me of "La Belle Questionneuse," I asked the maid going to bed whether the morning sun or the evening came into our chamber. "Both, ma'am," says she, "both morning and evening." Observe that the room had only windows one way, which a few hours convinced us were to the East, for, soon after six, the glorious sun visited our apartment and persuaded us to rise before 7.

The Smythe's too were up, and they and I attended 5 barges a little way up the river, whilst the careful Julia got the breakfast.

About 9 we departed from Henley, and at 1[1] arrived at the Angel Inn, Oxford, which I should first have made you admire from the top of the hill before you come into the city—the view is, indeed, very fine. No sooner were we arrived and had ordered our dinner, but we sent our credentials to Dr. King, who with great politeness waited on us immediately, but so august was his mien, so magisterial his air, that I thought we should be better without him, and considered him as one that was "*tout hérissé de Grec, tout bouffi de Science.*" But never was anyone more mistaken, for in the afternoon that he walked with us to a college or two, and afterwards conducted us to his own apartment to drink tea, this formidable, learned man became the best, the easiest companion in the world, told a thousand pleasant stories, listened to and entered into anything we would say, and for humbug and all manner of pleasantry, excels Ramsay in his best of humours.

With this incomparable Dr. King, this excellent old man, we passed all our time during our stay at Oxford. We were at his house by 8 in the morning, where we found the breakfast spread in a room perfumed with tuberoses and adorned

---

[1] Distance twenty-three miles, time four hours, or six miles an hour.

(I may say *adorned* because they were Vandykes and Sir Peter Lely's) with the heads of the Charles's and James's, Prince Rupert, Duke of Monmouth, etc. Presently the Doctor appeared, as gay and good-humoured as could be, and then came the Brown George (*alias* hot roll).

Breakfast dispatched, and everyone satisfied, which was the work of time and the reputed endeavours of several Brown Georges, we attended the Doctor to visit this or that College— for we saw almost all, as well as the theatre, the printing house, the public schools, the Bodleian Library, the picture gallery, the New Radcliffe Library, the physic garden. And we did not see them hastily, for we continued to walk from a little before 10 to a little before 2. And, in all the time we were there, we had never one sour day, so that we had many pleasant walks, on the banks of Isis and the Charwell—the latter called Maudlin Walks, as they belong to the College of St. Mary Magdalen. Christ Church Walk too, is very fine and the Mall of the place, but there was no company, no Collegians in the University when we were there, it being the middle of their long vacation and the deadest time of the year.

At two, we went to dinner in our Inn. Sometimes the Doctor dined with us; if not, we called upon him about 5 and spent one hour more in our inquisitive walks, and these of the afternoon were chiefly confined to buildings, as those in the morning were (as much as we could) in gardens and groves.

Soon after 6, we were again housed at the Doctor's, who gave us charming good tea, of which he drinks vast quantities. And, as to College bread and College butter—'tis indeed beyond compare! From teatime to supper was always spent in the most agreeable manner imaginable—that is, in the most easy and lively conversation. For our good Doctor knows everybody, is a particular friend of Lord Chesterfield's, as he was of Dean Swift, Dr. Arbuthnot, etc. About 9, he used to send for a bill of fare from his cook—that is, the cook of St. Mary's Hall—and indeed, they were extraordinary ones for their plenty and variety. From these we chose our supper, which he offered as heartily as we accepted, and about 10 we parted—he always attending us to the door of our Inn, not out of ceremony, but to have so much more of our company, for, says he, "Us monks ought to think ourselves happy when we can get into society. And, for my part, when I find that I don't relish (Oxford) company, I get upon my horse that minute, ride to London and see no more of books and colleges for three months." In short, my dearest, I was in love with Dr. King, and if you are to have a rival, methinks you will bear one of threescore as well as younger.

Our first excursion out of Oxford was to see Ditchley, where my Lady[1] was asleep, having been at a ball at Cornbury,[2] which saved all ceremonies between her and me, but deprived us at the same time of the pleasure of seeing Cornbury, which is fine *à l'ancienne* as Ditchley is *à la moderne*. From hence, then, we came back to Blenheim, which we had heard was not to be seen but between the hours of 2 and 4. 'Twas about half an hour past one when we asked whether we might have the favour to see the house. The porter said no, 'twas not two o'clock. So we moved off; and when we heard the clock strike, returned again, and were going to get out of the coach, but the porter bid the servant not open the door, for the bell had not rung. At length the bell rung, and he conducted us to the hall door, where we sat on the plinth of the pillars about ten minutes before any servant came to show us the house. At length, a dirty lad appeared and led us through the hall and saloon to the two rooms hung with tapestry; thence into the gallery, from whence the fine Titians are taken away, so there we were disappointed. We likewise went into the chapel, and then he told us we had seen all we could see. So we went and dined at Woodstock, ill satisfied with our cousin (for his Grace is the same relation to Mr. Smythe by his father's side as he is to you by his mother's) who, we thought not very polite to make his relations wait so long for a sight of his house, even after the hour he had appointed, and then not let them see it at last.

But I bestow more paper upon this subject than 'tis worth—

[1] Charlotte Lee, wife of 11th Viscount Dillon.
[2] At Cornbury was a collection of Vandykes, formed by the great Lord Chancellor Clarendon.

so, adding only that I was not at all pleased with Blenheim—nor the manners of Blenheim—I proceed to give an account of a more agreeable expedition, and that was to Kirtlington Park, a fine seat built by Sir James Dashwood. Here we found my agreeable friend, Miss Vansittart, who had prepared breakfast for us and shewed us the house. The butler waited on us afterwards to say Sir James and my Lady desired we would do them the honour to dine with them, which we civilly declined, being engaged to Dr. King. But we had observed in the eating parlour that our 4 covers were laid and, before we went away, Sir James and my Lady both came to us and with great politeness lamented they could not have the pleasure of our company. We walked over the building, which is, indeed, very noble; the gardens he is going to put into the hands of Greening, so I could not recommend North. I complimented them on their children, which are good, pretty ones, but not to compare with yours. As to Sir James—whether he looked particularly handsome that morning, I know not—but Mrs. Smythe confessed she was much smitten with him. For my part, I came off heart-whole, being possessed with Dr. King, with whom we spent the remainder of that day and the next morning, which was Sunday; then took our leave of him, he, as well as we, expressing much satisfaction in the week we had spent together and we assuring him of our gratitude and respect.

Set out from Oxford Sunday afternoon and arrived at Henley at 6. There, happy to a great degree in receiving my dearest husband's letters, which found me most agreeable employment for the whole evening; avoided our stinking chamber and rose early, being in haste to get to Englefield and see my sweet babes. Our company would have been glad to have stopped at Cliveden, but, as I wanted one of those with whom I had visited that place, I was sure it would have no charms for me and therefore voted to go straight home, which was readily agreed to and accomplished about 2 of the clock.

Thus ended our expedition to Oxford, which was extremely pleasant and attended with no cross accident, or inconvenience, not so much as a shower of rain. My share of the charges amounted to 8 guineas, including horses.

CHAPTER IX

FANNY'S JOURNAL, OCTOBER–NOVEMBER, 1748

BOXLEY,
7th October, 1748.

I NOW return to my journal. We left our sunny home at
Englefield on 22nd September, after dinner. Mr. Smythe's
coach-and-4 marched first, with he and she, Julia and I and my
son. Afterwards followed mine with my two daughters,
the two nursery maids and my own servant Mrs. Marshfield; and we arrived in London about 6. There we took
leave of our good friends the Smythes, and, as soon as Julia
and I had seen the children settled in Audley Street, we proceeded to Berkeley Square, the courageous Julia walking the
streets and defying the smallpox. There we found Charles,
almost spent and worn out in the service of the firework which
is to be at the peace,[1] his wife reclining on her couch, and your
mother, who I thought a good deal broke.

Next day we dined with the Fredericks, and on proceeding
home through Hyde Park, I met Phil Medows, as if he had
never moved, no more than the walnut trees. An explanation,
you may be sure, on both sides, and then:—"What brought
you to town" and "what brought you to town"—Why, said
he, he was come to attend Lady Frances in her lying in; was I
going to lie in likewise? I told him no; I had just laid in, in
private, and was come to take the air, as he might see. This
point settled, we agreed to spend the afternoon together, which

[1] The Treaty of Aix-la-Chapelle was finally signed on this very day,
7th October 1748. On 24th October, Sir Horace Walpole was writing:
"The peace is signed between us, France and Holland, but does not give
the heart joy . . . there has not been the least symptom of public rejoicing;
but the Government is to give a magnificent firework." A space of two
acres had been enclosed in the Green Park for the fireworks, with a covered
stand, 800 feet long and 76 feet wide, for the "nobility and gentry."

we did—in Brook Street. Present, Lady Frances and Phil, Mrs. Bretton, Mr. Fortescue Seaman, Mr. and Mrs. Frederick, Julia and I, who had all dined together in Berkeley Square. We spent the evening with Miss Grenville at my house.

Mr. Geary I enquired after, but he was married and gone to Polesden, where I addressed a congratulatory epistle to his bride, whom he has made very fine in diamond earrings, solitaire, and buckle. This is Norris's intelligence, who has been to see us since we came to Boxley and has resided near two months on board the *Prince Frederick*[1]—much to his discontent and still more to his poor wife's, who is a proverb with us by way of fondness, for no company, no servants, no nothing, can keep hands off. Julia has been inconvenient enough to seat herself between them sometimes, and then they kiss over her shoulders, which has diverted me much.

But, to return to my journal. On Sunday, the 25th September, we set out for St. Clere. Only 7 in the coach—that is to say, 3 babes, their mother, cousin and 2 maids, all *sans* hoop! Our march through the city was easy on account of the day.

At Foots Cray we were met by a servant on horseback, and a pair of horses with a postilion, for such was my father's pleasure, at whose feet we arrived at 3; Madame vastly gracious and kind, he commending the children for the finest that ever were seen, but not choosing to bear their noise (that is, their play, for they never cry) a minute. And your boy will tell you that "Grandpapa says I was born in a storm because I talk so loud."

Next morning we set out again, bag and baggage, for this place, where we arrived by dinner time—found my aunt, as well as her nephew and his lady, much as they all were when you were here last. My aunt (who being now in her 88th year, is really a miracle) is vastly fond of all the children and has always one or two of them playing in her room.

13*th October*, 1748. We have been to see Lady Romney who has lately lain in of a boy.[2] I carried mine, who towers

---

[1] Norris was still Captain of the *Prince Frederick*.
[2] Hon. John Marsham, born 1748, died young.

above all hers, both in height and learning, which is no small honour to him and me, since the eldest Marsham will be six years old next spring, and there is more pains taken with them than with most children. Nevertheless, your son beats him all to nothing.

Your son has also been to Church every Sunday and has behaved extremely well. Mr. Gore asked if he could. sing Psalms. He said no, but he could sing the *Rakes of Marlow*, if that would do. In short, he is a charming child.

14th October, 1748. This day twelvemonth we parted. I can shudder at the thought of it, but am thankful that my mind is now at ease and not as it was then, when I did not say much, nor desire everybody I met to pity me. But, when I returned to town, every creature said to me, "How you are fallen away" and I believed them. But I am since arrived at a great composure of mind—always think the best and never look on the dark side of the pillar, or raise devils. No, I always suppose my husband successful, triumphant, returning home with health, riches and honour. I suppose him vastly well pleased when he is come home: thinking his wife the best of all wives and his children the loveliest of all children. Thus, my dearest, I paint the scene and, fixing my eyes on so pleasing a prospect, I keep them free from tears, unless now and then a tender thought or a kind letter steal a few, almost unknown to me.

19th October. Mrs. Roche, Commander Brown's daughter, is going to be married to Capt. O'Hara, whom we are told intends to eat off plate, and has bought a very handsome service for that purpose. Without having the honour to know the gentleman, one may venture to prophecy that, with that Irish name and that Irish wife, he'll certainly come to the necessity of eating plates and all. I am, however, glad this jaunty widow is going out of the way of our poor friend Parry.[1]

[1] Later Admiral William Parry.

AUDLEY STREET,
8th November, 1748.

Your children are well and settled in winter quarters.

It is high time I should resume the pleasing custom of writing to my dearest husband, which has been for some time interrupted. But my dear knows I never write to him when I am in distress, and he will easily believe I have been in a good deal when I tell him I have lost my good, excellent old aunt! You know I have had always a very sincere affection and duty for her and it has been heightened, if possible, by her kindness to me, which she expressed by the last action of her life.

A few days after I wrote you last, which was the 19th October, my poor aunt was taken ill, but, as it was usual for her at this season, she made light of it, said 'twas a thing of course, and we, too, flattered ourselves 'twas nothing more. It confirmed us, however, in our resolution of going away on the 24th, because she did not love to have anybody see her when she is ill. So we parted, and it affected both her and me more than usual. I promised I would come to her again at Easter and bring the children for a month. This seemed to delight her, but still it was not without many tears that we parted, were kindly received at St Clere and, on the Friday following, the 28th, we (Julia and I) set out for Rooksnest, according to my promise to deliver her there into the hands of her parents, who had spared her to me for 6 months.

At Rooksnest, I was not at all happy or in spirits. We were a great company, but no society, for they played at Pharo, a most detestable game in my mind, which absolutely shuts out all talk. For my part, I played at Quadrille in a grave way with my uncle and aunt Evelyn and Mrs. Boone, the Pharo table consisting of Mr. and Mrs. Clayton and Mr. Boone and James Evelyn. The poor Julia (having got the Mumps) cherished herself by the fireside.

The Felbridge family stayed all night. We kept sad hours, but nevertheless I got up before 8 in order to return to dine at St. Clere. Mrs. Boone put into the coach—unknown to me—a very fine present for our son; a silver ship made in

India, a very curious thing, and has gone by clockwork, but the spring is now out of order. 'Tis still, however, a fine thing and, as I have told her, a present fitter for Prince Edward than Cousin Edward.

But I dwell thus long at Rooksnest, not caring to think of what happened e'er I got to St. Clere. At Chepsted my father met me and told me I had lost my aunt. She died that morning, 29th October. Mr. Gore had sent Thomas over to acquaint me with it and to insist on my coming there, for that I was joint Executor with him, and he would not open the Will nor order the funeral till I came, which I had in the utmost horror, and would have refused it, but my father said I must.

So I went there the next day. I won't tell you how much I suffered. You know me to have as much softness of disposition as would make me very miserable in a house where a dear friend lay dead, and where I had so lately seen her well, and giving me a thousand proofs of her kindness and affection. That she died with the same kind disposition towards me will be ever a satisfaction to me; 'tis a proof I did my duty and approved myself to her.

As soon as she apprehended her end was near, she declared she would make a Will. Mr. Gore said, "Is it possible, madam, you have no Will by you?" "Yes," she said, but it was old and she would make a new one. In short, she was quite uneasy till she had cancelled this old Will (which was entirely in his favour, I having only a legacy) and made a new one, by which she leaves all she had equally between her nephew and me, directing that if either of us died without heirs of our body, then it was to come to the other and their heirs. So, you see, she meant us and our dear boy all the time, giving Mr. Gore (who had swallowed all) only his life in half.

'Twill be small, very small, addition to our fortune, my love, but I own I set a high value on it as it expressed hers for me. As soon as ever she had made this Will, she was easy. She said no more on any earthly subject. Her senses left her in a few minutes, as if she had kept them together by force till this Will was signed, and, in about twelve hours after that, she expired.

11th November, 1748. Soon after I came to that dismal house, Mr. Gore gave me to understand that I should stay there till after the funeral. I told him 'twas impossible, and indeed, he was glad to let me go again when he found I could not be cheerful, nor was likely to be well long. In the meanwhile, we performed many shocking offices, such as ordering the funeral, ransacking closets, cabinets, etc. (You know how unfit I am for all this.)

After G. had read the Will, he flung it away, saying there was not so much left of his Grandfather's land as that it need be minced, and he seemed much offended, more I believe for the look of the thing to the people of Boxley, and not appearing to be sole master and heir, than that he could care about the land, which will yield hardly anything after we have paid off the mortgage.

I said nothing, resolving not to quarrel with him, which he, on his side too, seemed to guard against. So we remain good friends, without having had the least jar. He muttered again afresh when we came to find the old Will written in her hand, whereby she gives him everything, without any restriction or entail; gives me a legacy of £100, some pictures and all her china. All the good I could do him at Boxley was to serve him for secretary, in which employment I continued a day, and then he was glad to let me go, as I was not at all well. Getting to St. Clere revived me. However, I have not been quite recovered till within these few days and am not now in so good spirits as I used to be.

14th November, 1748. So on Sunday, 6th of this month (the day after my poor aunt was buried) I left St. Clere, where I had had all manner of satisfaction in the friendship and kindness of the master and mistress of the house. The latter, particularly, was vastly easy and comfortable, so that I could have liked very well to have spent another fortnight there—and I had your kind letter from St. Iago[1] to mump upon every evening; I received

---

[1] Santiago, Cape Verde Islands. The Admiral must have touched Santiago on his voyage from Madeira to South Africa, and this letter had taken nine months to reach London.

it the 30th October—but, without mourning I could not stay, as everybody knew my loss and D. of Dorset told my father he heard she had left me £1,500. In short, I removed hither on the 6th; brought my young ones in perfect health to town, and had the satisfaction to see all the servants I had left behind surprised at the children's looks and affirming they were grown fat and tall and more improved that they could have conceived it possible—all ready to eat Bess, who fell a-talking to them very familiarly.

My first care was to provide victuals for 'em, and, as I had had the precaution by letter to order chicken broth, that was soon ready, but not so soon as their stomachs.

I had no sooner lost these little agreeable companions and resigned them to their pillows than I received one more agreeable, viz: your large packet of letters. I have read 'em over and over, still finding new matter for joy and gratitude, for your affection and esteem for me and the repeated kind expressions you give me of it. After this, my love, will you say your letters are insignificant? Can anything be so significant to me as that my dear husband loves me, thinks of me every day, notwithstanding the vast multiplicity of affairs that surrounds him, that I possess his heart, his thoughts, his tenderest wishes. Can that be insignificant? Oh, no, my dearest, 'tis the most important news you can tell me. For that and your health I thank God with my whole heart, and pray for the continuance of them, as blessings on which the happiness of my life depends.

15th November. I was charmed to find my letters gave you such entertainment. My dearest Ned seemed over-joyed to see the characters of his dear, his faithful Fanny, and yet perhaps they did but faintly express her love, her sincere affection for him. I am happy, however, to think they were so welcome to you. As for your letters, I could dwell on 'em for weeks, answer them line by line and give you back kindness for kindness. But I must curtail these and many other *douceurs* I could bestow on my dear Admiral (Ned, methinks sounds too familiar for so great a man), for Mr. Cleveland informs me the *Dragon*—I would it were a flying one—is to sail forthwith.

I must, therefore, think of finishing my packet, or at least winding it up, and first I will give you an account of your family and friends, keeping your children *pour la bonne bouche.*

Mrs. Evelyn is in Grosvenor Square, waiting for the good hour, and intends to suckle her child herself. I can't think but she will make a bad nurse—at least, I know I would not hire her. But perhaps she may suit her own child better. I doubt it won't suit herself, but I wish I may be mistaken. She is extremely hoarse, but not quite a whisper as it was.

Mr. and Mrs. Frederick[1] are in Berkeley Square—he the busiest, she the idlest, mortal living. He is in the Green Park from 8 in the morning till 4 in the afternoon, has an office built there for him. The rest of the day he gives audiences, and worries his spirits and his person, till 'tis reduced to a shadow. Not so the large Mrs. Lucy. She prudently cherishes herself in bed till noon, at 4 walking gravely downstairs and at night as gravely up. Seriously, she has never been out of an afternoon but once to see me and meet the Smythes, though she is perfectly well: so are her son and daughter. Little Augusta is reckoned a fine child, but my little Bess spoils me for admiring any child. If you hum a tune, instantly she seizes her frock at each side and falls a-dancing. Frances, too, is a great dancer.

Mr. Glover made me a very civil visit t'other day, but the girls were both asleep and I could not prevail with your son to dance what he calls a "hornpike", which he does vastly well, but can't prevail with his modesty to exhibit before a stranger. I have seen him try when I have pressed it extremely, but he has come running back the first step, "Mama, I'm ashamed, don't ask me to dance." But he promises himself great pleasure in dancing before dear Papa. He would do anything for you, loves you excessively and remembers you perfectly. He draws ships for Papa to sail home in and houses for Papa to live in and, drawing a waggon once, he asked me whether I did not remember how Papa made him tilts to his waggon. By this and many other such histories, I know that lovely child has a very perfect idea of you and your actions, particularly those in which he was concerned. Amongst the rest, he has not forgot the

---

[1] Sir Charles Frederick, and his wife Lucy Boscawen.

whipping. He says then he was a naughty baby in coats, but now he is a man he's sure Papa won't whip him. You will be charmed with this angel. Oh, what a meeting shall we have if God continues to bless us! I can think of it for hours and I shall talk of it too till I forget all else I had to say to you—but I return to your family and come next to your Colonel[1] and his wife.

She came to see me of an afternoon and found me at home. I went there in a day or two after, but did not find her, since which she sent to ask me. I went, and found them *tête à tête* at Backgammon. The Colonel was very good-humoured and as civil (*à sa manière*) as if he had never abused me about my apprehending his boy's smallpox, which, as I learnt it clandestinely, I shall never take any notice of.

Colonel John is probably at Helvoet[2] waiting for an Easterly wind. When it comes, and he comes, I suppose 'twont be long before we have a new sister, in whose favour I am extremely prepossessed.

17th November, 1748. So much for your family. Now for a little more of my history, and herein I must tell you I have had, for your sake, a great present. Your Lieutenant Bemish (I may properly call him yours, since you made him one) is come home in the *Dreadnought* and waited on me one morning with a black boy, which he has presented to me. I declined it as civilly as I could, as indeed such a one is only an incumbrance to me, but he assured me he had got him on purpose for me and, as I saw he had clothed him in our livery very handsomely, I thought 'twould be wrong not to accept of him. He is a good-natured child, about ten years old. Your son took to him immediately and whispered he should be his servant. Accordingly, he walks out in the garden with him, plays up in the nursery, waits upon him at table, and 'tis quite "follow my heels, Jean Ruggbi."

I fancy Lady Anson[3] is not pregnant, as Mr. Glover told me

[1] Colonel George Boscawen.
[2] Helvoetsluys, Holland. He had been on the Continent in attendance on the King.
[3] Admiral Lord Anson never had a child.

she intended to dance at the birthday. I have been to visit her to-night, Lady Norris, and Duchess of Dorset,[1] and am returned home before 9, wishing my dearest husband was here; what would I not give for a *tête à tête* supper with him! How many more tedious days and nights will there be first, my love? Christmas twelvemonth, you say—but 'twas war when you said it—now 'tis peace. Won't that hasten my dearest home?

22nd November. Last week I sent to Brindley for pamphlets, etc., and took *Lettres Peniviennes*, which I had read at Englefield and knew to be pretty, charming. Indeed, I took likewise *Les Bijoux indiscrets*, thinking to read a bit here and there, and if I found them stupid, to send 'em back again. But my dear, what a book! I am ashamed of it! I have read it right through, and because I do not wish to conceal from you the worst actions of my life, I send it to you, to show you what a wicked book has engrossed your chaste wife these last two days. But it is you, my dear love, who have caused this vulgarity, for if I had not sought your amusement, I should not have amused myself with such an improper book. Here it is, then; and it will make you laugh. You are as great as Mangogul; could you think me as loveable as Mirza? I often think of your grandeur. Monarch as you are, how will you descend to private life again!

23rd November, 1748. I have been reading once more your kind, your affectionate letter. What a variety of sensations does it cause! One moment I feel happy, exquisitely so, when you tell me you love me even better since we parted; will never cease to love me; will never forget me till you forget yourself. This is a matter of inexpressible joy. The next minute comes tears on the representation of your uneasiness and misery—for vastly miserable I can perceive you was during your tedious voyage to the Cape. Many melancholy days you spent, many pangs and conflicts you endured, which you could not conceal from your Fanny, your other self. You ask for my pity. Think how that must move me, think how I must wish

[1] Grace, daughter of Viscount Shannon, married Charles 2nd Duke of Dorset, 1743.

not to give you pity only, but assistance. At length I had that happiness that the letters brought you by Hardwick seemed to be a balsam for all sores. Oh, if any bird would fly to you with my letters I should write all day long; you should never want that cordial. As it is, the most acceptable employment I can dedicate to you is the care of our dear children, and this is my study and the pleasing business of my life.

But what became of the woman that was like me? I'm afraid 'twas a handsome likeness, but am not at all alarmed. *Je crois que vous m'avez toujours été fidèle, et que vous le serez toujours.* Most wives would tell me I have great faith. So much the better, for I have but too many subjects of anxiety and care to bear the additional one of jealousy—an evil I should have been very susceptible of if I had had the least cause.

You must know I have fixed a day for our joyous meeting. It is the auspicious nineteenth of August! In the year forty-six we met on that day, why not in the year forty-nine? And last summer, too, on the 19th August, I received the first news of your welfare at the Cape and of the very acceptable letters which were arrived from thence. In short, 'tis a day I shall celebrate, and it can be no ways so worthily celebrated as by your presence. Come then, my dearest husband, come. I shall wait for the charming summons at Englefield Green, where I propose to reside again this summer, Hatchlands (which I still think of) being neither sold nor saleable. I liked my situation last year; I know all the faults of it, and indeed it has none but being very expensive, which I solve by the goodness of the air, which agreed with the children perfectly, and by there being so much garden for them to run and play in. I have left several things at Englefield, with an intention to return, such as Delft, china, glasses, etc. I have every week from thence a hamper of green-salads and roots, even mushrooms—having a bed there—and I am to have everything of that kind in great perfection next year and shall probably be there the beginning of May. Come then, my love; come before the mulberries are all gone. I have two fine trees that used to furnish them to Queen Anne. Let me reserve them next summer for a worthier guest.

(*At* 8 *p.m.*) I intended to have gone this afternoon to Phil Medows and Lady Frances, but I have spent it in a much more agreeable manner in talking to my dearest husband. Mr. Hume[1] came in as I had dined; drank some of his own tea with me; has stayed 3 hours talking over your expedition and revealing to me the secrets of it. But about your coming home he distracts me. I can't bear the thought of another winter first. I must not, I will not, believe it.

24th November. Contrary to my expectations—another sheet, but Mr. Hume says I shall be in time enough for the *Dragon* if I send my letters next week. If I had known so much yesterday, I had gone to the play, for, in the morning, Mrs. Frere came, tempting me with Othello and a stage box and the best dance and all that could be desired.

26th November. I write so much to you that I know not what I say, but believe I have not told you that His Majesty arrived in perfect health last Wednesday at 2 in the morning, at St. James's, where he was so little expected that 'twas with some difficulty he got into his apartment and, much more, that he obtained any food or fire. He landed at Kingsgate,[2] got a hired post chaise and came through without stopping any more than was necessary to change his equipages. I have not seen His Majesty—'tis a great affair for me to go to St. James's— but I have been at Leicester House, where I had great pleasure in hearing his Royal Highness talk of my dear husband with so much affection. I shall always love the Prince for the regard he expresses towards you. He would know all about your voyage, and I told him how tedious it had been, but at the same time how healthy. I then told him how unhappy you was not to be able to obey the commands his R. Highness was pleased to honour you with, but that there was no wine when you was at the Cape which would keep the passage to

---

[1] Mr. Hume was a director of the East India Company.

[2] Leaving Helvoetsluys on Monday at 10 a.m., he had landed at Kingsgate (four miles from Margate) at 10 a.m. the next day. He had been absent from England since May.

England; that you had visited every cellar there. He said you was very kind to think of him; and I all the while thought within myself "anybody less honest than my good Admiral would have sent you any stuff they could have got for the best in the world and, when it turned out bad, would have laid it to some accident in the voyage." Upon the whole, I wish you may be able to bring him some sort of present. I think he'll take it kindly, and you can't imagine how affectionately he speaks of you.

Her R. Highness' birthday was celebrated at Leicester House, and there was a ball that everybody commended for the best conducted thing imaginable. I saw nothing of it, but I fancy I shall go and pay my duty to His Royal Highness on the 20th January. It may be but fancy, though, for I hate to pay for fine clothes; I hate the trouble of buying them and, more, the trouble of wearing them. I have had but one suit of clothes since you went and that was the yellow foreign silk[1] you gave me.

27th November, 10 p.m. I forgot to tell you that I have been at the Opera with Charles Frederick and his wife. The former was much pleased, but Lucy and I were edified no more than could be expected from a reproduction in an unknown tongue. [2] They say the actors are extremely good, which may possibly be, but as I don't know what they aim at, I cannot rejoice in it, and, if I look at my book, then I lose their gestures. As to the music, 'tis worth nothing in my humble opinion, and the dance is ten times worse, for that is slow and serious—one step with arms extended and then half an hour before there comes another. In short, more likely to put you to sleep than to make you laugh. Upon the whole, my half guineas are safe till Oratorios begin. And, as to plays, Mr. Garrick is so crowded that I have no chance of seeing him, but when some charitable

[1] Actually, at an earlier reception in 1748, the Prince of Wales, noticing that some of the men present were wearing French silks, had commanded that no one should again appear at Court in French silk; but now that peace was declared this probably did not apply.

[2] Almost certainly one of Handel's Italian operas.

body provides a place and invites me to it—a favour I expect from Madame Smythe before 'tis long.

29th November. Your brother Jack brought his lady to breakfast with me and to see a house which he and I had pitched upon, after having spent two mornings in the disagreeable employment of house-hunting. This house is in Prince's Street, Hanover Square, next door to that which Lord Stair[1] lived in. I need not add then, "'tis a bad house." *Vous le comprenez assez.* A one-eyed room and several other faults it has, but then £100 a year, a pretty garden, stables for 6 horses, and 2 coachhouses, are you'll grant, perfections. In short, the young lady approved, so 'tis taken and I have been busied in adding some little ornaments and directing the furniture, etc. Methinks I hear you whisper "*je me moque*," but I assure you I am grown a woman of business. Taste I always pretended to and must own I shall be greatly disappointed if you do not approve that which I have displayed in Audley Street. But to return to Mrs. John. After this taking of the house, I went to wait on her in Mark Lane. That is, Jack carried me in the Royal landau,[2] and because these lovers should not wish me hanged, I chose an evening when there was business to be done between Mr. Surman and Charles Frederick (who is Jack's trustee). Of course the latter must otherwise have been absent from his lady, who seemed much pleased with my visit, as did her father, who is very clever and a very polite man. So that I might be polite too, I invited him and his daughters to dinner, gave them a very elegant one, our company being only Jack, the 3 Surmans and Charles Frederick and wife, which, with myself made 7—just the number I choose at table. I won't trouble you with my bill of fare in the exact order it was. Let it suffice that I had soup, fine dish of fish, salmon and smelts, turkey, brawn, oysters, etc., partridge

[1] John Dalrymple, 2nd Earl of Stair, died 1747. A General and diplomatist, he was Commander-in-Chief of South Britain in 1744 and General of Marines, 1746.

[2] The one-horse Royal broughams to be seen in London to-day, patiently threading their way through the maze of motor traffic, are a survival of this privilege to "the ladies and gentlemen of H.M.'s Court."

ragout, fricassee, asparagus, mushrooms, mince pies, blanc manges, jellies, fruit, etc., etc. Everything extremely good of its kind, well dressed and well served. Everybody praising it, and, what pleased me better, eating very heartily. In the evening some company, and I had two tables at cards.

I like Miss Surman extremely. In short, I think Jack's a very happy fellow. I suppose he'll think himself still happier this day se'ennight when he may enjoy this fair lady's company of nights as well as days.

So much for the marriage of your brother. Now for the marriage of your mare—an affair about which I have been very anxiously concerned, I assure you. She was carried to the Great Park in May, in order for the nuptials, but with great trouble (I heard a month after) of her coyness and coldness. At length, however, by opportunity, importunity and assiduity the lover prevailed, of which I hope there will be proofs five months hence. But, in the meanwhile, I must tell you her history. I took my lady bride home to Englefield after the hay was in and after I had had the fences all round the two meadows secured. By way of a companion she had old Rockwood, whom she enticed and corrupted, taught his old limbs to jump over the gate, and so eloped. Upon this, scouts were sent to Egham and Staines, where the turnpike would have stopped them; Old Windsor, Wraysbury, and as far the other way as Virginia Water they were cried, but to no purpose. The Park, you may be sure, was the first place we enquired at, but all the gates said "No". However, we had great dependence upon the races at Ascot Heath, where we expected to see someone mounted upon our strays; and there indeed, though we did not see them, we heard of them, that they were in the Park, discovered that morning. So the next day they were brought home, and Lady Grey was confined to the stable. As to poor, stupid Rockwood, he was very well content in the field when he had not this madcap to entice him.

30th November, 1748. And now, my dear love, I think I may close this enormous letter. Mr. Mostyn, whom I had the pleasure of seeing yesterday, seems to believe you will be at home next May. This I doubt or, rather, despair of, but in August—sure, my love, in August I may be happier than I can express or you imagine. You say you will be excessively so if I love you. Depend upon it then, dearest husband, for I love you with all the tenderness, and even passion, that you can desire. Methinks it will be another wedding, and we shall live to see more than one honeymoon. Come then, my dearest, come to this fond wife, to these sweet children. Heavens prosper your voyage. Give you a safe and speedy return. Bless you with health and honour, love and peace. But—I can never express all my wishes and thoughts concerning your return; charming visions which entertain me every day.

Adieu, then, accept my love, my kindest, sincerest affection. If I knew anything else worth your acceptance, with how much pleasure should I send it but no, they tell me there is nothing. So adieu, once more. With tears I take my leave.

Ever your faithful wife,

F. BOSCAWEN.

CHAPTER X

THE ADMIRAL IN INDIA

FANNY'S hopes of her husband's early return were soon to vanish, for they had made no allowance for the very dilatory methods of Whitehall.

The peace of Aix-la-Chapelle had been ratified on 7th October, and Fanny had taken it for granted that the orders for her husband's return were already on their way. Actually however, it was not till the beginning of January that a frigate was sent to the Admiral with an "express" letter from the Admiralty, informing him of the terms of peace, instructing him that the French were to restore Madras to the British flag, and ordering him to remain on the Coromandel coast till this had been completed. In point of fact, therefore, while Fanny was weaving plans for welcoming her husband home in the summer of 1749, there was not a chance of his return till the spring of 1750.

The first horrid suspicion that her dreams could not come true began to take shape on the 23rd December—just in time to spoil her Christmas fun. On that day a young sea-officer called Captain Hugh Palliser—a name we shall meet again in the course of this story—presented himself at 14 South Audley Street with very unwelcome news. He was sailing, he said, in ten days' time with sealed orders, to be carried "express" to the Admiral, and any packets she wanted to send to her husband should be ready by the end of the month.

Fanny's picture of Captain Palliser's call is so vivid that she must be allowed to tell the story in her own words:

23rd December. An express from the Admiralty to you! Do they expect, then, that you are to be found in the Indies six months hence? What becomes of the pleasing dreams I have had about August! They vanish; and I feel as uncomfortable as people who have dreamed of happiness and wake to misery. I am low-spirited. You will find it plain enough in this dull letter, which is to be conveyed by the *Sheerness*, Captain Palliser, whose politeness I have reason to commend.

He has been here this morning, and, as I never saw him before, introduced himself by telling his errand. I desired the children should see the man who was to see their father. So, because they were eating their pudding, I carried him to them, and he admired their good looks and good appetites. He asked your son what he had to say to you, who answered, with his chops full, "I want Papa at home!" He then asked him if he would go with him, to which your son consented without the least demur, which was a great expression of his love.

But this Captain Palliser makes me angry with all other captains that have gone before him; for whenever I have been summoned for letters I have always asked "Is there nothing I can send which would be acceptable to the Admiral," and have always been answered, "No, nothing at all; he has everything in plenty." But now Captain Palliser tells me that cheese and ham would be welcome. These you shall certainly have, asking your pardon, my dear love, that this is the first time you have had any little present from me. But how monstrous it is that I have sent letters by 7 or 8 ships and could never send you a few cheeses and hams till now. I can't bear to think on't. It disturbs me. So adieu for to-day.

Christmas, we can imagine, in the face of this news, was a very dull festivity, for Fanny's journal continues:

25th December. I wish you a merry Christmas, my dear love, or rather I wish you many future ones, for I suppose this won't be a very joyous one to you, no more than to me. This is the second Christmas we have spent asunder, and you have flattered me it shall be the last. So have I hoped, too, nay, even depended; but this ship's being sent quite sinks my spirits.

Last night, being Christmas Eve, we dined with Lord and Lady Falmouth.[1] Judge whether we did not wish for another of the family to grace the feast. I'm sure I did, and heartily joined in the first toast, which was "Success and a safe return to the Admiral."

26th December. Yesterday I spent at my father's, as usual. Carried his grandson to wish him a merry Christmas. Brought him back at 7 o'clock, for you know I can never trust anyone in a coach with my children but myself.

More tiresome news was to follow, for on 28th December we read—and the story shows that shopping in London two hundred years ago was a very uncertain affair:

28th December. I've had a great disappointment. I sent Beuvregny to Mr. Potts to order him to pack up a dozen hams for the East Indies, and he sends me word there is not a new ham in town, nor won't be these three weeks, so that 'tis impossible. But 3 immense cheeses are gone. I wish they may be acceptable—and that they may meet you coming home. If I did not think *that* possible I should be too unhappy.

Weddings in the eighteenth century had nothing in common with the public parade of a London wedding to-day; for Fanny's journal of the 28th December goes on to speak of the marriage of the Admiral's brother, Colonel John Boscawen, who, as we have already seen, was marrying a Miss Surman. Jack, it will be remembered, was Equerry to the Duke of Cumberland, and a Colonel in the First Guards, and his future father-in-law was an Essex landowner, as well, apparently, as a prominent merchant in the City:

Jack has been here this morning, and I have taken leave of a

[1] Her brother-in-law and his wife, at 2 St. James's Square.

free man. Your brother Nick, who is to tie this durable knot, came with him. Both dine in the City to-day, and to-morrow repair to some church there (I don't know which); and as soon as the mystical ceremony is over they all go down to Mr. Surman's house in Essex, where the nuptials are to be celebrated. Sir Charles and Mrs. Frederick[1] go down to visit them the next day. Jack presses me to go; but I'm sure I won't till after Saturday, which is the day I send this letter to Portsmouth.

Fanny was still only 28 years old at this time; she had already been separated from her husband for fourteen months; her latest news of him was eight months old; and the fortunes of his squadron since he sailed away from the Cape were utterly unknown. She was now facing the prospect of at least another year of loneliness, and try as she would she could not refrain from pouring out her distress. The sparkle had momentarily disappeared from her writing; but it is an interesting coincidence that after meeting, on the first page of this letter, a man whose name, in association with two famous court-martials, was to be notorious for a generation, she describes, a few pages later, her first meeting with Admiral Byng, and speaks of her instant antipathy to that unfortunate officer, whose name and tragic fate are so well known.

29th December. Well, here I am again, my dear love, but in no brighter humour than before. I think of but one thing. It goes to sleep with me, and when I wake again, there I find it. All the account I can give of my present uneasiness is that, whereas I had taken it into my head (perhaps without reason) that you would be at home next August, I now as strongly imagine (I hope with less reason) that you will come neither in August, nor September, nor October. Such capricious animals we are, and how can we help ourselves? When these fancies take possession of one, there's no getting rid of 'em.

[1] Fanny did not bestow the title of "Lady" upon a baronet's wife. "Mrs." Frederick was her husband's sister.

Now perhaps if I was to meet Mr. Hume, and he was to speak some words of comfort to me, that is, tell me a few lies, I should be easy again. At present I think of nothing but the twelve, perhaps fourteen, months we are yet to live asunder. Then I think of your coming into the Channel in the blustering winter months.

After we had drunk tea at home to-day as usual, and between 7 and 8, I sallied forth to make some visits, and at Gammer Stukeley's I met Admiral Byng, who seems to me a mixture of coxcomb and f——, if you'll allow a judgment upon an Admiral. He had an undressed frock, very richly embroidered with silver, which in my eyes is a strange dress, and his discourse and manner pleased me no better than his garb.

His Royal Highness the Duke arrived in town yesterday and has given Jack Boscawen leave of absence for 4 months. The Royal children at Leicester House are going to act a play in which your nephew, Fred Evelyn, has a part. It is Cato and I believe I can recollect the principal performers:—

CATO	Masr Nugent.	PORTHUS	Prince George.
JUBA	Prince Edward.	MARCUS	Masr Madden.
SEMPRONIUS	Masr Evelyn.	SYPHAX	Lord North's son.
LUCIUS	Masr Montagu.	HEAD OF	
MARCIA	Lady Augusta.	MUTINEERS	Prince William.
		LUCIA	Lady Elizabeth.

All these are, I'm informed, to be instructed by Mr. Quin, to whom they make a handsome present, and their dress, I'm told, comes to thirty guineas, so that 'twill be some expense as well as honour to those who accompany their Highnesses.

31st December. I begin to be in the hopes that I shall have a companion in the house, whom I shall like mightily. I have invited Miss Vansittart, who was with me in the summer, and she gives me hopes that a petition to her mother will succeed. 'Tis very few people I like well enough to set up a bed for them, but I think she will answer my expectations, for she is a very sensible girl, with the easiest temper I ever met with. She was with me ten days in the summer, during which time it did not happen to us to make but one excursion, yet she was as gay and good-humoured as if we had seen all the people in the world, and she is, indeed, remarkably good tempered.

As for news, my love, I know none. Be not anxious, dearest husband, about your children. Only trust in Providence for a blessing on a mother's care, who will be the happiest woman alive when she sees this dearest husband and these lovely children embracing one another. To this point tend all the wishes of your most affectionate faithful

F. BOSCAWEN.

This letter of the 31st December is the last of Fanny's letters to India that survives, and she now disappears from our view for more than a year. So here for a little we will take our leave of England, and follow the fortunes of the Admiral on the Coromandel coast. His fortunes, it must be admitted, should rather be classed as misfortunes, for the record of this Indian expedition is a record of unrelieved failure. Luckily, however, no shred of blame for the failure was ever allotted to Boscawen, for throughout his service in the Navy, the Admiral possessed the confidence not only of those above him but of all who served under his command. His high sense of duty, his dauntless courage, his integrity and single-mindedness, his burning patriotism and complete subordination of personal interests to the interests of the service were known to everybody. A stern but kindly disciplinarian, he was loved and respected by all who knew him personally, and there was something in his charm of manner which silenced, where he was concerned, the envious or malicious tongues of those less fortunate than himself. Not only in the East Indies, therefore, but on two subsequent occasions when an undertaking in which he was concerned did not turn out as successfully as expected, it was at once accepted by all parties that, with the means available, no one else could have done as well as Boscawen, and from no part of the country was there ever a note of criticism.

A popular favourite, without a thought of seeking popularity, his reputation was safe in the keeping of his countrymen. Boscawen could do no wrong.

It will be remembered that the Admiral's first task, after leaving the Cape of Good Hope, was to seize the Island of Mauritius, provided this could be done without endangering his chances of capturing Pondicherry, which was always to be regarded as the main object of his voyage.

Leaving Table Bay on 8th May, it was not till dawn on the 23rd June that Boscawen's squadron made the coast of Mauritius. Coming to anchor in a small bay about six miles from Port Louis, the Admiral spent the next three days in close reconnaissance of the coast. No information had been given to him of the possible strength of the enemy and their defences; and the intelligence which he now accumulated was that the French garrison was alert, that there were several strong ships in harbour, that owing to the presence of reefs a landing was only possible at a few sandy beaches, and that all these beaches were defended by works and guns. Boscawen consequently decided that "the reduction of the island not being the principal design of the expedition, and as an attack on it would certainly be attended with considerable loss, the attempt should not be made." No one has ever questioned this decision, though it was subsequently learnt that the garrison would not have been strong enough to man all the defences, and that a general attack, carried out with vigour, would probably have met with success.

The voyage from Mauritius to India was completed without incident, and the whole squadron arrived at Fort St. David on the 29th July, six days under eight months after they sailed from Spithead. It was just at this time that, far away in England, Fanny was in tortures of anxiety through her footman catching the smallpox.

Very unfortunately none of the Admiral's Indian letters, which brought such happiness to his wife, are still in existence, and as this is not the place to embark on a detailed study of the military operations, the story of his campaign can be told in a few words.

On arrival at Fort St. David it was found that, owing to the approach of the monsoon, only two months could be counted on for active operations in the field. Preparations for the siege of Pondicherry were therefore pressed on with vigour, and three ships were dispatched to blockade the town from the sea. As the Admiral had insisted on the provision of ventilating-pipes to the holds of the transports before he left England, his troops were in good health when they landed, and counting the local troops on the spot his whole force amounted to some 3,500 European soldiers and seamen, 150 gunners, and 2,000 native auxiliaries of doubtful value. Pondicherry, which lay some twelve miles to the north, had been ably fortified by a skilful Swiss engineer called Paradis. Its guns were heavier than any in possession of the English; its garrison consisted of 2,000 Europeans and 3,000 natives; and its commander was M. Dupleix, who had already proved himself an able and resourceful leader.

In less than a week Boscawen had completed his plans, and on 8th August, under the broiling sun of Southern India, along the roughest tracks imaginable, the march of his ill-trained and inexperienced army began. Boscawen himself, in the unaccustomed guise of Major-General, marched at the head of his men.

The siege, unfortunately, was an unexampled failure. The English engineers, on whose advice the "Major-General" had been instructed to rely, were found to be utterly ignorant of their duties. Major Goodere, of the Artillery, on whose experience he chiefly counted, was killed; Major Stringer

Lawrence, his best infantry commander, was taken prisoner; and one of the very few officers who really distinguished themselves was the young Robert Clive, who had only recently left his office desk to become an Ensign in the Company's service.

"If," wrote Clive, a few years later, "there be any officers or soldiers in India remaining of those who were at the siege of Pondicherry, experience must have convinced them how very ignorant we were of the art of war in those days." It only remains to add that at the end of two months' fighting, during which the attacking forces lost over a thousand Europeans, while the losses of the defenders amounted to less than 250, the arrival of the monsoon put an end to the operations, and Boscawen was obliged to raise the siege and return to Fort St. David. There, in the month of December, news reached him of the armistice signed in May, but he was ordered to remain in India till peace was finally ratified.

Even in times of peace however, the expedition was dogged by misfortune, for on the 13th April, 1749, a violent hurricane struck the port of St. David, and the Admiral's flagship, *Namur*, together with two other vessels of his squadron, were lost with the greater part of their crews. Providentially the Admiral himself was ashore, for of the 600 men on board the *Namur* less than 50 were saved.

At long last, in the month of September 1749, Captain Palliser arrived with his "express" from the Admiralty. Madras was thereupon handed over to the Admiral; and every other stipulation of the treaty being duly complied with, Boscawen and his squadron sailed for home on 19th October.

The only recorded incident of their return journey, probably provoked by the deadly monotony of the voyage, was a duel fought when the squadron arrived at the Cape, between the Captain of one of the men-of-war and a Lieutenant of the

Marines, in the course of which the Lieutenant was killed and the Captain so badly wounded that he had to be left behind.

To Fanny, who had dreaded the thought of winter gales if her husband's return were delayed, the last two months of waiting were fraught with real anxiety. According to Smollett's *History*, the month of February was ushered in by such a tempest as filled the populace with fear and consternation; and on the 8th of the month the people of London were still more fearfully alarmed by an earthquake which shook all the houses with such violence that the furniture rocked on the floors and pewter and porcelain rattled on the shelves. Nor was this the end. On the very same day in March, Londoners were "affrighted" by a second shock, even more violent than the first. Many persons, roused by this terrible visitation, started naked from their beds, and ran to their windows and doors in distraction, for the concussion was so dreadful as to threaten the dissolution of the globe. The general fear of a third shock was widespread, and was increased by the warnings of a fanatic soldier, who publicly preached repentance, and prophesied that another shock, on 8th April, would totally destroy the metropolis. According to this picturesque historian, the churches were thereupon filled with unaccustomed crowds, the streets no longer resounded with the noise of brutal licentiousness, and the highways leading out of London were blocked by the coaches of the well-to-do, who were fleeing to the country for safety. "In after ages," he adds, "it will hardly be believed that on the eighth of April the open fields that skirt the metropolis were filled with an incredible number of people, assembled in chairs, in chaises and coaches, as well as on foot, who waited in the most fearful suspense until the return of day disproved the truth of the dreadful prophecy."

The Admiral did not escape these winter storms, and half

his squadron became separated from him in their passage up the Channel. But six months after leaving Fort St. David he dropped anchor at St. Helens on the 14th April, 1750; and though, alas, there is no existing record of the joyful meeting with his family, we can rest assured that their cup of happiness was full. The world was safely at peace. The long years of anxiety and separation were over. Summer had come at last.

PART II

SUMMER

Covered with ripening fruits, and swelling fast
Into the perfect year, the pregnant earth
And all her tribes rejoice.

JAMES THOMSON.

CHAPTER XI

FOUR YEARS OF PEACE

WITH the British Navy reduced to eight thousand men, and peace restored to the world, there seemed to be little fear of Admiral's Boscawen's services being wanted again at sea, and he and Mrs. Boscawen settled down to the happy home life for which they had yearned through eight long years of separations. As Member of Parliament for Truro since 1742, the Admiral was at last able to take his seat at Westminster, and found the House engaged in domestic legislation. He and his wife continued to live in Audley Street; but they were in active treaty for the Hatchlands Park estate, near Guildford, and in the autumn of 1750 they at last succeeded in buying it.

For the summer of 1750 they rented, for the enviable sum of four guineas a week, a furnished house at Tunbridge Wells, with stabling for eight horses, and the comfortable proviso that if they kept it on for three months the total rent would be only thirty-five pounds. Tunbridge Wells was then at the height of its fame as the summer playground of London society, and it was there that Fanny's acquaintance with Elizabeth Montagu, which had begun the previous year, ripened into a friendship that lasted all their lives. Mrs. Montagu, writing to Lady Medows in 1749, had said: "I think Mrs. Boscawen a very sensible, lively, ingenious woman, and she seems to have good moral qualities. We often pass the evening together, partly in conversation, partly in reading." And Lady Medows had replied: "I think of Mrs. Boscawen as you do; and I expect you will be fond of the Admiral. His cool courage, his firmness, good nature, diligence and regularity, with his strong sense and good head, make a great character."

Lady Medows's opinion of her nephew is a proof of her own perspicacity; for the same high opinion of his sterling character was held by all who knew him. In 1751, at the age of 39, Boscawen was appointed a Lord Commissioner of the Admiralty,[1] and a few weeks later an Elder Brother of Trinity House. At the Admiralty his wide experience, clear brain, and capacity for hard work, were invaluable. Even when new governments came into power, and insisted upon a clean sweep at the Admiralty Board, one exception, at least, would always be made: Boscawen would always be asked to remain in office. So high, indeed, as time went on, did his reputation stand in the eyes of the public, that his name on the Board was regarded as a guarantee that all was well with the Navy. In time of war, he would be absent from England for many months on end, in command of some special enterprise that was almost invariably successful. But as soon as his mission was done, he would return to Whitehall; and from 1751 to the day of his death he remained a Lord Commissioner.

From a domestic point of view, there were two events of outstanding importance in Fanny Boscawen's life in 1751. In the spring, she and her husband moved into their new home at Hatchlands; and there, on 11th August she gave birth to her second son, William Glanville Boscawen.

Thus, for the next three years, though war clouds were beginning to darken the continental horizon, the Admiral and his wife continued to live an idyllic existence. Their winters were spent in Audley Street; their summers in the country, where they threw themselves with zest into all the delights

[1] The other members of the Board were Lord Anson, Lords Barrington and Duncannon, Wellbore Ellis, Hon. T. Villiers, and Adl. W. Rowley. J. Cleveland was Secretary.

of farming, in an age when farming really paid its way. The Admiral, it is true, had to spend a part of every week at the Admiralty. But he would drive to London in his curricle— the distance, via Epsom, where he changed horses, was only thirty miles—and as his week-ends often lasted from Thursday to Monday, it would seem that official duties—in times of peace—did not interfere too much with his country pursuits.

Whether from choice or necessity, it is not for a mere man to guess; but the fact remains that women of the eighteenth century differed from their descendants in the reign of George VI in one outstanding particular: they usually looked their age. Probably, in those days, when Bond Street consisted only of private houses, and "beauty parlours" were unknown, it was physically impossible for a woman of 45 to look as young as she did at the age of 30; so nobody bothered to try. In attempting, therefore, to picture Fanny Boscawen in 1752, we have got to remember that she herself, at 33 years old, had already begun to regard herself as a woman of mature age. Nevertheless, from the freshness of her letters, it is very hard to imagine her as anything else but young; and we can see her in summer-time at Hatchlands as a slight little figure in a muslin dress with a pattern of scattered flowers, and a big straw hat with ribbons under her chin. Hoops, according to contemporary fashion-plates, had greatly decreased in size, and a garden dress was probably made with large side panniers.

But sorrow and Fanny Boscawen were never parted for long; and the four and a half years which followed the Admiral's return from India were the longest spell of happiness she ever knew. These happy days, moreover, were already coming to an end. In the autumn of 1754 she was seriously ill for several weeks, following the birth of a stillborn daughter; and six months later the Admiral was again at sea, on active service.

147

The last letter but one of this happy period is dated 29th September, 1754, and gives a vivid picture of daily life at Hatchlands. The eldest boy—it was before the days of preparatory schools—had been sent to Eton at the age of 9 in 1753. The Admiral, on his way to Newmarket races, is staying a few days at The Grove, near Watford, with his Admiralty colleague, Thomas Villiers,[1] the future Lord Clarendon. Fanny, expecting her confinement in a few weeks' time, has remained at home, and is supervising the farm; and there is just a trace of nervousness about her health:

HATCHLANDS PARK.

Sunday, 29th September 1754.

I return you thanks, my dearest husband, for your agreeable letter from The Grove. Your company was good, but I cannot picture you amongst all those chatterers. Monsieur le Comte de Brooke, I suppose, was making up for Madame la Comtesse,[2] who, I think, is always silent and not at all a Capel.[3] We must hope that the *nouvelle mariée* is "breeding," since she is indisposed.

By your description of The Grove it should be a desirable place, and I have often admired Mr. Villiers in getting it. I've a notion he would be Prime Minister were he to *wish* for it, but in the meanwhile he's a much happier man. I hope Lady Charlotte will recover, and am glad the Villiers-Hyde[4] is so fine

[1] Thomas Villiers, son of 3rd Earl of Jersey, then a Lord Commissioner of the Admiralty, married in 1752, Lady Charlotte Capel, daughter of 3rd Earl of Essex by his first wife Jane, daughter and co-heir of Henry Hyde, last Earl of Clarendon and Rochester. He became Baron Hyde in 1756 and Earl of Clarendon in 1776.

[2] Francis, 8th Lord Brooke, was created Earl Brooke 1746. He married, 1742, Elizabeth, eldest daughter of Lord Arch. Hamilton. Their daughter Louisa married William Churchill, Esq., of Henbury, Dorset.

[3] William, 4th Earl of Essex had just (August 1754) married Frances, daughter of Sir Charles Hanbury Williams. He was a brother-in-law of Thomas Villiers (see note 1) and his bride was probably the *nouvelle mariée* referred to, as the Essex property, Cassiobury, adjoined the Grove.

[4] Lady Charlotte Villiers's son and heir, Thomas, was 9 months old.

a fellow. I like your companion to Newmarket—that is, I fancy you like him, and that is the same thing.

I did not write to you yesterday, for want of matter rather than time, for I was alone all day. 'Tis my fault if I am so this evening, for Mr. Greenhill[1] (at Church) offered to come home with me, but I told him I had a letter to write to you by the night's post and should be glad to see him some other time.

Here is a Dame Smith dead, mother to that handsome John, as well as to my son's friend George, who was crying so desperately at his cottage door when I went to Church that I longed to try to comfort him with a bit of money.

Woodroffe was at Guildford yesterday to spy the market, and reports that good wheat fetches £7 and no more. To-morrow he proposes to attend Bookham fair to see how lambs go. The teams are still employed in dung cart, as the term is. Tom Pride[2] is as well as can be expected.

Here is a letter[3] from your son, by which it will appear that he does not know the difference between the phrases of "entering into the eleventh year of his age" and "being eleven years old," which, however, I have explained to him, permitting him at the same time to purchase *Robinson Crusoe*, not without a view of making myself acquainted with that worthy personage —an honour which I am at present destitute of.

I have an answer from Dame Owsley,[4] who *don't choose it.* That is, Isaac is not at home, and all her farm-servants are going away, some at Michaelmas, some at old.[5] In short, she can't stir a foot, it seems. *Tant pis,* yet, as to health, I am full well as you left me, and walked with much ease to myself as far as the woods this morning. I would like an interview with Dr. Sandys; perhaps 'twould make us both easier. Supposing I go up next Saturday and so come down with you (for now, surely, there's no more danger of violent heat). But then, what will you do with your curricle? Give me beforehand your

[1] The Rev. Joseph Greenhill, Rector of Horsley and East Clandon, and a prolific theological writer, was the local parson.

[2] Tom Pride was the name given to their negro page, see page 124.

[3] See page 150.   [4] Mrs. Boscawen's old nurse, a farmer's widow.

[5] I.e. "Old Michaelmas." It was only two years since eleven days were cut out of the calendar in September 1752.

advice on this proposal, and tell me whether you think the journey will be as hurtful to my body as the Doctor may be satisfactory to my mind.

Here comes Tweedle[1] from a ride (with Beck[2] in the coach) in the common fields, which I permitted him to take when I came from Church, Tom trotting on one side. He's vastly good and grows pat, I think. We've cut his hair round his forehead.

Adieu, très cher. Does the post come in every day at New-market, or only 3 times a week?

EDWARD HUGH'S LETTER

ETON.
Friday, 27th September, 1754.

DEAR MAMA,

I have just received your kind letter with great pleasure, in which you have put that I am eleven years old this birthday, but I am only ten.

As I have read out all the English books that I have, I should be glad if you would let Mrs. Gregory buy me *Robinson Crusoe* or *Telemachus.*

Pray give my duty to Papa and love to my brother and sisters when you see them.

My cousin joining with me in duty to you and Papa,
I am your most dutiful son,
EDWARD HUGH BOSCAWEN.

Fanny's last letter of this period, written four days later, contains her first reference to Mrs. Montagu, and her house at Sandleford, near Newbury. Fanny's condition at this time was obviously sufficient "reason" to prohibit a bumpy journey of forty miles, despite the boasted comforts of the newly-invented post-chaise, which Mrs. Montagu had described as "the nearest sensation to flying I ever experienced."

[1] Her son William, aged 3 years.   [2] An old gun-dog.

Thursday.

But, my dear, what can have become of all my letters? Two ought to have arrived at Newmarket before you, that is, by Sunday's post; yet you write on Tuesday, and do not mention them. Is it that you have not sent to the post-house, nor the said house made any advance to you, or is it that you imagined I was silent all that while? My father would tell you that, if that was your conjecture, 'tis plain you don't know me yet, for that I must cackle to somebody. Amongst those somebodies you have always the preference, though that, perhaps, is a privilege not to be envied you.

I have wrote to Mrs. Montagu to tell her I was alone, and exhort her to direct her new post-chaise hither, that I may see it, and make her see my new Walk. After which, we may exchange approbations, if we see cause. I tell her, as an inducement, that, had I a post-chaise, I would certainly get into it and go to Sandleford, but for a REASON. She answers me that I make a sort of Old Bailey excuse, unbecoming my rank and dignity. I find she is very well, and Mr. Montagu recovered; but all the answer I can get out of her as to coming to Hatchlands, which I told her "she might if she would," is to require me to read my sentence backwards, like an Oracle, viz: "she would if she might," and that then I might give it more credit than any oracle ever deserved.

'Tis fine to-day again; the rain's entirely gone off and the glass rises. Woodroffe is gone with two waggons to Walton. The carpenter is very busy about something, I don't know its name, but there's a brace of 'em, made of deal.

I shall be glad to see the plan of Lady Essex's house, and still more so (I fancy) to see the elevation of it upon Admiral Boscawen's lawn.[1]

I have nothing new to tell you in respect of the laws of motion, only I know I shall put my own person (at least) in gentle motion on Saturday and, giving myself the whole day, propose to arrive in Audley Street before 'tis dark. I hope I

---

[1] The Boscawens were already planning to build a new house at Hatchlands.

shall have the pleasure of receiving you Sunday night, or Monday at farthest.

Nothing could be less judicious than carrying any sort of rheumatic to Newmarket. I'm sure 'tis like carrying coals to Newcastle and that you might easily have accommodated yourself with rheumatics of all sizes on the bleak heath at 6 this morning. But I desire you would repulse all further solicitations with the stern answer of a great coat or a flannel waistcoat, and take care of yourself if you would oblige your affectionate wife.

F. B.

The Admiral's affectionate wife, however, was not exactly practising what she preached. Her own journey to London was certainly injudicious; for after returning to Hatchlands she was suddenly taken ill, and it ended in a stillborn child. Luckily there were no serious complications, and at the end of November she and her family went up to London for the winter. But she did not return to Audley Street, for Admiral Boscawen had just been allotted the official residence in the Admiralty recently vacated by Thomas Villiers and his wife. The Audley Street house was consequently closed down, and Fanny moved into the Admiralty, which continued to be her London home for the next six years.

Meanwhile the sky was darkening, and the days of peace were numbered. On the continent of Europe the peace of 1748 had never been regarded as more than a temporary truce, forced upon the contending Powers by sheer exhaustion. France was still longing for the humiliation of England, and had spent the last few years in building a new fleet. It was rumoured also that France and Spain, perhaps with the assistance of Maria Theresa and Saxony, were preparing for another war with Prussia; and it was soon to transpire that Russia, too, had joined this powerful alliance.

For England, however, the immediate concern was the

danger to her American colonies; and as Admiral Boscawen was soon to find himself *en route* to North America, it will be well to take a glance at the situation in that country in 1754. The events of that year were the beginning of the struggle as to whether North America was to become the land of an English-speaking or a French-speaking race.

Up to the middle of the eighteenth century the English colonists had been content to colonize little more than the eastern fringe of the continent;[1] and though the virgin country to the west of the Alleghanies was regarded as King's territory, they had taken no steps to occupy it. The French, on the other hand, though far fewer in numbers, were pursuing a forward policy. In firm possession of Canada in the North and Louisiana in the South, they owned the two main gateways to the interior; and the St. Lawrence and the Mississippi were ready-made roads which beckoned them to the heart of the continent. They had already established a chain of missions and trading-posts from the Great Lakes to the Gulf, and were laying claim to the sole ownership of the valley of the Ohio. Up in the north, though New England troops had captured the French fortress of Louisburg, at the entrance to the St. Lawrence, in 1745, it had been handed back to the French at the peace of Aix-la-Chapelle; and on the borders of Nova Scotia the French had erected forts in British territory, and were even encouraging their Indians to murder English settlers.

In 1749 a number of Virginian colonists, trading as the Ohio Company, had been given a Royal grant of land in the Ohio Valley, on condition of settling a certain number of families there, building a fort, and maintaining a permanent garrison. This work had begun, some trading stations had been opened, and the site for a fort had been chosen at a fork of the Ohio,

[1] See sketch map facing page 154.

now covered by the city of Pittsburg, when in 1753 the news arrived that M. Duquesne, the new French Governor of Canada, was taking active steps to exclude the English from the valley. Travelling south via Lake Ontario, a force of 1,500 French had established one fort on Lake Erie, at the point now marked by the town of that name, and two more to the south of it, and had ejected some English traders from their stations on the Ohio.

The Governor of Virginia, Mr. Robert Dinwiddie, there-upon took a step which undoubtedly influenced the course of the world's history. He selected a young officer, not yet 22 years old, to carry a message to French advanced headquarters, demanding the immediate evacuation of English territory. The young officer's name was George Washington. After a month's difficult journey by mountain and jungle tracks, he reached the French post at the beginning of December. The French commander received him with native politeness, and promised to forward the demand to M. Duquesne. He added, however, that pending further orders, his present task was to eject every Englishman from the Ohio basin, and by God he meant to do it. Washington returned to Williamsburg with this reply in January 1754.

Meanwhile a small colonial force of forty men had set out to build and occupy the advanced English post at the Forks. But the day after this post was completed, several hundred French arrived in front of it in a large flotilla of canoes, and demanded its instant surrender. The tiny garrison, out-numbered by twenty to one, could only comply. The French occupied the position, enlarged the fort, and called it Fort Duquesne.

Before these facts were known, the Governor of Virginia, who had already been authorized from home to meet force with force, had decided to treat the French reply to Washington

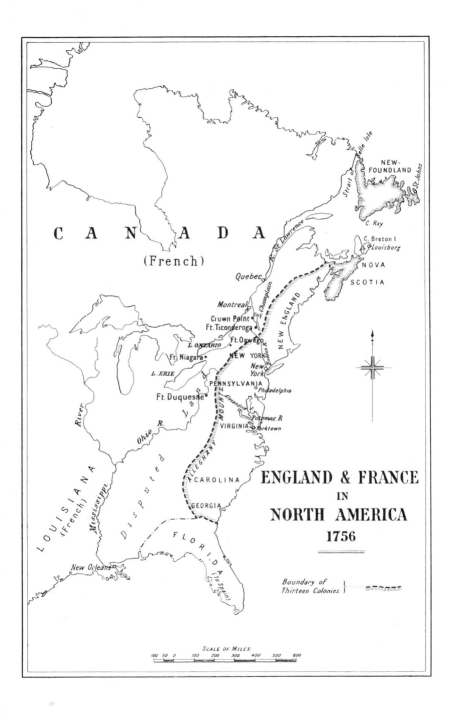

ENGLAND & FRANCE
IN
NORTH AMERICA
1756

Boundary of
Thirteen Colonies

SCALE OF MILES.
100 50 0   100   200   300   400   500   600

as a declaration of war. With some difficulty he had raised a force of 300 men to strengthen his advanced post, and had promoted Washington to the rank of Lieutenant-Colonel to take command of it. Washington started west a few days before the fort fell; but before his journey was half completed, he met the returning garrison, and learnt of the capture of the fort by a thousand French and Indians. Pausing only to send back a message for reinforcements, he pushed boldly on; and hearing from a friendly Indian that a small force of French was advancing towards him, he rushed their camp and put them to flight with loss. It was Washington's first engagement, and his fighting spirit can be judged from a letter he wrote next day, in which he remarked that "the whistling of the bullets made a most charming sound."

Realizing, however, that nothing more could be done till reinforcements reached him, Washington then fell back to another post in rear, where he was joined by an independent company of locally enlisted regulars from South Carolina, under a Captain Mackaye. This officer, holding the King's commission, could not, or would not, take orders from a provincial colonel, so he camped his men apart. Nor would he allow his men to help the Virginian militia in the "menial" task of road-making, on which they were actively engaged.

Washington's force was now 400 strong. But there was much sickness, and provisions were runnng short; so after a council of war it was decided to fall back to a more convenient site. Here, at a point not far from the present Uniontown, a new fort was begun; and owing to the extreme need of the men they called it Fort Necessity.

Meanwhile a force of 900 French and Indians was marching east from Fort Duquesne. They attacked Fort Necessity on 3rd July, and after a sharp resistance Washington made his first and last surrender. He was allowed to march out with the honours of war; but the French flag was now supreme to the west of the Alleghanies.

The situation was serious, but most of the English colonies remained supine. United action by the colonies was as yet an impossibility. Pennsylvania, New York, and New Jersey refused to co-operate, or even to admit that any danger existed; and only from New England could Virginia at first obtain a promise of support. Finally, however, the Governors met in congress to frame a joint policy; and after a long delay, the English Government decided on the dispatch of two regular battalions to assist the colonial garrisons. A senior English general was also to be sent from home, with orders to take command of all the troops available, to clear the Ohio valley, and to drive the French from all their posts in British territory. At the request of the Duke of Cumberland, the officer chosen for this difficult mission was General Edward Braddock, a hard-swearing martinet, 59 years of age, with no previous experience of colonial warfare. Commodore the Hon. Augustus (later Admiral Viscount) Keppel was to accompany him to Virginia with two fifty-gun ships of the line; and Captain Palliser, whose acquaintance we have already made in these pages, was to escort the transports from Ireland with two frigates. Sailing up the Potomac at the end of February, the whole squadron dropped anchor at Alexandria, where no King's ships of that size had ever been seen before.

Meanwhile at home the full extent of Louis XV's ambitions in North America was gradually becoming known. It was learnt that a strong squadron was fitting out at Brest to rein-force the French garrisons, and there were even reports of contemplated attacks on Boston and New York. In these circumstances, in March 1755, the government decided on a further effort to protect the American colonies. Two more battalions were detailed for this service, and it was resolved to fit out a squadron of eleven ships of the line for American waters. Edward Boscawen, lately promoted to the rank of Vice-Admiral of the Blue, was selected for the command, and he was categorically instructed to attack the French squadron wherever it should be met. The French Ambassador in London, who was politely informed of these instructions as soon as Boscawen had sailed, replied that the King his master would look upon the first gun fired at sea as a declaration of war.

Once more, therefore, Fanny Boscawen was to endure the anxieties of those who sit at home while their husbands are on active service. But the secret of the Admiral's destination was closely guarded, and even she was not allowed to know, until he had actually sailed, that anything more was intended for him than a cruise in home waters.

CHAPTER XII

THE ADMIRAL SAILS FOR AMERICA, 1755

ADMIRAL BOSCAWEN started off from the Admiralty in his own coach-and-four, to take command of his squadron, and was accompanied by his old friend, Savage Mostyn, lately promoted to the rank of Rear-Admiral, whom he had appointed second-in-command. On arrival at Portsmouth, as the *Torbay*, which was to be his flagship, was still on passage from the Nore, he lodged for a few days with his former flag-lieutenant, Charles Brett,[1] then in charge of the dockyard.

The day after he left London, Mrs. Boscawen resumed her habit of keeping a journal, and sending him large sections of it whenever a chance occurred. For the first ten days or so these packets were addressed to Portsmouth.

England and France, it must be remembered, were still officially at peace, and even Mrs. Boscawen did not yet know her husband's destination. It is plain, however, that despite her apparent spirits, she was now alive to the risks of his latest mission. Her first letter opens with an amusing account of her son obtaining three days extra holiday from Eton, by applying too late for a seat in the Eton coach:

ADMIRALTY.
8th April, 1755.

Good morning to my dear love. I hope he has slept well, in a well-aired bed and warm room.

Here is your son, who, when he told you he had given all

[1] Charles Brett eventually became a Lord Cr. of the Admiralty and member for Sandwich.

the money he had to the Eton coachman, did not inform you what service the said coachman was to perform. Nevertheless, had he bribed him ever so high, he could not have made him more agreeable amends, for when Wakeham[1] went to bespeak your son's place, he told him he could not take Master neither Tuesday nor Wednesday. Thursday he had a place at his service. Wakeham, not content, desired to see the books, and saw 6 boys set down for each day, but represented to Mr. Bluff (or Bruff) that if they were little ones, his gentleman, being also little, might make a seventh. Mr. Bluff replied that 'twas true the gentlemen would crowd in to come up, but he durst not propose to them to take a seventh going down. So here we are, and here we must remain till Thursday. You'll tell me I rejoice, but you'll wrong me. *Tout au contraire*, I have even had thoughts of hiring a post-chaise for to-morrow, but for him to go quite alone in it would be rather too stately, and too costly, proud and melancholy. Neither perhaps should I be quite easy to trust to a chance postillion. But, I assure you I am almost as sorry as he is glad.

Now for your cook. I sent to Dr. Garcourt's for the person in question, who has hired himself to Sir Edward Hawke. I should first have told you that I spoke to Mr. Villiers' cook, who assured me he could by no means have the honour to serve you, as he should not have quitted Mr. V.'s service but to attend his Majesty to Hanover, for which he is strictly engaged. These two disappointments made me turn my thoughts to the Swiss, who just then luckily came to know my pleasure. I told him the £50 was the great objection. He stood stiffly to it, so that I could not offer him a more considerable abatement than 40 guineas, which I told him was two and forty pounds. This, when he had considered some time, he accepted, but called it two and forty guineas, and I could not beat the jumble out of him. So 42 guineas (including the ship's wages) is what you are to give Mr. Augustin Faesch. When I tell you that you are likewise to pay his travelling expenses to Portsmouth, I am afraid you will reckon I have made a bad bargain, but I protest I could not get him any cheaper. I send you enclosed

[1] The Boscawens' new butler.

his own writing. That same "pr: take" is, I fancy, a claim which he lays in to a share of prize money.

Yesterday I did not go out, and went to bed, according to your order, at 12.

To-day (very perverse, you'd say) I rose before 9 and took a walk with your two sons in the garden before breakfast. The reprieved was in good spirits, you may believe, and the little one ready to jump over the wall to the soldiers.[1]

Adieu, mon très cher. I could chat much longer to you, but I believe the dispatches are sealing. Compliments to Mrs. Brett.

Wednesday, 9th April. I hope my dearest got better repose in his Inn at Petersfield than *sa chère moitié dans son lit déserté.* I won't write to you so late another night—it keeps me awake and sets my thoughts upon the uncertainty of your present expedition and the slippery paths of glory, for as the poet says:

> High on the mountain's lofty brow,
> 'Mid clouds and storms has GLORY fixed her feet;
> Rock'd by the roaring winds that blow,
> The lightnings blast it, and the tempests beat.

High as it is, and difficult of access, I do not despair of your attaining the summit. Whether I desire you should now make any fresh efforts towards it is another question.

I have few anecdotes to recite for this day, nothing having yet passed but a note from Lady Hester,[2] with civil inquiries after you and me. Another from Mr. Cleveland to thank me for brown bread, and a bill from our gardener in Audley Street, demanding a guinea for a year's allowance. Such, and no greater, are the events of this day.

But you, my dear sir, what eventful history have you not to tell? Your highwayman, quite an adventure; Mrs. Fuller's accouchement, *un chronique scandaleux*; and Mr. Beverstock's escape from so many keepers might form an episode in the history of Jonathan Wild.

The demand of Lady Essex's plans I have already made in

---

[1] On the Horse Guards Parade.   [2] Wife of William Pitt.

writing, and shall send it by my son, as soon as he has dined. T'other son received discipline again this morning. Nevertheless, he has been mighty affable ever since, playing here all round me. I was trying new nightcaps for his inoculation, observing he must have his hair cut off. Then says he "Little *May*, I must have a vig as *Pay* has got."[1]

10*th April.* Your agreeable letter, my dear love, made the best part of my breakfast. I am obliged to answer it in brief, for my Aunt Evelyn and Julia have swallowed up my entire mornings. They are just gone, and it is 1 p.m.

Your son is at length departed. 3 Eton "comrogues" beside him in the coach, among 'em Medows and Mr. Henry St. John Berkeley Miller. All *these last* professed they would depart on Wednesday, but yesterday they called here and said they could not get a place on the coach till this morning. Your son was very jolly, and had bestowed all his tender tears on dear Papa: none were reserved for to-day, I assure you.

I dine to-day at Mr. Luttrell's, and must dress myself at all points for the misses' ball.

Yesterday I went nowhere but to my opposite neighbour, where, to oblige Madame, I sat down to half guinea cribbage with Mother Nugent and lost a shameful lot of money. Ah! *l'on ne m'attrapera plus.*

Lady Folkestone has sent to me to go with her to St. James's to-morrow. I shall go and make my lowest curtsey to His Majesty for his kindness to you, and I cannot make him a greater compliment, considering my drum in the afternoon. I suppose I shall be tired to death.

My Virginia nightingales are arrived, and most charming creatures. They have already sung to me. They are to live in my bedchamber, and indeed I shall love them. I have sent a thousand thanks to Mr. Spry,[2] but, as to the man that brought them, I did not know how to thank him properly for the journey from Portsmouth. *Je lui donnai pourtant un ange, & il parut bien content.*

[1] Obviously the small son's names for his parents.
[2] Captain (later Rear-Admiral) Richard Spry was one of Boscawen's captains.

11th April. So far, my dear sir, from expecting a letter from you, I am very sensible of your goodness in writing at all. In return, I have to compliment you very sincerely upon your daughters who (*foi d'homme d'honneur*) appeared last night at Mrs. Roberts', the eldest dancing like Mme Auretti, the youngest looking like the Duchess of Hamilton. In short, they are lovely girls. There's absolutely a degree of perfection that is almost ridiculous in Fanny's dancing. I am not sure I ever saw anybody off the stage dance so well. As to Bess, she had two Provence roses expanded upon her cheeks by the heat of the room, terrorism, etc., by which means (and you can't imagine what they did for her) she became neither more nor less than the most beautiful girl I ever saw.

I have been at Court with Lady Folkestone. His Majesty spoke to neither of us, for there were many people, but the Duke did, and Madame Emily[1] asked me if you were gone.

Au reste, mon cher, your youngest son did me the favour of his company at dinner to-day, *tête à tête,* upon a chicken. Having drunk your health, I advised him to drink that of brother Boscawen. He did so, and, leaving something in his glass, he returned again, took it up and said, "Now I'll drink myself, shan't I?"

Adieu, très cher, I must go and assist a little in giving my rooms the airs of a drum. *Aimez-moi toujours, et croyez que je suis vraiment à vous.*

Indeed, I shall remember your lesson and never again defer, till the *Black Week* itself, sending for places in Mr. Bluff's coach to Eton.

12th April. Hébien, jamais je ne vis tant de chats noirs. Jamais je ne vis tant de chats gris. I should have had you singing that refrain if you had been of our party yesterday. I can count above 80 that came. How much, then, am I obliged to 40 who did not come. A crowd there was, that's certain, for where there are a quantity of misses they *will* make a crowd at the door; but there were always seats in the outer and inner rooms, and even 3 vacant chairs in the great room, besides window seats, for it was too hot to let down the curtains. Everybody

---

[1] Princess Amelia, daughter of George II.

admired everything, and Lady Charlotte[1] protested she hardly knew her house again; the whole extremely well conducted, well lighted, though I say it that, etc. An inexhaustible flow of very good tea continued the whole evening. The best lemonade I ever drank, and in vast quantities, with great variety of biscuits of every kind.

Enough of such nonsense—let us talk of the *Torbay*.[2] I heard the wind was East sometime yesterday morning, possibly long enough for her to get out of the Downs. Then you'll say, she put back again when it became West. I lament therefore, for I figure to myself you would be more at home, more easy, and more comfortable on board your floating castle. Besides, I long to have you see her and tell me you approve her.

Mr. Luttrell sets out for Portsmouth to-morrow and with him goes a very sincere friend of yours[3] who, though a lady, I recommend very strongly to your memory and affection, because I durst answer for her that she will give you the first place in hers. I don't know that she will make you any professions of her particular regard, but if you'll consult her looks, you'll plainly read it there.

I have your most kind and welcome letter, for it brings me that which I wanted most, viz: an account of your health. Pray ride as much as ever you can, and leave the unimportants, even the importants, to somebody upon whom the well-being of the nation does not depend.

I must dress and go and dine at my father's, so *adieu*. Here is culprit, fixed upon a chair, without power of descending from it, occasioned by some misunderstanding between him and his pudding. He is pure well, and recovers his strength and activity *à vue d'œil*.

I have paid a year's ground rent to Sir Robert Grosvenor.[4]

[1] Lady Charlotte Villiers.

[2] The Admiral's new flagship, which had not yet arrived at Portsmouth from the Nore.

[3] Fanny's miniature.

[4] The ground rent for 14 South Audley Street. Sir Robert Grosvenor, 6th Baronet, died August 1755; his eldest son Richard was created Earl Grosvenor in 1784, and his grandson Robert, Marquess of Westminster in 1831. The Dukedom dates from 1874.

Monday, 14th April, 1755. Mrs. Montagu is amazed at my receiving a letter from you every day. *Moi, au contraire,* I could not tell how to behave myself yesterday for want of a letter, and was saucy and vain enough to hope I might possibly have one enclosed in Mr. Cleveland's packet, who, I'm told, receives advices from the ports of a Sunday as well as on other days. But the day passed without this consolation.

I was told I ought to go to Leicester House and I fancied I would go, till I saw a lovely sunshiny morning. I thought 'twould be profaning it to carry it into a crowd; so after Chapel I walked in the Admiralty garden and Park. By so doing, I saw Mr. Thomas Villiers-Hyde, etc. etc. who is really a good, pretty, blue-eyed boy, like Villiers. I dined with Mrs. Montagu, and there likewise spent the evening.

To-day I dine at my father's and spend the evening at Mrs. Stanley's. Lady Hester invited me, but I was engaged as aforesaid.

The coach arrived here about 2 yesterday, and all well. I shan't use it to-day, having hired my chair for a guinea a week, of which this is the last day.

We have got a good place for Monsieur Henri, so I shall soon be *sans cuisinier,* and perhaps, during the first days of Tweedles' sickness,[1] *sans appétit.*

15th April. I have a melancholy tale to tell you, melancholy in itself and in its consequences too, for since one of my nightingales is dead, there remains no visible reason that the other should live. The cage is in my bedchamber; and, every morning, while I put on my cap, it is placed in the window near me, where the meat, the water, the sand is changed, and Wakeham is called for to produce his fresh turf, for every morning he goes into the Park to cut a fresh turf for these pretty fellows, whose loss I lament.

'Tis sufficient that the other side of the paper is dedicated to grief. Let this begin with joy, which I heartily offer to you on the subject of the *Torbay's* arrival, which pleased me

---

[1] Billy, alias Tweedle, who had had fever at Easter, was to be inoculated for smallpox as soon as he was well enough.

inexpressibly. If Capt. Colby[1] is in love with her, I suppose she beat the *Dunkirk*.[2] So may she always beat everything that contends with her.

Lord Poulett[3] was to have made a motion in the House of Lords to address His Majesty not to go abroad. But as his Lordship did not summons the House yesterday, as was expected, it is concluded that he thought better of his motion. And now the lie of the day is that he has persuaded the Lord Mayor and Aldermen to address his Majesty to the same effect. If they do, I would advise Great George, our King, to issue a Proclamation forbidding the said Lord Mayor and Aldermen to eat any custard on their next Feast day.

Did you hear of a conference between the King and Lord Chancellor? The latter humbly represented how much his Majesty's absence would be regretted *this* summer and how wrong a measure it appeared to him. "What then," subjoined his Majesty, "don't your Lordship think it reasonable I should see my country seat once in two years: I know your Lordship goes to yours every summer?" "Yes, sir, but not in term time." This is the history—I'm not sure I do it justice.

You must cause to be read by your Chaplain the 35th Chapter of Ezekiel. It is a prophecy against Mount Seir, and Lord Chesterfield interprets it is that very same Monsieur whose name only rouses the metal of every good Englishman.[4]

16th *April*. Thank you kindly for giving so cordial a reception to the young woman Mr. Luttrell carried with him. You will take her to your bosom. You safely may. She will not be a serpent there, but rather a dove, whose gentle fondness you may recline upon, herself desiring no greater happiness than to be able to procure you any.

You ask me after my drum. As to attendants, I had one of His Majesty's Beef-eaters by way of a porter, and one of His

---

[1] Captain Charles Colby was Captain of the *Torbay*.

[2] Another ship of Boscawen's squadron, commanded by Captain the Hon. Richard Howe (later Admiral of the Fleet Earl Howe).

[3] John, 2nd Earl Poulett. He made a motion in the House of Lords a few days later, but no one seconded it.

[4] The parallel is well worth reading.

Royal Highness's footmen (not in his livery) to usher upstairs, which left Wakeham and Tom at liberty to obey me here, and Charles by way of Mercury. Lord Anson was not invited, fearful that I could not get a guineas-table; besides, my lady was ill of a swelled face. Mr. Cleveland senior did not come; junior did. By way of young men (a species you seem to think I was deficient in) proceed to count two Mr. Rowleys (they prove much, you'll say). Well, go on, and count Capt. Tryon, Evelyn, Medows, Fred and George Evelyn, Will Burrell, Colonel Frederick, besides Peter Junior, Mr. Clayton, Mr. Medows, Mr. Evelyn, Colonel Gray, and Mr. Villiers. These are all of the best age, I must admit, for they are your school-fellows. But what will you say if I tell you that a lady (who was at my drum) declared t'other night in company that of all the drums she was ever at, none ever was so agreeable and so well conducted as Mrs. Boscawen's; that all rout-makers should take a lesson of her, for that so much politeness, accompanied with so much ease, she had never observed in anybody. In short, that I did the honours in a certain way that was agreeable and attentive to everybody, and yet (seemingly) with great ease to myself. As I do not think this character quite the first in life, I venture to transcribe it without great arrogance.

It speaks well for the degree of secrecy maintained by the navy at this time, and for Fanny's unquestioning acceptance of naval discipline, that despite her privileged position as wife of the commander of the departing expedition, she still had no idea when it was going to start, or whither it was bound, or how long her husband was likely to be away. On this day, 17th April, however, she apparently received a letter from the Admiral, telling her he would be sailing with the first fair wind, begging her to keep up her spirits, and expressing some little anxiety about his small son's approaching inoculation for smallpox. The shock of his imminent departure, even though it had been daily expected, was great; and Fanny writes:—

17th April. 2 p.m. I have just received your second letter, my dear sir, and you must excuse me if it shortens mine. I feel no more than what every English heart ought to feel for your safety! I pray God Almighty to preserve you, to bless you with health, and grant you success. May every circumstance of success attend my dearest dear Lord till he returns to the faithful arms of his most affectionate F. B.

I must beg you not to be uneasy about the child. He is in the most desirable state for inoculation that can be. Mr. Hawkins felt his pulse, said he wanted no bleeding, no purging, but a little rhubarb, and he assures me that in all his practice he never remarked a more favourable run of inoculated patients, not one having yet had it full. You may depend upon my care. I shall seldom be out of doors; but to-night, alas, I have promised Miss Speed and Vansittart to go with them to Ranelagh. You may believe my choice would have been a more solitary walk this evening. I shall write on till the East wind points the last *adieu.* May I ask where?

In my Chamber at 11 *p.m.* Housed at this *early Ranelagh* hour, how can I better employ the forty minutes which he permits me to sit up than in conversing with my dear departing friend. It will not be long that I can enjoy this pleasure.

Being tired and low-spirited, I made my misses come the Westminster way, set me down first, and be content with my coach to conduct them to their respective squares, for I had Miss West (self-invited) as well as Miss Speed and Vansittart. The two former sung to me all the way home.

The company at Ranelagh was rather numerous than splendid. My Lord of Falmouth would make me comprehend all the chances, all the algebraical theory, of the present lottery.[1] *Trop obligée* you know, for at all times I am pretty indifferent to such subjects, and to-night, particularly, I could not have talked to any mortal but Mr. Cleveland; for, as to his Lordship, I would not communicate to him what I knew of your sailing orders. He had a vassal with him, who I imagined would make

[1] The Government was running lotteries as a means of raising money, instead of increasing taxation.

himself considerable at Lloyds, or the Exchange, to-morrow morning, by knowing the news so much sooner than anybody else.

I have been summoned upstairs to assist at the solemnity of poor Billy's rhubarb, for the pretty cur was asleep when Burges sent it. I have not been able to get it all down—he reached so. However, as 'tis prescribed, I shall attempt the remainder to-morrow morning, but now the sweet soul was so sleepy and tired, and tried so honestly to do his best to oblige "May," the little stomach heaving all the while, that I must have had a heart of flint to torment him any more.

A letter at this time of night! *Mon dieu*, what does it bring? Counter-orders and you don't sail? No! Well, I am pleased that you seem pleased and in spirits about your orders. But October, alas! I was not prepared for that. This morning I counted it had been but a Channel service, but God's will be done. So your valuable life is preserved to me and your country, go where you can do it best service. I am, and I boast of it, the wife of your honour as well as of your person, and no riches, no acquisitions would delight me like additional laurels, glory and reputation to my dear Admiral! Whom God's guardian providence vouchsafe to accompany in all dangers and difficulties.

You bid me not mention your orders. You see what occurred to me before I had that injunction; therefore, if you think proper to let me into any other part of your destination, you may equally depend upon my silence, without one hint, or one shrug, or one look of important knowledge; and do not fear to terrify me, for whether you *undertake* anything or not, do I not know that they who go down to the sea in ships and occupy their business in great waters are exposed to various perils and danger? Yet, at the same time, I reflect and humbly trust that you are safe in the hand of One Disposing Power. To His Gracious Providence I commit you, and rest ever with the utmost tenderness of affection, yours,

19th April. I have received two letters from you to-day, my dearest love. How much am I not obliged to you for letting no opportunity slip without giving me the pleasure to hear from you. It is indeed a pleasure, and I know not how I can so well express my gratitude as by wishing to resign it. Yes, I am disinterested enough to wish you may sail to-morrow, before anybody dreams it is possible for you to be half ready. Methinks I should like to hear the wise heads in the City cry, "Why his ship was in the Downs but t'other day. Well, nobody but Boscawen could have done so. Oh sirs, for dispatch, ay—and for anything else—he's your man." For you must know, my love, *que quand il s'agit de vos louanges,* I am not content with those of the Senate only. No, I must have the popular, nay even the vulgar, applause. It puts me often in mind of Pope's verses on the Duke of Wharton:—

> "Born with what e'er might win it from the wise,
> Women and fools must praise him or he dies."

That is just my case, so once more *quoi qu'il m'en coûte,* I wish you with great sincerity (and, I'm sure, great disinterestedness) an East wind to-morrow morning.

I am jealous to have heard nothing of the elegant entertainment on board the *Torbay,* but you reserve it perhaps to entertain M. Hocquart *pour la troisième fois.*[1]

I have a notion you told me of a map of America that was in the house. Whereabouts is it?

To-night I repaired to Lady Hester's, where I have lost 3 guineas, and that it was to Earls and Countesses was no manner of satisfaction. 4 tables *d'un extrême beau monde,* and very much *le pays ennemi*: Lady Caroline Fox,[2] Lord and Lady Hillsborough,[3] Mr. and Mrs. Ellis,[4] etc., etc. Fat Will desired to shake hands with me in sign of amity. I told him, with all my heart, for that having beat him I was quite satisfied.

[1] This, as will be seen later, was an amusing prophecy. The Admiral, it will be remembered, had captured Capitaine Hocquart twice during the last war.

[2] Lady Caroline Lennox, daughter of Duke of Richmond, married 1st Lord Holland, 1744.

[3] Wills, 1st Earl of Hillsborough (later Marquess of Downshire), married Margaretta, sister of 1st Duke of Leinster.

[4] Wellbore Ellis, a Lord of the Admiralty.

Madame Ellis took no more notice of me than if I had been an inhabitant of Crutched Friars. Not so Monsieur. He was very civil and enquired after your health. I said I heard from you this morning and you was well. *C'est tout!* The King goes, *dit on*, to-morrow se'ennight![1]

April 20th, Sunday p.m. Pray Papa! Pray to God to bless us,[2] for we are inoculated. This day exactly at noon it was done; no fuss, no rout, no assistance. Nobody with me but the servants. I held the child myself and so effectually employed his eyes and attentions (by a bit of gold lace which I was putting into forms to lace his waistcoat) that he never was sensible of the first arm. For the second, he pretended to wince a little, but I had a sugar plum ready, which stopped the whimper before it was well formed. And he is now (Mr. Hawkins gone) tattling here by my bureau with some cards and papers, etc., for the weather is so very hot that I reckon the chief service I can do him is to provide him such amusements as will keep him still and quiet. So that, instead of waggons, carts and post-chaises, we shall deal altogether in mills, pictures, dolls, London cries, and such sedentary amusements. The nurse-maids are both inoculated, too.

I have now, I think, two great stakes! My husband sails, my child is inoculated; both in the same day. There is but one way to look. Towards the blessing which can protect on the fields of battle, or on the bed of sickness! I desire you to be persuaded that I am composed and that I strive to be so, instead of raising (as you sometimes, not wrongfully, accuse me of) phantoms to terrify my imagination. As to my dear husband, I consider that he is just where I wish whilst national affairs are thus situated. For would I not have you at the head of a Squadron? Should I choose to have you neglected and forgot, whilst a Hawke or a Byng or an Osborne claimed the attentions of three Kingdoms! No, *j'aime trop votre gloire!* Go

[1] George II started for Hanover on 28th April, and embarked at Harwich for Helvoetsluys that afternoon.

[2] I.e., her small son. It was customary to speak of a child in the first person plural.

where that points, but let me see you again in health and safety,
I pray God.

Mr. Cleveland was so kind to come to me to-day, and to
him I did vouchsafe to talk of your sailing. He thinks it will
happen to-day. I wish you may, and let this 20th April,
Gracious God, be propitious to both our undertakings!

I believe I must conclude, lest you tell me I talk too much
on both these subjects.

While these last entries were being written, the Admiral
had already sailed for Plymouth, where he arrived on the
evening of the 24th April. Here he embarked his two battalions
of infantry and one hundred tons of water in casks, and, after
a delay of twenty-four hours, due to a shortage of water-casks
and the consequent necessity of making them while he waited
(it is said that thirty coopers made casks for sixty tons of watei
in that time) the squadron sailed for America on the 27th.

ADMIRALTY,

24th April, 1755.

This fast from writing to you, as well as hearing from you,
does by no means agree with me. You will say the first part
of my abstinence is a penance of my own imposing—I do not
acknowledge that. To be sure, there was an appearance of the
contrary on Tuesday last, but I beg my love to believe that it
was a day without a minute at my disposal. Mr. Cleveland
came in soon after I was up: to him succeeded Mr. Gore,
Mr. Glanville, Mrs. Jones (with her rent), Mr. Hawkins (with
our plaster), Mrs. Anstey (whom I turned out, in consideration
that she would come back and dine with me). At 1, I was
obliged to repair to Kensington. I say "obliged," because *you
bid* me take the air, and I had never been able to do it because
of my cold. I brought back 5 happy and pretty misses; was
no sooner dressed than dinner was served; could not write
after dinner because of Mrs. Anstey. Before 6 she walked off,
and we repaired to Drury Lane, where I found myself much
more interested in the scene than I imagined. Coriolanus's

brave and noble spirit I could make out to be a certain Admiral. The Volscians were the French, and I myself had the choice of Virgilia's or Volumnia's character. I chose the latter, and wept when she wept, but far be it from me to carry on the comparison and suppose the English can ever be so ungrateful to you as the Romans were to Coriolanus. Descending from these heroes, we had Jobson's stall just in our corner, at which the young ones laughed so immoderately that I believe we disturbed his work. You may think I was obliged to attend through all the transformations, and till every man had his mare again. Then I attended the young Bisshopps home, so that it was almost twelve when I got home with my little rakes. Then I could only beg of Mr. Cleveland to tell you we were well; and so all hands to sack, whey, and to bed. Bess lay in your place, and next morning both returned to M'am Bear.[1]

And here is good Mrs. Owsley, who has come to nurse Billy, which I'm sure you'll rejoice at, as does your son, who has been in raptures and undertakes to do the honour of the house to her: never sees a coach, but he calls for Mrs. Owsley to partake of the entertainment. He wants her to lie with him, and, in short, is vastly fond of her, which will be of great use to us.

And now, although I have a long story to tell you of Sir John Elwell, etc., and how they took two highwaymen and let them go again, yet I must not do it, for the hour is come.

But thank you I must, and will, for my nightingales. Guess what was my surprise to-day, when I returned from Lee, to see my poor widowed cage again replenished. *Ah, mon cher, que vous êtes obligeant!*

29th April. If I did not know that my dearest husband required no other expressions of gratitude than those of the heart, I should be quite at a loss for some that would be adequate to the obligations he had laid upon me—your letter to our son, your frequent and kind ones to me, can only be returned, as I mean to return them, by devoting my thoughts and actions—my whole life—to your service, as far as lays in

---

[1] Mrs. Bear's Polite Seminary for Young Ladies in Kensington.

my power. Your children and affairs must now engross this
attention, but the time will come, I hope, when my gratitude
may be expressed more personally to you and consequently
more agreeably to myself. Meantime, be assured it is very
sincere and can never end but with my life. Yes, my dear
Mr. Boscawen, you have made me happy by your kindness,
you made me proud by your esteem, and I value both too
much not to make it my chief point in life to preserve them.
It has pleased God to restore me to everything I ever had
(except youth), to render myself agreeable to my dear partner,
and surely I will employ it all with earnestness to that purpose,
happy if I can so make him any sort of amends for the
burthen I have been to him, and which he bore with a degree
of temper and patience that deserves greater rewards than 'tis
perhaps in my power to bestow. Yet, a tender friend, a faithful
servant, are comforts to every man that possesses them. Such
you shall always possess in me and, while I am my own, I
will be yours. Yours! to every purpose of friendship, assistance
and consolation through the rugged paths of life. I am charmed
to find it your opinion that your son is also likely to contribute
to this end. I pray God he may! And, in return for the advice
you gave him—advice so kind and flattering to me that I could
not read it without tears of joy and gratitude—I will most
carefully inculcate, as indeed I have ever done, principles of
the most profound duty and most respectful affection to so
good and worthy a parent as you are! God grant you may
live to see your children's children and to enjoy as much
satisfaction in the sight as ever man knew! I think there cannot
be a more rational sort of happiness in this life than a virtuous
offspring: to see creatures that (under God) we have been the
instruments to produce, become useful to society, and ornaments to human nature.

> "This sure is bliss if bliss on earth there be.
> May't be the lot of my dear Lord and me."

Though I am sure you will join me in this wish, yet you may
possibly like that I should end my preface and begin to tell you
a little the history of other things and places, besides that of

my own heart, which indeed you seem to entertain such a notion of as I need by no means endeavour to change or amend. *Allons donc*—you shall have my journal first, and that of my dear little baby, and then the more general occurrences that have happened since I wrote last.

It was Thursday night, as I remember. Friday I stayed at home all the morning: had a visit from Sir John Elwell: talked *almost my* fill of Portsmouth and you, and at 3 consigned my sprightly little fellow to Mrs. Owsley and went to the Pay Office for Miss Pitt,[1] with whom I walked to Buckingham Gate. There we found my coach, which conveyed us to Chelsea College, where we met with a very cordial reception and a very good dinner. Admiral Boscawen and success to him, was the first toast, and I am not sure sober Mr. West[2] himself did not propose it should be a bumper. With them we remained in friendly conversation, enlivened with some songs of Miss Pitt, who has a pretty voice, till near 9, when my coach came and reconveyed us to the Pay Office, all by the light of the moon. We found there Mr. Pitt, Lady Hester, and Harmony, for two charming French horns were playing in their anti-chamber, who, as soon as I appeared, changed their air and entertained me with " See the Conquering Hero Comes." I accepted the omen and could not resist the pleasure; so, dismissing my coach, I stayed near two hours, then home to bed.

Saturday about noon, I went to Kensington to fetch my girls, who were to bestow on Mrs. Clayton the vast treat of 2 days' visit. Accordingly I brought them to Brook Street, where I had them taken measure of for turn-stays by a very skilful operator, for Fanny's collarbones and breast grow visibly awry. There we all dined together with Mrs. Boone and cousin Nanny. At six, we all repaired (that is, 3 mothers and 4 misses) to Drury Lane, where in a stage box and very cool, we beheld *Richard the Third* and *Tommy Thumb*, after which I conducted my daughters to Mrs. Clayton's bedchamber

[1] Mary Pitt was living with her famous brother. William Pitt had not yet become Secretary of State, but was carrying out the duties of Paymaster General with an integrity hitherto unknown in that office.
[2] Gilbert West.

and then Mrs. Boone and I repaired to our respective ones. All this while Tweedle continued as though nothing had happened to him.

On Sunday he drooped a little, yet not so as to hinder me (after seeing Hawkins) from going to Chapel. I walked to that of Duke Street to avoid Mrs. Capel Hanbury, who has not had the smallpox, and sits in our closet. Yet after Chapel was over, she was the first person I met in the Park and made me walk with her to show how insensible she was to fear on my account. I had an assignation near Buckingham House, but the faithless mortal never came. It was no other than sister Lucy, who I do not admit into my house (the measles spreading all over her house, but pretty favourable), so I had appointed a meeting in the Park, where to the great annoyance of myself and 500 more short and long personages, a sudden storm of hail rushed in upon us. Chair there was none, and I took shelter among many others under the trees. There I was hospitably protected for some time, but at length, my friendly elm having got its load, discharged itself upon my hat and the flaxen periwig of my unknown neighbour; we had perfect sheets of water fell upon us, so that an open exposure and defiance to the storm was more eligible. Accordingly I sallied forth, and arrived at home soaked, obliged to change clothes and hose.

God Almighty bless and prosper you wherever you go. Remember always with your usual tenderness your very affectionate, faithful and obedient wife.

CHAPTER XIII

LETTERS TO AMERICA, 1755

ADMIRALTY.

May 15th, 1755.

On Saturday se'ennight, the 24th instant, we propose to be at your honour's seat at Hatchlands Park in Surrey. Then (I flatter myself) our happiness will be as complete as it can be, wanting our two dear Edwards, our honoured and much beloved father and our dear comrade brother. Of him I do not hear one word of holidays at Whitsuntide, but as to the girls, they have been at home these 4 days, to the inexpressible joy of William, whom, however, I do not allow them to run over, *tout à leur aise*, for the poor merchant is weak, as you may imagine, the inoculation treading so fast on the heels of that ugly fever which he had at Easter.

It is 7 p.m., and I have had at dinner two Messrs. Cleveland only. Madame is at Lee, and when the gentlemen come up to the Board,[1] they willingly dine with me, as they are at liberty to retire to their post-chaises the moment they have dined. I make no fuss with them, but contrive that the bell shall ring as they step into the house, assuring them I have not waited a moment. To-day they had a very good soup, some mackerel, ham and Hatchlands' chickens, cold mutton and salad (which is Mr. Cleveland's favourite dish), and apricot tart. They had claret, madeira, jellies, oranges, etc., and departed in little more than an hour after they came in. This sort of treatment encourages them (as I guess) to promise me they will eat their victuals here while I stay in town.

[1] The Admiralty Board. Mr. Cleveland, the Secretary, who lived at Lee, had a younger son in the Navy, who, thanks to his father, was promoted Captain at the age of 18.

To-morrow I dine with the great Adair, at the particular desire (I believe) of Lady Rowley,[1] who is so fond of me that she can't live without me, and asks me to dine and sup with her every day of my life. Last Tuesday I did both, and kept very good hours, too. Sir William seems entirely to approve this *belle amitié* of Madame's. I'm a violent favourite with him, too. And, on Sunday next, I dine at Lee, together with the said Mr. Adair and Sir Wm. and Lady Rowley, who both declare they'll go in my coach for the sake of my company. I am invited to their country seat and what not.

I have hired a housekeeper, which has most excessive recommendations and is, besides, niece's niece to my quondam *Gouvernante*, Mrs. Hayward of awful memory. The person I have taken is very young, which perhaps I chose on purpose to make my court to those who do not like "Grey Cat."

22nd May. To my dearest and best I dedicate a second folio in the midst of all that hurry which attends and precedes the arrival and despatch of the waggon. Mine is arrived this day. To-night we load; to-morrow, very early, the waggon moves, and at 8 the damsels in the stage coach, together with Wakeham (partly for want of a nag, and partly because that said Wakeham is ill and very infirm), and on Saturday I go with my 2 daughters, my little son and the 2 inoculated maids. I don't know whether you will commend my foresight, but it came into my head to order Woodroffe[2] to bring up some charcoal and some wood in the empty waggon, considering well that, when the waggon comes up at Xmas time, it will be loaded, and incapable of bringing either of these commodities. They all arrived accordingly and Wakeham has deposited them in a vault for the year '56.

Hatchlands, 25th May. I am now to congratulate my dear love on the happiness of his little wife and little family on their safe arrival at this verdant mansion. We got here yesterday evening before sunset. At Leatherhead all hands had as much

1 Wife of Sir William Rowley of the Admiralty Board.
2 The bailiff at Hatchlands.

tea, milk and bread and butter as they pleased. Messes of warm milk were likewise ready when we arrived, after which to wash and to bed, and to sleep exceeding sound. A pigeon was proposed to me at 9, and I had not the heart to refuse it. I went to bed, however, before 11 and rested well, though I did not forget that I wanted the partner of my chintz bed. I should tell you, though, that I eat green peas and heard the nightingale or ever I eat my supper.

To-day, being morning Church, we could not attend Mr. Greenhill, but walked about, my two companions, Mistress Runaway and Mistress Sparaway, being as delighted as colts turned to grass, plucking up the cowslips and longing for the oak apples. I will say nothing of my Walk, but as to the growth of the plants, and the difference of their appearance since last year, I won't anticipate, but please myself with fancying that my dear companion will take a walk with me in it or ever the leaves fall. Yet, should that be happily the case, he'll know nothing of my spring beauties, so I will just deign to tell you that I have purple lilacs, yellow laburnums, white Gelder roses *comme des Susannes ou Nanettes*, fine red cinnamon roses, delightful double thorn blossoms; and my double flowering cherries and peaches assure me they have done their duty (witness their remains though I would not come to see them). Indeed, I'm come as soon as I could, having brought Billy with a plaster upon each arm. The rogue dined with me to-day and eat his plum pudding and asparagus so heartily 'twould have done you good to see him, and me a great deal to have seen you see him.

The afternoon was spent partly in conference with Woodroffe (who makes out a very good state of affairs) and partly in causing a general delivery of all the chairs and stools *alfresco*. Then to drink tea, and *puis* to separate the hay from the straw in my own apartment, drawers, etc., in which laudable employment I was in the midst, assisted by Mrs. Mary and counter-assisted by my two daughters, when behold Mrs. Lane and Mons de la Vergne. They had walked from Horsley, but would have no tea or refreshment.

"Well—when did you hear from the Admiral?" "So and

so." "Well, so you write to him ever." "Yes frequently." "So then, pray tell him that I am here at Horsley and that as long as I stay I'll be the comfort of your life, d'ye hear—don't forget to tell him so." *Mais vous, mon cher*, don't you believe a word of it, unless you substitute the word torment in the room of comfort and then there may be some truth in it. For she stayed two hours and made me a poor miserable hearer of all the *monstrous* behaviour of I don't know who, etc. I would fain have talked of Portsmouth to Mons de la Vergne, but it could not be. She would not let either of us put in one word endways, and yet you'll say, to silence Mrs. Boscawen and a Frenchman is a pretty hard task—yet, I assure you, she accomplished it.

9th June. Billy is now perfectly recovered, I thank God. Purging discipline all over, but *my* discipline to begin, for it has been slackened so long it is unknown how perverse and saucy we are, and how much we deal in the words won't, can't, shan't, etc. To-day he would not eat milk for breakfast, but the rod and I went to breakfast with him, and though we did not come into action, nor anything like it, yet the bottom of the porringer was very fairly revealed and a declaration made by him; indeed he could not but say it was very good milk.

Miss Pitt[1] is with me, and a very agreeable, easy companion. I can tell you exactly the life we lead. I rise at $\frac{1}{2}$ past 6. Here I must interrupt myself while you have recourse to Jemmy Moke,[2] but I shan't bate you a little of it. I have done it near a fortnight and I don't doubt I shall continue it as long as the fine weather lasts.

The first employ is to feed young ducks and chickens, of which I have 40 under the laundry window eastwards. The ducks are large enough to deliver up to the pond, being no longer crows' meat. Then I visit Mrs. Farr (your honour's housekeeper), order dinner, and talk of household affairs. By the way, beef is 4*d.* a pound, and they threatened me with 4$\frac{1}{2}$*d.* when first I came, and made me pay that price for one sirloin. Then I proceed to the *bassecour*, talk to one and another,

---

[1] Mary Pitt.　　　[2] *Je me moque.*

find out whether the teams are gone, follow them, and discourse with Woodroffe.

In all this, I am accompanied by your two daughters, who are called every day at 6 by Nannie Humphreys. This (in respect to Fanny) is done by doctor's orders. He bid me send her out every morning in the early dew that she might outgrow the difference (not inconsiderable) that there is between her two collar bones. And this helps to account for the prodigy of my morning hour. Now and then we go to the village. *Enfin*, our walk seldom ends till after 9, by which time we discover Miss Pitt walking before the door; then to breakfast with what appetite we may, and truth, 'tis no small one. We breakfast in your dressing-room. When 'tis over, Miss P. retires to her own devices and the girls remain to read and work. And, while they work, I write. Here they are at this moment sitting by me, hemming pocket handkerchiefs for Mr. Billy's coat pocket. They desire their duty to Papa and, not content with so reasonable request, they keep prating on and talking to me, just as well satisfied as if I heard them.

At 1, we walk together as far as the grove in the Walk, where we commonly find Miss Pitt, who accompanies us home and we just get a clean apron (for I comb in the morning) before the clock strikes 2 and the bell rings, for Mrs. Farr is very exact, but, I think, not much of a cook.

After dinner, all hands to feed the chickens, then to walk and then to settle in my dressing-room, where I am the worker and Miss Pitt the reader. This continues till near 8, when the girls go to bed, and we take our evening walk, which is generally out of the Park. Another conference with Woodroffe, then to supper exact at 9, *puis la conversation*, and so to bed at 11. *Voilà notre vie.*

The affection which Fanny Boscawen won from all her friends, and the delight they found in her company is reflected in a letter which she received about this time from Elizabeth Montagu. Writing from her house near Newbury, on 19th June, Mrs. Montagu began:

" 'When the mower whets his scythe,
And the milkmaid singeth blythe,
And every shepherd in the dale
Under the hawthorn tells his tale,'

there am I, and no longer in the sinful and smoking City of
London. This happy change was brought about on Tuesday,
by very easy and speedy measures. We got into our post-
chaise between 10 and 11, arrived at Maidenhead bridge about
1; were refreshed by a good dinner, and amused by good
company. . . . I have not for these ten years been so early in
the season at Sandleford, and it appears therefore with greater
charms. It cannot afford to lose any of its natural beauties,
as it owes none to art . . . but my dear Mrs. Boscawen may
turn it into a Paradise when she pleases. When may I hope
to see her here."

Mrs. Boscawen, however, was too busy in her own paradise
to tear herself away. On 1st July she was writing to her
husband:

We have been once at Lady Onslow's and once at Mrs.
Lane's, which is all the visits we have made, which gives two
teams constantly to the farm.

I don't know whether I told you that Charles Brett's wife[1]
is with me, though sure I must, for she has been here these
three weeks. Charles brought her—stayed 2 days. Clements
came with them and returned with Charles, who is expected
again in ten days to reconduct his lady. I like her mightily, and
make no manner of stranger of her. Tim[2] has been to see her
and stayed 4 days here, and when she goes away, Lady Smythe
succeeds immediately to her chamber. So that you see, my
love, I am in no danger of being melancholy for want of
company.

I cannot get my friend, Mrs. Montagu, and I doubt I shan't,
consistently with my plan, be able to go to her, so we shall
hardly meet till January. I reckon Lady Smythe will stay

[1] See note, page 57.   [2] Timothy Brett of the Navy Office.

with me till I go to Portsmouth; you know how comfortable she is to me.

I shan't be able to go to St. Clere after the month of August, yet my father writes me in a very low style which grieves me. He says he goes down the hill remarkably fast. God forbid he should be near the bottom. When I cast my eyes on his young family, there arises such a cloud of mischief from the loss of their father that the continuance of his life is most desirable!

All the world goes to Portsmouth, which disposes of many a slice of my mutton. To-day, Jack Warde and his wife came on the return from a visit to Capt. Denis and his, at Gosport. They came in only to ask me how I did, and bid their coachman walk the horses, but I assured 'em I should not be able to answer that question till after they had eat some roast beef. I did not add one morsel to my dinner, which consisted of a soup, some mackerel, beans and bacon, roast beef. *Puis*, a Rouen duck, tart, lobsters, and prawns from Capt. Dilke. We sat down to dinner a few minutes before 2, as 'twas afternoon Church, but did not go thither and gave Mrs. Warde some tea. She took her leave (seemingly much satisfied) between 4 and 5.

Next Wednesday the Prince of Wales, the Duke and Prince Edward, all the Lords of the Admiralty and Mr. Cleveland, go to Portsmouth, where has resorted all manner of Lords and Commons.[1] I hope the rage will be over before I go, for I love society but hate crowds.

This is a long pull from Easter to Election. I believe I shall break it by a dinner at Eton with my son and a night's lodging at Sunninghill with Lady Hester, but if this takes place it must be before haying time, and, if Woodroffe would believe me, he would mow directly, for the grass rather loses than gains.

Meanwhile, on the other side of the Atlantic, Admiral

---

[1] About this time there was a naval review at Spithead, and Lord Anson gave a big entertainment on board H.M.S. *Prince* for the Duke of Cumberland, which was attended by 1,200 guests.

Boscawen had fought a small but momentous action off New-foundland, and had fulfilled his wife's prophecy by capturing "*pour la troisième fois*," a French man-of-war commanded by the luckless M. Hocquart.

Louis XV's preparations for reinforcing his North American garrisons had been on an even larger scale than the English Government anticipated, and the fleet, which eventually sailed from Brest on 2nd May, consisted of ten men-of-war carrying troops, five troop transports, and an escort of nine more ships of the line. Of this escort, however, six ships returned to Brest as soon as the fleet was well on its voyage.

When news reached London of the sailing of so large a fleet, urgent steps were taken to strengthen the English squadron, and on 11th May six more ships sailed for America under Rear-Admiral Francis Holburne. But they did not join Boscawen till 21st June, and they were then too late to be of any assistance.

Admiral Boscawen, knowing nothing definite about the strength of the French forces, or of the date of their sailing, reached the mouth of the St. Lawrence at the beginning of June, and continued to cruise in that neighbourhood, waiting and watching for the enemy. Constant fogs[1] reduced his mission to a mere game of chance; but on the 6th June, when the weather cleared, the British squadron saw four French line of battle-ships, and immediately gave chase. For a time the French disappeared in another bank of fog; but two days later three of them again came into view, and after a brisk action, the *Alcide* (with 800 troops on board) and the *Lys* were both captured, but the third managed to escape. The commander of the *Alcide* proved to be none other than the unfortunate M. Hocquart—the Admiral must have greeted him almost

[1] Cf. King George VI's experience on his voyage to Quebec in the spring of this year, 1939.

as an old friend—and from him it was learnt that the rest of
the expedition were ahead of him, and had probably entered
the St. Lawrence by way of the Straits of Belle Isle, which no
ships of that size had ever used before. This turned out to be
true, and though the Admiral continued to cruise off the
Newfoundland Banks till after Holburne reached him, not
another French ship was seen.

By this time, towards the end of June, all the crews of
Admiral's Boscawen's squadron were being ravaged by fever,
and so many deaths were occurring that the Admiral left
Holburne to watch the entrance to the St. Lawrence and proceeded with the original part of his force to Halifax. But the
fever continued to rage, even in harbour; and for several weeks
to come the squadron was out of action.

It was not only in the extreme north, however, that fortune
was favouring the French in the summer of 1755. Down south,
in Virginia, after a succession of interminable delays, General
Braddock had started off with a column of 2,000 men, to clear
the French from the Ohio valley and capture Fort Duquesne.[1]
Quick to realize merit, he had appointed Colonel Washington
as his personal assistant and A.D.C., but his bullying manners
had already gone far to estrange the sympathy of the Pro-
vincials, while his insistence on "parade-ground discipline"
had lost him the support of the majority of the friendly
Indians. Transport was deficient, and the march of the long
column through jungle country was painfully slow; but on
8th July, Braddock advanced with 1,200 men to attack Fort
Duquesne. The following morning, when still some miles
from the Fort, disaster overtook him. His long, straggling
column was suddenly ambushed by a force consisting of one
hundred French and several hundred Indians hidden in the
forest on their flank, and was literally cut to pieces. Braddock

[1] See sketch map, facing page 154.

himself, after showing conspicuous bravery, was mortally
wounded, sixty-three of his eighty-nine officers became
casualties, and more than two-thirds of the men. The remainder broke in panic, and all the English guns, ammunition,
and baggage fell into the enemy's hands. Washington, whose
own courage was superb throughout the engagement, had
two horses shot under him and four bullets through his coat,
but despite the complete rout of the column, he rallied some of
the men and carried his wounded General to safety. His own
report to the Governor makes gloomy reading: "We were
attacked," he wrote, "very unexpectedly, I must own, by
about 300 French and Indians. Our numbers consisted of
about 1,300 chosen men, well-armed, chiefly regulars, who
were immediately struck with such a deadly panic that nothing
but confusion and disobedience of orders prevailed amongst
them. The officers in general behaved with incomparable
bravery. . . . Our poor Virginians behaved like men, and
died like soldiers—only 30 left out of 3 companies. . . . In
short the dastardly behaviour of the English soldiers exposed
all those that were inclined to do their duty to almost certain
death, and at length, in despite of every effort, broke and ran
like sheep before the hounds." Braddock, whose ignorance of
Indian methods of warfare, and refusal to listen to the advice
of provincial officers, had been largely responsible for the
catastrophe, kept his courage to the end. With his life ebbing
away, his last recorded words were: "Who would have
thought it. . . . We shall know better how to deal with them
next time."

By this defeat, the frontiers of Pennsylvania, Maryland and
Virginia were left in insecurity; and owing to lack of co-
operation between the various states, to the apathy of some of
them, and to the inefficiency of the English generals who were
sent from home to help, three whole years were to pass before

the situation was restored. The local state of affairs in the autumn of 1755 can be judged from a letter to Admiral Boscawen by Robert Dinwiddie, Governor of Virginia. The Admiral had of course heard the news of the Braddock disaster, and when, in September, he found himself still chained to Halifax by the outbreak of fever in his squadron, he had helped the Virginian government with all the powder and small-arms he could spare. The Governor had replied as follows:

November '55.

To ADMIRAL BOSCAWEN,
I had your letter of 11th September, with 500 barrels of powder and 400 small arms, which supply was very seasonable, as our magazine was quite empty, and I had no arms for the new levies. I now, on behalf of this colony, return you sincere thanks for this necessary supply for his Majesty's service.

The French and their Indians on our frontier have done great mischief in robbing and murdering our back settlers. There are now 1,500 in Pennsylvania, perpetrating the most egregious villainies. I hope it will rouse the people in that province from their lethargic indolence, and with resentment and spirit [cause them] to grant proper supplies to the necessary expedition.

I sincerely wish you great success in all your operations against the common enemy, and for the service of our King and country, and remain, etc., etc.,

ROBT. DINWIDDIE.

On the New York frontier, the military situation was not much better. A force under Colonel Johnson had defeated a French detachment near Crown Point, but an American expedition against the French fort at Niagara had completely miscarried. Only in Nova Scotia was the situation improved. There, thanks to the energy of Massachusetts troops under Colonel Monckton,[1] supported by a small naval force under

---

[1] Hon. Robert Monckton, son of 1st Lord Galway.

Captain John Rous, R.N., the French had been driven from all the forts which they had erected in British territory.

In England, meanwhile, the news of the capture of the *Alcide* and the *Lys*, which arrived in the middle of July, was at first regarded as a victory. Few stopped to realize that, thanks to the ill-luck of fog, Boscawen had done either too much or too little, and that England, as usual, was utterly unprepared for the war that was now inevitable.

The Secretary of the Admiralty himself drove down to Hatchlands to be first with the news of Admiral Boscawen's exploit. He assured Fanny that her husband would be home in a month; and Fanny, wild with excitement at all this good news, at once arranged to go to Mrs. Brett at Portsmouth, to await her husband's return. No one yet knew of the disastrous epidemic which had laid his squadron low, and which would delay his return, first for six weeks, and eventually for three months.

Elizabeth Montagu managed after all to pay a visit to Hatchlands in July, and arrived there the day after Cleveland had brought the Admiral's news. She brought Mary Pitt back with her for a second visit to Fanny, and there is a charming picture of Hatchlands and its happy mistress in a letter which she wrote to her husband a day or two after her arrival:

We were received by Mrs. Boscawen with the most joyful welcome, as we found her in great spirits on account of the taking of the two French men-of-war. M. Hocquart has been taken twice by Mr. Boscawen in the last war, but did not surrender himself in this engagement till 44 men were killed on board of his ship. Mr. Boscawen writes that he lives at great expense, having eleven French officers at his table, whom he entertains with magnificence. . . . The Duke of Cumberland declares himself well pleased with Mr. Boscawen for his enterprise. . . .

I walked round the park this morning. It does not consist

of many acres, but the disposition of the ground, the fine verdure, and the plantations make it very pretty. It resembles the mistress of it, having preserved its native simplicity, though art and care has improved and softened it, and made it elegant.

Even on 1st August neither Fanny nor the Admiralty had heard of any hitch in the Admiral's plans, for on that day she wrote to him:

My dear Love, I have had repeated assurances from Mr. Cleveland that no opportunity whatever of writing to you will occur before your arrival at Portsmouth, where, God willing, I hope for the pleasure of embracing you. *Dieu sait avec quel transport.*

Thus assured, I stopped the current of my nonsense, for so it would have been in Mrs. Brett's house, where I should have grumbled had you *purred* over my letters while I might otherwise have enjoyed your conversation. But, last post, Mr. Cleveland wrote me word I might send you packets by a ship which had some chance of meeting you (though uncertain). So now, in hopes to amuse a few hours of your voyage, I send you whatever I have scribbled.

Your daughters I carried to school last week; two Roses, much grown, quite healthy and (dancing excepted) I trust they lost no time by playing truant a little with Mama, who attended them early and late with instructions, admonitions, reading, working, writing, etc. Billy is *un des* pretty rogues *d'Angleterre*; stout, robust, bold and comical. "Wants Pa to come home," and "he won't know me in breeches though."

Thus, I praise God, our hero will find his little Ithaca in a good state; his faithful Penelope, though void of suitors, and truly not much versed in work or web, yet equals Penelope of old in tenderness and faithful attachment to her dear Lord!

Ah! *Pour la troisième fois Monsieur Hocquart—quel bonheur!* Mr. J. Cleveland himself came hither with your letters, and I think I have never been happier than when I received them. I could neither eat nor sleep for 3 days and yet lived so well upon joy that I have grown fat ever since.

ELIZABETH, DUCHESS OF BEAUFORT
Mrs. Boscawen's younger daughter
(*From the painting at Bill Hill*)

You are the universal toast of all England, and Mrs. Montagu says that before you go upon an expedition you should get fresh laws made against drunkenness. Your countrymen (and I can assure you, some women) are charmed with you. God send you safe home, and with more laurels, since you desire them, but indeed those you have got content everybody but yourself, and you are here looked upon as the Deliverer of America!

How shall I descend from the hero's wife to the goody farmer, and tell you, as indeed I can, that all things have flourished under my administration. My hay was all got in delightfully and stacked the 28th of July. The rick is no bigger than usual—I told you of 6 weeks' drought; but then my aftermath is admirable, oceans of rain having fallen the minute my hay was in. My turnips are all sowed and on fine seasons. The 2 pastures in the Park I caused to be rolled again and again soon after the aforesaid rains fell, though I had repeated assurances from Mr. Woodroffe that 'twould do but a small matter of good. Your Snip is well, your colt thrives, and all the cavalry seem in excellent order. My Walk is charming, but I wish I could persuade all the choicest flowers to wait for my *Berger*. I have the finest piece of barley in the parish, and forwardest by a fortnight—not a weed for love or money— and I am proud therefore. Thus all things go well, and nothing is wanted but you!

Come then, dearest love, and let me make it the business of life to try if I cannot make some amends for the fogs and ice with which your great and noble designs have been over-clouded and chilled. God grant you may meet with no clouds on shore; with me you shall have nothing but sunshine.

Faites bien mes compliments à M. Hocquart. Dites-lui que je serai charmée d'avoir l'honneur de le recevoir ici, et de lui montrer la bague que je porte toujours, et qu'il reconnaîtra.

Adieu, my dearest love. God grant you all blessings, and to me that of receiving you in my arms!

Fanny reached Portsmouth in high spirits on 10th August, expecting her husband's return with the first fair wind. She was all unconscious of any change of plan; and, in the letters that follow, there is something very pathetic in the picture they conjure up—the Admiral's young wife daily taking up her post on Southsea Common, gazing across the Solent, and "spying for sails around St. Helen's Point," when all the time the ships for which she was waiting were lying in harbour, stricken with fever, on the other side of the Atlantic.

PORTSMOUTH,
24th August 1755.

Here I have been this last fortnight, my dear love, in daily, hourly, expectation of the greatest pleasure this life can give me—the joy of seeing you arrive safe. As I think of it all day, and dream of it all night, so I cannot well sit quiet in my chair if anyone rings at the door, without running to the window to see who it is; for I have upon this occasion learnt all my old vivacities, and am what my father would call as great a fool as I was 12 years ago. I was much more reasonable and quiet at Hatchlands; but here, at Portsmouth, I breathe nothing but the *Torbay's* return. It has taught me a Jacobite health, and we drink "Happy and Speedy" twice a day.

I shall not chat with you long, my dearest life. On the contrary, I am not without fancies of seeing you this blessed day—blessed then it would be. I shall go as soon as Church is over to Southsea Common to stare at St. Helens, which is my daily entertainment, and much the most agreeable I meet with here.

As to Julia,[1] what I promised to tell you is *une petite bagatelle*: she is married, that's all.

One word more and I have done. The girls I heard from yesterday and they are well. Tweedle I heard from on Friday and he is well. As to your son and heir,[2] I have no words to describe what he is. At this place I hope you will see. For that purpose, you must come this week, for his school begins

---

[1] Julia Evelyn, her cousin and oldest friend, had married James Sayer, Esq., of Richmond, and Old Palace Yard, Westminster.
[2] Now 11 years old.

on Monday se'ennight. I shall, therefore, send him hence on Sunday for, piquing myself on great exactitude in fulfilling your will during your absence, I would by no means keep him even till Tuesday morning. He is vastly good and vastly agreeable, not only to me but to everybody. He knows every ship at Spithead, harbour and dock, their names, rates and Commanders, and he is very communicative of his knowledge and often astonishes his hearers. Portsmouth has entirely taken from him the shyness he used to have, he is speaking to everybody with all the freedom, but none of the pertness, of knowledge.

Just now I have had a quarrel with Mrs. Brett. Judge between us. She said the best time for you to arrive was to-morrow, when we are to sail in the yacht with Mrs. Hughes, and that it would be far better than your coming to-night. To this I did not agree, but protested I thought this very evening the best time; and having very gravely pronounced this maxim "that you should never defer till to-morrow that which may be done to-day," *Madame se moque de moi, mais honi soit qui mal y pense.*

Adieu! A short adieu let it be. Spread all your sails, catch every gale, and fly to the faithful arms and tender heart of your most affectionate and entirely devoted

F. Boscawen.

After six more days of this breathless expectation, the bubble of Fanny's happiness was pricked by the arrival of a frigate with the news that Admiral Boscawen's squadron would not, after all, arrive till the end of September. To Fanny, apparently, the Admiral wrote that he "dared to suppose" that she would be as disappointed as he was at the unexpected delay. To this Fanny replied:

Portsmouth,
30th August, 1755.

You suppose, my dearest love, that I am as impatient for your return as you can be. Indeed you can venture to suppose this much and more. You cannot be so impatient or so intent upon one point, having so many important ones to think of, as I am, who have had no other point in view these many days but our happy meeting, which has been all my thoughts by day and all my dreams by night. This being the case, you must not be angry if I perverted the design of your last kind letter, and suffered that to give me pain which you meant to give me pleasure. To confess the truth, I could not read it without a pain in my stomach, grief of heart and loss of sleep, for I had so *depended* upon your coming day by day (having very brisk Westerly winds) that a month more seems an age, and to pass it here I cannot. Not that my hosts are not very kind to me, but that this place of all others would be most irksome after such a disappointment. For here is the sea, and here are ships; and men of war come in daily, but not the ship which my eyes have ached in looking for every day upon Southsea Common, spying for sails around St. Helen's point. This was my favourite occupation, but Othello's occupation's gone, so I go too! Mr. Edward to Eton and I to Hatchlands, where I shall see my dear little fellow; examine the state of my harvest with fear, for we have had severe and frequent rains; see to that which remains, and stay at home while all hands, and all hoofs, are employed to get it in; keep good hours, and try whether, by early rising and going to bed, I can secure such an *embonpoint* as will render me pleasing in the sight of my dearest lord. These will be my pre-occupations for the next thirteen days, and I shall return here on the 12th September to take up my post once more by the side of the sea, whither my eyes and my hopes will be continually turned. *Venez donc, mon très cher, et ne me faites point resentir pour la seconde fois cette peine cruelle d'aspettare non venire.*

But this is your birthday,[1] my love, and we have kept it. Pray God send you many happy and fortunate days, and me the joy of contributing to your felicity! We have drank your health in bumpers, but your son has most distinguished his zeal. He got a flag and flagstaff, which he erected in the garden. Then was Tom[2] dispatched with all the money in

[1] The Admiral's birthday was the 19th August, old style, 30th August, new style, see page 243.

[2] Their negro page.

Ned's pocket, to procure serpents at Gosport. A castle was built, in each battlement of which was an Indian Cracker mounted. These Charles Brett furnished, and finally we have a battery of 8 brass cannons mounted on wooden carriages. All this has been happily discharged, to the great delight of Mr. Edward.

After we were come back from the Commissioners, they entertained me with a Concert of Music, consisting of hands, and really very good ones; an Italian Arrigoni was first fiddle, and the whole was calculated merely *pour l'amusement de Madame l'Amirale.* So much consideration does it give me to belong to you that I meet with the greatest respect from all ranks and degrees of people. My friend, Mrs. Montagu, says if she was about to travel over England just now, she would take the name Boscawen, believing it to be the best travelling name in our island.

The uncertainty of this scrawl's reaching you makes me stifle many subjects which I could treat upon at large. War is most in my thoughts now, as being most my concern, since, as we are told, 'tis actually begun, the Captain here having orders to sink, burn and destroy—horrid words! God send us happily and honourably out of it, and, as my dear Admiral began the war, so God grant his noble achievements may make the peace and he himself live many years to enjoy that peace!

I can hardly end my letter better than by the hearty prayer on the other side, and I will not talk to you of Gen. Braddock, for it is a story that you did not hear without grief and indignation, indeed there has not been one so dishonourable to the English name these many a day—how I pity the poor officers! As to the General, he too, is most to be pitied if by any omission of his this disgraceful calamity happened. I hate to think of it and will say no more on such a painful subject. Where would have been America but for you?

It is strongly reported that Spain is ours and will not go off to the French side. Something tells me, methinks, that we shall yet humble France and bring her Navy into this port.

At least I must hope that you will succeed in all you undertake, and be as happy at sea and on shore as is wished by her whose study it shall always be to make you so, and who is, with inexpressible tenderness and attachment, your most affectionate, faithful wife, friend and servant,

F. BOSCAWEN.

Meanwhile, in America, owing to the virulence of the epidemic which had attacked Boscawen's squadron, he had been forced, day after day, and week after week, to postpone his departure from Halifax; and instead of reaching Portsmouth at the end of September, it was actually the beginning of October before he set sail. But no warning of this delay was ever to reach England; and from 30th August, when news was received that the Admiral expected to arrive "at the end of September," not another word was heard from him till—six weeks overdue, and having lost two thousand men from sickness—his fever-stricken ships crawled wearily into port on 15th November.

One does not need to be very tender-hearted to be filled with real distress at the thought of the weeks of suspense that were waiting for Fanny Boscawen, when, all unconscious of this new delay, and brimming over with happy expectations, she arrived for the second time at Portsmouth on 12th September. During those next two months of suspense—a suspense that was shared by the whole country—Fanny remained with the Bretts, scanning the Solent by day from Southsea Common, or tossing in bed by night with fear at her throat. And as week followed week without a shred of news, her mounting fears were magnified by the evident uneasiness of the Admiralty, the extravagant rumours that spread from mouth to mouth, and the growing concern of the public at the apparent disappearance of the naval hero of the day.

Fanny's friends were all in deep distress for her, but could do nothing in the world to help. Mrs. Montagu, in a letter to her (Mrs. Montagu's) sister on 10th November, said: "What gives me most concern is Mr. Boscawen's delay; the Admiralty do not know where he is or what he is doing. He may be gathering laurels, but they are so deadly a plant that I could wish he was at his inglorious fire-side. I am very uneasy for that poor woman Mrs. Boscawen, who is still at Portsmouth. If any accident should happen to him I should go post to her."

But on 15th November all these anxieties were happily forgotten; and a few days later, in a letter from Hatchlands Park, Fanny was describing the scene of her husband's arrival to her newly-married cousin, Julia Sayer:

HATCHLANDS PARK,
20th November, 1755.

I should not have fail'd to impart to you the news of Mr. Boscawen's arrival (in the belief of its giving you pleasure) if I was not sure the public papers would give you the intelligence sooner than I could by post, as an express was sent away to London before Mr. Boscawen landed at Portsmouth, and after he *did* land I do assure you 'twas next to impossible for me to find *le quart d'heure de l'écritoire*; for our mansion, upon the Admiral landing, became immediately a FAIR through the concourse of officers and others that came to congratulate me. Amongst them, as there were the French gentlemen Monsieur Hocquart and Monsieur L'Orgeril, late captains of the *Alcide* and *Lys, vous jugez bien qu'il me fallut faire les honneurs de ma patrie.*

This lasted till Tuesday 3 o'clock, when Monsieur Hocquart handed me into my coach, and I set out with the Admiral, his small son, and our attendants for this place. We halted that night at Petersfield, and arrived here yesterday to dinner. This morning at 6 the Admiral and his secretary proceeded to London, whither I propose to follow him in a few days, when I hope to wait on my dear cousin as well.

Your affectionate

F. B.

The "mansion" referred to by Mrs. Boscawen will have been the Commander-in-Chief's house in Portsmouth Dockyard; while as for M. Hocquart, we can confidently assume from this letter that he had now been made prisoner, *pour la quatrième fois*, by the charm of the Admiral's lady.

CHAPTER XIV

THE SEVEN YEARS WAR, 1756

A POSSIBLE reason for the more than friendly interest which Englishmen of the present day are inclined to take in the English of the eighteenth century, is to be found in our recognition, in the men of that period, of many of our own absurd peculiarities.

In 1755 the English people, as soon as they realized that their colonies and their world trade were threatened by a continental Power, clamoured for immediate war. Reckless of the fact that, in recent years of peace, the fighting services of the country had been allowed to fade away; that only three regiments in England were fit to take the field; and that the nation was quite unready to meet a foreign invasion, they trusted their lucky star to lead them to victory. Nor was their sublime, if apparently crazy, confidence unjustified. The war which began officially in 1756 was the most important that England had waged since the days of the Spanish Armada. For the first eighteen months of it—as in the circumstances was only natural—the nation's arms sustained such a chain of disasters that the Government and the people were overwhelmed with despondency. But then the tide turned; and a succession of victories followed, which raised England to the topmost pinnacle of power. When the war ended in 1763, it left her undisputed mistress of the seas; her American colonies were safe from foreign aggression; her new empire in India had been founded; and she was owner of the lion's share of the trade of the world. In the achievement of these successes, though he died from his exertions at the age of 49, Admiral Boscawen was to play a highly honourable and unforgettable part.

So great had been the popular indignation at the news of French pretensions in North America, that in July 1755, the announcement of Boscawen's mission to prevent the arrival in America of further reinforcements, and of his capture of the *Alcide* and the *Lys*, was received with acclamation throughout the country. Heartened and urged forward by this approbation, the British Government, without counting the cost, took another step forward, and dispatched a squadron to the French coast, with orders to sweep up all the French mercantile marine that could be found, and by capturing as many French sailors as possible, to hamper the future mobilization of their fleet. Three hundred vessels were taken, and they and their crews of 8,000 men were interned in English ports.

Arising out of French reactions to this behaviour, which in English eyes was justified by French hostile action against the American colonies, but in the eyes of France was nothing short of piracy, King George II became nervous for the safety of Hanover, and pressed for the grant of subsidies to continental States for the protection of his home country. The Duke of Newcastle obtained Parliamentary sanction for these subsidies, and William Pitt and Legge, the Paymaster-General and Chancellor of the Exchequer, were both dismissed from their posts for opposing them.

It happened, therefore, that when Admiral Boscawen returned to the Admiralty in November 1755, a situation had arisen which is not unfamiliar to modern ears. England, having thrown down, or taken up, the gauntlet—the distinction is not important—and engaged in active hostilities, was at last beginning to prepare herself for war. France, on the other hand, whose preparations were much further forward, was taking active steps to invade these islands. An army of sixty thousand men was assembling at the channel ports; squadrons were fitting out at Rochefort and Brest—luckily hampered, however, by the recent loss of eight thousand seamen; and there were so many reports of vast numbers of flat-bottomed boats being held in readiness to ferry the army across, that the incompetent government of the Duke of Newcastle was frightened out of its wits. New regiments were in hurried process of formation; military camps were opening in Kent and Sussex; fireships and floating castles were being anchored in the mouths of the harbours; and most alarming of all, the inhabitants of coastal areas had been warned, in the event of invasion, to drive all their horses and cattle twenty miles inland.

These alarmist measures almost led to panic in the southern counties; yet service in the armed forces was so unpopular that, despite the offer of large bounties to recruits, not enough men could be obtained by voluntary enlistment to man the fleet or fill the ranks of the regiments now to be formed. The upper classes and the merchants had cried for war; but the troubles of the American colonies, and the cause of world trade, were of no more interest to the illiterate masses of eighteenth-century England than the troubles of Europe to-day can be to the population of the Middle-West of America. Recruits for such a cause could not be found, even when the enemy was apparently knocking at the door. The press-gang had to be used to fill the fleet, while to provide a military force to protect the coast, Hessian and Hanoverian mercenaries were hurried across from the continent.

In addition to the reports of an imminent invasion of England, repeated warnings arrived from government agents at the beginning of the new year that the French were fitting out an expedition at Toulon, possibly for service in North America, but more probably for the invasion and capture of

Minorca, which, with Gibraltar[1] and Nova Scotia, had been ceded to England by the treaty of Utrecht in 1712. For the moment, however, the Administration had no eyes for anything but the threatened blow at the heart, and every available ship was kept in home waters.

Actually, as regards the risk of invasion, the moment of England's greatest weakness was in the last month of 1755, when many of her ships of the line, which had been laid up for years, were still unready for sea. With the turn of the year, more ships continually became available, and it was clear that the French could not afford to risk a large army in flat-bottomed boats until they had gained at least a temporary command of the Channel. The English plan of defence was to blockade the French fleet in Rochefort and Brest, to patrol the Channel with cruisers, and (in order to placate the merchants) to allot a few ships for escorting convoys of traders. With this object, a squadron was sent to watch Brest in January; but when news arrived that a small force under M. Perrier had managed to elude their vigilance and sailed for the West Indies, and when, in addition, most positive information was received that the main French fleet meant to break out on 4th March, to cover the invasion, the English squadron there was strongly reinforced, and placed under the command of Sir Edward Hawke.

By this time, it would have been equally possible to spare an adequate squadron to deal with the Toulon force. But very unfortunately, it was not till the second week in March that it was at last agreed to dispatch a squadron on that important mission, and that the command of it was entrusted to Admiral John Byng, of most unhappy memory. Even then, the ten ships allotted to Byng, with three others already in the Mediterranean, would not assure him of any numerical

[1] Gibraltar was captured by the English in 1704.

superiority over the enemy; and so much delay occurred in getting his squadron fitted out for sea that he eventually did not sail till 6th April.

The orders issued to Admiral Byng make it plain that the Admiralty were not yet sure whether the Toulon force was intended for Minorca or North America. He was to proceed as quickly as possible to Minorca, but on arrival at Gibraltar he was to find out whether the French squadron had proceeded through the straits. If it had, he was to take it for granted that it was bound for Louisburg; the threat to Minorca would then have disappeared, and he was to dispatch a portion of his squadron to reinforce the British ships already in American waters. If the French squadron had not passed the straits, he was to embark a battalion of the Gibraltar garrison, and to hurry to Minorca, and if the island had already been attacked, to use all possible means in his power for its relief. If no attack had yet taken place, he was to proceed to Toulon, blockade the port, and so protect both Minorca and Gibraltar.

These instructions, for which Admiral Boscawen, as a member of the Admiralty Board, may have been partly responsible—though it is more probable that the First Lord issued them on his sole responsibility—were perfectly clear, and there can be little doubt that they were still capable of execution. But Byng was ever prone to recognize difficulties. Dissatisfied from the first with the small size of his squadron; looking with envious eyes at the ships he was leaving behind him, as they idly lay at anchor at Spithead; disgruntled by what he considered the avoidable delays that had occurred in fitting him out for sea, when he finally started out on his ill-omened voyage he was already half defeated.

Meanwhile, in the southern counties, the approaching arrival of the Hessian and Hanoverian troops, though looked upon as a mixed blessing, was restoring an uneasy confidence, and in London itself gaiety was reappearing. "The Duchess of Norfolk gives a great ball next week," wrote Horace Walpole on 25th March, "to the Duke of Cumberland, so you see that *she* does not expect the Pretender, at least this fortnight." But Fanny Boscawen, for one, was not allowed to enjoy a rest from anxiety. In the middle of April, five months after her husband's return from America, he was appointed to the command of England's main fleet, in relief of Sir Edward Hawke, and at the end of the month he sailed for the Bay, to assume his new appointment. Fanny left London at the same time, and returned to Hatchlands with her small son for the summer. Here, for a moment, she disappears from our view, for her next existing letter to her husband is dated 4th October.

At this point, therefore, as Admiral Boscawen, and consequently his wife too, were connected to some extent with the fate of Admiral Byng, it will be convenient to follow the fortunes of that very unfortunate officer on his way to the Mediterranean.

The French had decided from the first to besiege the Island of Minorca, and it is often asserted that the threat to invade England was merely a cloak to hide their real intention. If that is the case, the ruse succeeded well. Not only did the naval reinforcements for the Mediterranean sail from Portsmouth two months later than they need have done, but the War Office had taken no steps to place the garrison of the Island on a war footing. True, the fortifications of St. Philip had been greatly strengthened since the English gained possession of the Island in 1712; so much so that after the fall of the citadel the French admitted that, had they known its strength, they would never have undertaken its capture. But military stores were deficient; the Commander-in-Chief, Lieutenant-General Blakeney, was in his eighty-second year; and, of the four regiments of infantry under his command, all four colonels and a large proportion of their officers were on leave in England, and only started on their return to the island with Admiral Byng's squadron. But the record of a certain Major Cunningham would adorn the pages of any story of chivalry. This officer, who had been chief engineer at Minorca, had lately been superseded, and was at Nice, on his way home to England, when he heard for certain that the armament at Toulon was intended to attack Minorca. Knowing the many deficiencies of the citadel, and its inability to withstand a long siege, he at once disregarded his recent supersession; and after laying out all the money he was master of, being about £1,600, in the purchase of necessary stores, he hired a vessel, shipped the stores on board it, and landed them safely on the island before the French arrived. He played a gallant part in the defence of the citadel, and his knightly action was subsequently rewarded with a lieutenant-colonelcy in the Guards.

The French invading force, under the Duc de Richelieu, sailed from Toulon and Hyères on 13th April, and appeared off the island on the 18th. The English garrison thereupon retired into the fortress of St. Philip, and the three men-of-war in harbour, under Captain Edgcumbe, after landing all the men they could spare to reinforce the garrison, made good their escape and arrived safely at Gibraltar. But though the French effected an unopposed landing, their investment of the citadel was slow. They were obliged to send to France for more guns and material, and they were still awaiting their arrival when, a month later, Byng's relieving squadron hove in sight.

Admiral Byng's passage from England had been delayed by contrary winds, and when he reached Gibraltar on 2nd May, and heard from Captain Edgcumbe that the French had landed at Minorca, he at once made up his mind that his task was hopeless. This opinion was confirmed by the Governor of Gibraltar, who refused to obey the Government's order to send a battalion of troops to reinforce the island, on the grounds that even if Byng could land them, they would only swell the numbers that would eventually have to surrender, and that their absence would endanger the safety of Gibraltar. Nevertheless, in compliance with his instructions, Byng sailed for Minorca on 8th May; but it is plain from the dispatch, which he sent home from the Rock before sailing, that he had already accepted defeat. Reaching Minorca on the 19th, he engaged the French fleet, which was slightly stronger than his own,[1] the following day. But after an inconclusive action,[2] he decided that he could do no more, and, without attempting to land the officers and reinforcements whom he had brought out from England, or to get in touch with the Governor, he left the island to its fate, and returned to Gibraltar.

The English garrison of Minorca held out for another five weeks. But in the meantime the French were enabled to strengthen the attacking force with impunity, and on 27th June the garrison surrendered.

In England, as soon as news of the French landing was received, five more ships, and more reinforcing troops, were sent to strengthen the relieving force, and these sailed from home on the 20th May. But when, in June, the Government heard, through the Spanish Ambassador in Paris, of the action fought at Minorca on that date—an action which the French had magnified into a victory—Admiral Byng was recalled and Sir Edward Hawke was sent out to relieve him. Eventually, when Byng reached home at the end of July, the news of the fall of Minorca was known to the world, and so great had

[1] The French fleet had a total of 800 guns to the 834 of the English, but some of them were of heavier calibre.
[2] English losses, 43 killed, 168 wounded; French losses, 41 killed, 181 wounded.

been the public outcry against the Admiral, that he was placed under arrest, and, hissed and jeered at in every village he passed through, was taken under escort to Greenwich to await trial.

Meanwhile, Admiral Boscawen, who had left England in April, was still in command of the main English fleet, blockading the French coast at Brest, and there he remained without relief till the beginning of November. Throughout those six months the French squadrons made no attempt to emerge, but a large number of trading vessels were captured by the English fleet. Boscawen himself, with his high sense of duty and self-sacrifice, can have had little sympathy for Byng. Thirty years before, when, as a boy of 15, he first sailed for the West Indies in H.M.S. *Superbe*, he had heard the bitter comments on that officer, lately a lieutenant in the *Superbe*, for getting himself transferred to another ship to avoid the rigours of service in tropical waters. But Boscawen was anxious, above all things, not to sit on Byng's court-martial, or to act in any way as his judge, and was hoping against hope that the matter would be disposed of before he returned to England.

Fanny, on the other hand, as her journal for October discloses, was thinking it high time that her husband should be given a little rest at home:

HATCHLANDS PARK,
4th October, 1756.

If you have the day in your mind for our meeting, my dearest love, I'm afraid you have not calculated so justly but that you will be forced to make a new reckoning. For one Commander to cruise six months *sans relâche* is a great deal more than can be expected. I suppose I might add more than ever was performed yet by any Admiral. How, therefore, or in what terms of begging and beseeching, they will ask more, I know not, but I am told that Admiral Hawke is sent for home with his Squadron, and that, till the said Squadron is safe in the English ports, you will be desired to remain off Brest, as the only person that can *deter* the French from coming out and attacking Sir Edward Hawke as he passes through the Bay!

I see I judged right in believing I should make my court to you by offering to stay here till after Christmas, which I shall do very willingly and very happily, I hope. You may always dispose of me *selon votre gré*, and then you may rest assured that it is *selon* mine.

The Parliament meets the 18th November. I hope you will be able to keep your word of giving them a little of your company, but I doubt it.

You did not send me Titcher's letter enclosed, and (what is worse) you forgot to tell me what those *two wants* were which you suppose it difficult for me to supply. *Au reste, mon cher*, when I see Colby, Titcher, and your other followers and friends are so strongly attached to me, and so lavish in my praises, I cannot help flattering myself that you think your choice of a wife happy in that point—in your public character. For, when I hear of a Lady An-n[1] who gives the Sea Officers an account of her *friseurs*, and a Lady Lyttelton[2] who entertains the literate of her table with the wonderful cleverness of her French lap-dog, I cannot but reflect with indignation how much 'tis in a woman's power to distress a brave or a learned man amongst his own society and friends, at his table and round his domestic hearth, from whence a man should draw the best sources of social felicity, ease, comfort and satisfaction. My dearest love knows that no guests are so welcome to me as his FRIENDS, whom, therefore, I shall seldom fail of pleasing, because I desire to please, which will generally succeed without the help of many other accomplishments. And, indeed I flatter myself that all your friends who know me, love me; which at first they were inclined to for your sake, but have since confirmed it for my own, and for that strong attachment which they perceive I have for you.

[1] Lady Anson.
[2] Elizabeth, second wife of Sir George (afterwards Lord) Lyttelton, whom she married in 1749, was daughter of Field-Marshal Sir Robert Rich.

Thus, I presume sometimes to look forward to future years, when you will be wrinkled and I shall be grey. Place each by the other's side in our warm, well-built mansion, surrounded with these your old friends; each will have his neat cabin to the rising sun; a large room and a good fire for all to assemble. We shall talk of old stories, admire the young plants, our sons and daughters. Set them to dance, or laugh round about a commerce table, with good cheer, good hours, good humour and good wine. Perhaps we may yet add *a little tiny* one, which though last, won't be least beloved—the plaything of the house. If such should be your old age, my love, shall you think it tedious? No! far otherwise! but—we can answer for none of these things, and must take the best of the present moment. So let us use it, however, as not to poison with one uneasy reflection those pleasing scenes which may be, through the bounty of an all benevolent Master, allotted to us.

Thus I think aloud to you, my dearest friend and partner, and it is with great joy that I read in your last letter so kind an expression on your side as that you communicate to me your most secret thoughts on men and things. It always was my ambition to possess your confidence, for in so doing, I'm sure to possess your esteem. When I say confidence, I do not mean to extend it to those articles of which King William said to my Lord Marlborough, "You have told your wife, my Lord. So did not I mine." Doubtless in public life there must be secrets which no man ought to impart to the wife, even of his bosom and most intimate affections. But what I mean is that general, unreserved confidence which one friend owes and uses towards another, of whose truth, of whose love, of whose fidelity, he has had long and undoubted proofs. That friend of yours I am, and that confidence I will never abuse, for there can be no link which binds one friend to another beyond those which bind me to you. Affection (even the first affections of my young heart), gratitude, interest, duty, honour—all attach me in the strongest degree to be yours to the last moment of my life, the greatest happiness of which I derive (under Heaven) from you, and would willingly return by contributing as much to your happiness as my powers will permit. Sometimes I wish them greater. Sometimes I wish I had beauty to please you. But then, perhaps that beauty might have produced a youth of folly, an old age of cards. Those who are adorned with it often neglect to adorn their mind and their heart. And yet, these are a much more lasting and inexhaustible fund of happiness than merely a polished form. The one can but please the eye, the other extends to every faculty of the man. Upon the whole, you see, I would fain pass myself off upon you as a useful and a pleasant appendix to your state in this life. But my judgment, or rather, my self-flattery, is nothing. You must think me so too, or I am not the happy woman I take myself to be.

And now I will end this interesting conversation which I was insensibly led into—not merely, I hope, for the sake of talking of myself, but to talk of you and with you. *Revenons à nos moutons.* I have sold a load of new wheat for £10.10.0. I have let the fall of this year of Gaston Copse to Mrs. Delver at £4.4.0. per acre. And of this I must take the entire merit to myself, for when I proposed that price to Mr. Woodroffe he quite laughed at me, having himself (when I was at Portsmouth last year) sold the fall for £3.15.0 per acre.

I am vastly glad you have been so well supplied with turtle. I think the two clubs at White's should send you all theirs. I can't consent to take your pineapple. *No thank you*, I had rather send you a great bundle of bergamy pears which old Betty presented to me the other day and told me 'twas all she had. "But why don't you keep a few for yourself Betty? Don't you love pears?" "Yes, my lady, I love pears, but I love you better." This was truly the poor old creature's answer. She often asks after our Brave Admiral, and when I told her yesterday you was well, would be home soon and stay here till Xmas, she gave a great jump for joy by the help of her broom.

I am vastly glad you have a scheme to avoid Byng's trial. Mine is to make Forbes[1] President. 'Tis the only service he can do, you know. We talk now no more of Byng than if he

---

[1] Vice-Admiral the Hon. John Forbes.

was not. Two months ago every third word one spoke was Byng.

If you wish you were bound for England, my love, judge you whether I do not join in that wish. Pray tell me as soon as you determine to steer that course, *malgré* the injunctions of the *Tree*,[1] for I do most desperately smell a rat from that quarter.

I shan't send this letter to them, so I may express how much it astonishes me that Lord A. should not have wrote to you. That Cleveland is angry at your anger is very likely, but that his Lordship should adopt his Secretary's resentment—that is surely very unworthy and would tend to confirm a vulgar opinion that Cleveland is Lord High Admiral. T'other day his son Archibald was made a Captain and John Cleveland told me Lord Anson had done it unasked by his father. Truly it is unfit, I think, while Randall is a Lieutenant. The boy is but 18, I believe. This looks as if Cleveland really had that influence which people give him over our superior.

6th October. The wind is excessive high to-night.

Knowles[2] well fulfilled your prophecy concerning him. I'm told he has been shut up with Lord A. continually since he came home. And now, I suppose, this working brain is to relieve you. It diverts me to think what difference Cleveland and his patron will find between Knowles and you. I figure to myself he'll have a thousand projects and ten thousand wants, and plague 'em to death. At which I shall laugh in my sleeve.

I don't know what to say to my friend Father Bower[3] (as you call him), but that I love my friend Mother Montagu so

---

[1] The Board of Admiralty.

[2] Charles Knowles, Vice-Admiral of the Blue, relieved Admiral Boscawen in November, but returned for the winter early in December, leaving only a small force to watch the coast. He was much blamed for leaving so early, as immediately afterwards the French squadrons put out to sea, and two large convoys of trading ships returned to Brest in safety. See also Chapter XVI.

[3] Archibald Bower, author of *History of the Popes*. There is a very interesting letter on this subject on pp. 1–5 of the 4th Volume of Mrs. Montagu's letters, published 1813.

well that I had rather he were not such a rascal. She does not believe he is, or, if she does, she conceals it even from me, who, for my part, am by no means so staunch on his side.

But I am got to my 4th sheet, so must make up my packet or it will exceed weight. God bless you, my dearest life, and send you safe to the arms of your faithful and affectionate,

F. BOSCAWEN.

The children are all perfectly well, I thank God—myself never better. I danced 4 hours at farmer Evelyn's harvest home, and was so well after it that we have agreed there must be some mistake in my register and that I am about five and twenty. *C'est le bel âge, mon cher.*

HATCHLANDS PARK,
14th October, 1756.

8 p.m. The eve of my departure for Portsmouth.
I give you, my dear love, what is left of me, after paying, ordering, rummaging, directing, etc. "What!" you will say, "are you then going to India?" *No thank you Papa, only but just to Portsmouth,* but still a world of little affairs have occcurred to me. Affairs of the farm, of the garden, of the house. Directing Woodroffe to cheat Jo Gill of all the rotten dung— the said Jo to be content with long dung. Then a chapter of apples and pears. Then (to Waite) a chapter of honeysuckles and laurels. Then to old Betty to make war upon the thistles in the Park, if any yet remain. Then to Mrs. Whaley, for within-doors, shifts, rubbers, and kitchen tablecloths to cut out, lest my damsels degenerate into idleness, which is the root of all evil. Then *one* has a little bill, and *t'other* would be glad of a year's wages; then old Bronze wants some money, and Master Taylor must have the land tax. Then I must muster the brick carts;[1] and I have also with my own hands composed a table for their regulation in my absence. This table has been highly commended by Master Waite, 'tis very useful, he says,

[1] They were already making preparations for building a new house at Hatchlands.

and will save a great deal of trouble. *Tant y a* that I have been most excessive busy this whole day, *mais à présent me voilà, hors d'affaire et toujours votre très humble.*

I had a letter to-day from your son to announce to me his march out of nonsense into sense—a happy remove that! I have wrote to congratulate him.

I had a charming letter from you on Tuesday, my life. I return you many thanks for it—perhaps I may answer it— perhaps my head may run so upon seeing you that I shan't prevail with myself to talk till I can be heard. I know not how it is, but my rage for writing to you, which has been one of the greatest pleasures I have enjoyed this summer, goes off insensibly as the time approaches of seeing and conversing with you. I fancy it is, that as writing is the natural relief of absence, so when the absence seems as it were, ended, that relief becomes less necessary, for now that I am going to Portsmouth methinks *je touche au doigt l'heureux moment de votre arrivée.* I can't tell you with what impatience I long for it. I would not have you know it. You are so kind to me that you might hasten, and leave some *courageux* behind and afterwards repent it.

But why am I so vain to fancy I stand in the least com-petition with *les devoirs de l'honneur?* No, 'tis enough for me to know that I occupy the place immediately after them, and that, your public service once performed, and your ship in due time arrived in port, you can then be all impatience to fly to me—witness the 15th of last November, when neither the night, nor the drunken coxswain, nor nothing, could detain you one instant from the longing arms of your faithful Fanny. Let her prescribe to you two things in relation to your present arrival (neither of them, you'll say, absolutely within your power). The one is to come before the 7th of November, the other to arrive in the morning, lest she be terrified with the thought of a boat from Spithead in the night season, and in the dark. How I long for that day; but I will talk no more of it, nor think of it just now, for if I do 'tis impossible for me to talk of anything else.

I have received the favour of a most polite letter from Mr.

Pitt,[1] to announce to me the birth of his son.[2] *À propos* of the said Mr. Pitt, you wrong him indeed when you attribute to him the 4th letter to the People, for it is the joint letter of Messrs. Beckford and Charles Townsend, or at least universally said to be so. Besides, I have another proof (but I don't know what stress you will lay upon it). It is this: I had fancied one of the Monitors had been wrote by Mr. Pitt. His sister told him my opinion, upon which he bid her assure me that he had wrote nothing, nor would write anything upon the present uneasiness. Do you believe him, my love? I own to you I do: but, you'll say, I have great faith. It is certain I believe that he has had great offers, and that the plan was to have *settled matters with the Opposition* before the meeting of Parliament, but he has hitherto refused all. Why, I know not, as the Ministry could not settle with these opponents and orators. They have turned towards Leicester House, and there they have made up matters. Earl of Bute, Groom of the Stole to His R. Highness; Lord Rockingham, Master of the Horse; Lord Bathurst, Treasurer; Lords Euston and Pembroke, Lords of the Bedchamber; Messrs. Monson and Nugent, Junior Grooms of do.; Simon Fanshaw one of the Green Cloth. But now, the best of the news remains behind, and it will give you pleasure to hear that John Evelyn is also Clerk of the Green Cloth to the Prince. 'Tis a secret as yet, however, and not yet declared. And your cousin of Claremont contrived to do this thing for him with the worst grace that was possible. Lord Godolphin[3] insisted upon something, and the Duke of Newcastle haggled for an hour with our farmer, but the other saw through him and, believing something good was at the bottom of the dish, blowed off the froth that was first presented to him, with great disdain. The salary of these new Green Cloths is £400 per annum.

[1] William Pitt, later 1st Earl of Chatham.

[2] John Pitt, 2nd Earl of Chatham, was born 10th October, 1756.

[3] Francis, 2nd Earl of Godolphin, was son of Sidney, 1st Earl, whose sister, Jael, was Admiral Boscawen's grandmother. He was therefore the Admiral's first cousin once removed.

15th October, 1756.
ALTON, 11 *a.m.*

I am so far happily arrived on my journey, having set out at half-past five. But you'll tell me I have lost my way. *Point de tout*, sire, for I am going to Winchester to see the Hessian Camp. Charles Brett meets me at the Chequer in that city this afternoon. How polite he is! To-morrow we proceed to Portsmouth.

I think, meantime, you'll commend my diligence for being in the coach by half-past five, and getting a cow milked, too, that Master William might have a can of milk, sir, before he set out. We put a pillow into the coach, but there's no such thing as sleep in his eye. As soon as we got here, we put him down in his bed, and covered him up most neat, darkening the room; but he had not lain five minutes before he called out that the bed had no posts, that 'twas a silly bed, and that he did not want to lie in it, but rather to see those pictures that hung in the passage. And this speech he accompanied with corresponding acts, for he produced both his boots and then ran away as hard as he could drive. He is now making a great riot in the galleries.

Mr. and Mrs. Frederick, after their very long visit here, departed the day before yesterday to Burwood. I named the day for them, choosing to leave myself one day quite alone. However, as it is decreed that I shall not dine alone at Hatchlands, so Botham came the day we went, and yesterday the learned Jos Greenhill tapped at the door just as Mr. William and I were sitting down to a very good dinner. As soon as 'twas over and my walnuts cracked, we parted.

You tell me I shall not brag of my savings this year. Why no, not much. But then, I am very clear of debts. I have had extra expenses too. What pay you have to receive as Admiral and Commander-in-Chief, I know not, but of your Michaelmas salary I have borrowed fifty guineas, for John Cleveland made me a visit last Saturday and that sum was convenient to me. As to your Midsummer Quarter, it was so shabby a one I did not meddle with it. The whole sum was paid into Child's shop, consisting of £160, as I remember, but I have Child's receipt, in whose book there is a balance of £10,000 in your favour *sans* interest; besides the money lately vested in 3 per cents, I think he has bought 11,000 Stock for you, but am not quite sure. When I was in town last, I took up at Child's myself £100, which is the largest sum I have had from him at one time. But according to my father's maxim, I have spent as little as I could, consistent (I must add) with your *gloire*, for I have kept a very good house, and I have had abundance of people in it. The Fredericks consisted of 8 souls—consequently as many mouths—and stayed with me 11 weeks!

PORTSMOUTH, 20*th October*. My discourse was thus broke off by dinner, and now I should very gaily (having your letter of the 12th) proceed to tell you the remainder of my journey —the Hessian Camp, Winchester Cathedral, Charles Brett, who came to meet me, my safe arrival at this place, etc., etc. But this day I have received a letter from Mr. J. Cleveland, imparting that in Council it had been determined you should *not* come home as soon as was intended. This news has struck me dumb, and I cannot talk to you any more of journeys or pleasurable events. I wish this delay may be less painful to you than it is to your affectionate

F. B.

The postponement of Boscawen's return was probably connected with an acute cabinet crisis which had recently arisen in London. It was not only the fate of Minorca that had enraged the nation at this time, and made them shout for a victim. Distressing news had also arrived from the American Colonies; and though Byng might be made to bear the whole blame for the disaster in the Mediterranean, he plainly had nothing to do with events in America. Yet there, too, the French had won important successes. In May, the Earl of Loudoun had been sent out to America as Commander-in-Chief, and had reached New York in June. But on 9th August, before he had collected a force to oppose the French, M. Mont-calm had captured the English frontier station of Fort Oswego, on Lake Ontario, with one hundred guns and large quantities of stores; and all the English flotilla on the lake had fallen into his hands. In addition, a small French squadron had recently captured the British man-of-war *Warwick*, sixty guns, in the West Indies.

In these circumstances, realizing that the Administration was tottering, Henry Fox had recently resigned his post as Secretary of State, and the Duke of Newcastle was endeavouring to persuade William Pitt, whose burning patriotism and well-known integrity had won the confidence of the country, to fill the vacant office. But though, as mentioned in Fanny's next letter, it was at first believed that Pitt had agreed, the report was unfounded, and Newcastle himself tendered his resignation in the last week of October.

21st October, 1756.

It is Assembly Day, and I have prevailed with Mrs. Brett to go—I cannot. I stay at home with Charles, and plead a cold. In truth, a heartache. Nobody knows the news which hurt me but Charles Brett and his wife. Everybody else expects you in with the first fair wind. Would I did so too, and I will explain that wish. It is not selfish—no. My love for you is too generous, too noble (let me say) not to take in the considera-tion of your honour. I have, therefore, been very sensible to that which has been conferred upon you in being thought the only Commander the nation could trust in that which is undoubtedly the most important post. I have been easy (though I may have felt the first smart) and I have been happy. But now the case is changed, and your health is concerned. You are not made of iron, and if you have borne a 6 months' cruise, so much the less are you qualified to stay out any longer. You say it is cold—I am sure it is stormy. You will have no fire—you can now have few refreshments. Can I suppose your health will for ever resist under these disadvantages? That is my care, and if on that head you can make me easy, why—though my eyes ache to see you (if I may so express myself) I will be content with this measure, provided it pleases you.

If you are satisfied with this new (and unexpected) order to *remain* out, so will I be, as well as ever I can. I will pray God for your health and success. Your love I will not doubt of. I defy all length of absence now. There is a root of affection for me in your heart that I know will never be fairly out of it. But, my love, tell me what you will be pleased that I should do. If you would have me go back again, I am ready, and will write for my horses the minute I receive your orders. If you like better I should stay, I will stay—and see no sign that my hosts are weary of me. I have not the least choice *where* I am now, without you; so speak frankly and I'll obey punctually.

And now, my dearest love, Good night to you—I cannot gabble. My head is full of disappointment, *mon petit cœur aussi*, and 'tis natural it should be so, for can I love you as I do and not wish to see you sometimes? Especially when you have filled up the measure of your duty to your King and country. I afford them their part—you know I do—but that performed, may not I have my turn? And who shall satisfy me that your health will for ever resist the sea life?

7 *p.m.* I must come to you again, though I believe it were better if I could get you out of my head a little. But here is news—Mr. Fox out, Mr. Pitt in his place. If it be better for this poor country, I am glad of it—if not, why no. It is Mr. J. Cleveland that tells me this news and adds the D. of Newcastle remains as he was,[1] and that whether the head of the Admiralty will remove or not is not determined. I hope you will not move from the Admiralty just now, for I am sure the public wants your head as well as your arm. And, as to private considerations, I would not willingly turn out of my

---

[1] This news, as we have seen, was inaccurate. The Duke of Newcastle's resignation was accepted in November, when the Duke of Devonshire accepted office with Pitt as Secretary of State.

house till I have got one to put my head into.[1] When new Hatchlands is built and furnished, then, if they choose to send their brave Cincinnatus to his plough, why well! I'm sure I can live with him year after year without desiring once to see London; but, in the meantime, surely they will have more pity upon the State than to affront its bravest and best officer in time of war and action. If it were peace, they might lay you and all your prowess aside—now they cannot.

22nd October. As I dream of you almost every night, I wish these visions of my head, rather of my heart, would represent to me *how* you receive this prolongation of your cruise. If it be occasioned by expectation of Men-of-War coming out of Brest, and if you believe it, this expectation will gild the pill, and, *tout entier à la gloire, vous oublierez la pauvre petite femme.* But, if nothing of this kind is in view, you'll think of these green willows and wish yourself on shore, *comme dit la chanson.* My contrivance therefore is (and I'm sure you'll like it) that you should meet and take Mons Perrier and Co., and escort them to this port, or ever these orders (which trouble me) are dispatched to you.

And now, my love, being in better humour for scribbling than the two preceding days, I will answer some parts of your two last letters. Did I tell you that before I left home I saw the buck wheat thrashed? And a fine quantity there was of it—enough to save us a world of barley if Mr. Woodroffe does not borrow it for his own hogs, to whose benefit and emolument I suspected he had an eye when he caused it to be thrashed in his own yard instead of the field it grew in, which is the custom in Kent. But he told me the field was so soft and his yard so hard that there was no comparison between the two places, and this, I must own, was true, for there had fallen a great deal of rain just before 'twas cut, and the spot he thrashed it upon was a hard chalk. I hope he will be alert in getting in sand and brick with the broad wheeled waggon, for the Common is so torn up with the brick carts, that very soon it will be impassable with narrow wheels.

[1] The Audley Street house had been let for a term of years.

The K. of Prussia's first *aide-de-camp* being come with his Master's account of the battle to our Royal Master,[1] I shall send you herewith the *Gazette* on that occasion.

You will, on the other hand, lament the loss of Oswego, especially if it be true that there was taken with it such an immense collection of provisions as will victual all Canada. O fy, O fy, when will our luck turn? I have melancholy thoughts for poor England. I know little of the matter, 'tis true, but this I know: my country's ruin makes me grave.

I have been out twice in the chaise and saw 150 sail come in from the eastward; also the *Namur* and *Guernsey*, so Colby is going off, and, indeed, they ought to sail to-day for the wind is fair and this convoy to the Mediterranean is large and important, since there are naval stores, shipwrights, etc., for Gibraltar. It is supposed that place will be besieged by the Spaniards in the spring, and that they are on the point of declaring war against us.[2] Silly Dons, it is not to their interest to join with the perfidious French. They would find more of their own good faith amongst us. Should this event happen, we shall have our hands full, my love, shall we not?

I am very sorry for Mostyn. How deceitful are appearances! Would not one think him the pleasantest man in the world to live with? I am excessively happy to know it is not thus with you. Your officers love you and obey you with pleasure. Your example and your friendship at once teaches and rewards them. If this war lasts, you'll form a set of officers—a little Navy of your own making. If one would set oneself to reflect how much good you do your country abroad, perhaps one would be ashamed to wish you at home by your fireside. Yet—all work and no play won't do neither, my love. *Venez donc; jouer avec votre joli petit garçon, et causer avec votre chère petite femme.* What would I not give to know the day when this will happen; and yet, perhaps if I knew it,

---

[1] Frederick the Great, knowing that Maria Theresa, in an effort to recover Silesia, had joined an alliance of Austria, France, Russia and Saxony against himself, had taken the initiative, and in a lightning campaign had overrun Saxony and captured Dresden.

[2] Actually, Spain did not come into the war till 4th January, 1762.

I should not sleep a wink to-night. 'Tis 11 p.m. and you'll chide if I gabble any longer.

I must tell you though, while I think of it, that we dined and supped with Sir John Ligonier[1] the Tuesday before I came here. There were his 3 *Aides-de-camp*, George West, Hotham and Clinton (son of the Admiral). Hotham you know is a favourite of mine, but he yielded to his master, for 75 is a dangerous age, you know, to me, and I am apt to fall in love with persons so qualified. Accordingly, Sir John Ligonier won my heart that day, and his *Aides-de-camp* went off only with my money. He's a charming old man, that's the truth on't; polite, conversible, easy, free and very cheerful. So we spent a very pleasant day and came home by the light of the moon, which rose late.

I have regretted Capt. Holborne.[2] So young that his life should have been reserved for a better occasion, poor man.

Goodnight to you, my love.

23rd October, at 1 *p.m.* I have been out this morning in the chaise with Mrs. Brett to see the new lines, etc., and take an airing. At our return, we stopped at Miss Busshell's, where a gentleman, whom I judged to be Capt. Digby, came to me and said he was going to you, and desired my commands. I asked him to come hither, but he said he was engaged and should sail this evening. It seems he sailed this morning out of the harbour, rather on a sudden, for Mr. Brett told me yesterday that he would not sail before Monday. Nevertheless, I wrote yesterday to Titcher to get apples, onions, potatoes, parsnips, oysters, and what else you might want, and, as he sent me word he had ducks for you, I have sent him a coop. And Mr. Titcher acquaints me he shall get the whole ready to

---

[1] General Ligonier, later Field-Marshal, Viscount, and Commander-in-Chief.

[2] The *Dispatch*, sloop, Capt. Holborne, chased and came up with the privateer, *Prince de Soubise*, eighteen guns, in the Bay, and fought her for two hours. The privateer boarded the *Dispatch* twice, but was beaten off with loss. Capt. Holborne, who behaved with great gallantry, was wounded in the head by a jagged stone fired instead of a bullet, and died soon after the action.

embark by to-morrow morning; but if Mr. Digby sails this afternoon, how will that be? I must bustle about this very instant, and for that purpose, my love, I must take my leave of you.

Adieu, then; perhaps a long adieu! At least I shall think it long after I have had the pleasure to DEPEND upon seeing you in ten days. Don't be uneasy lest I fret myself—for I am used to disappointments. I flatter myself that you will continue well, that is the chief. And now and then, of a sunshiny day, I can persuade myself you will be successful at the last.

My constant prayers go with you, and I am, with the greatest truth, fidelity and tender affection,

Entirely yours,

F. B.

I hope it won't be long before I shall hear my sentence—that is, the length of your absence. Make no scruple of my going to Hatchlands, if you choose I should. I can have Miss Vansittart or Augusta Evelyn, and Portsmouth loses its principal charm when I cannot look to St. Helen's with the eyes of hope and expectation.

27th October. I hate to tell you fibs, and yet I have when I told you Mr. Pitt was Secretary of State. Yet John Cleveland wrote to me on purpose to announce it to me—would not one think he would know from his father, the great Adair, etc., etc.? And so now, how matters stand with our Ministry I won't pretend to tell you, lest I utter falsehoods, which I much dislike.

I can tell you some rumours, viz.: Lord Temple, first Lord of the Tree (that would be curious).[1] Whether, after all, Lord A. will be out, I dare say you are better able to judge than I am, and so I will not pretend to talk politics, for I really believe the present system is so uncertain that it is not well understood even in His Majesty's Palace, much less in His Majesty's dockyards.

[1] Richard, Earl Temple, was Lady Hester Pitt's brother. He knew nothing of the sea, and had never held office before; hence Fanny's surprise.

28th October. I have a letter to-day from your son at Eton, who is well and likes Pliny, he says, very well. I did not tell you that I had presented it to him in your name. He adds that when he has gone through Pliny, he desires to have *The Preceptor*. I don't know what that is, but it sounds like a sober demand and a proper.

Do you remain stubborn about fire this cold weather? I can't imagine what you do to warm your *pingys* now and then. For my part, I had rather have a short allowance of meat than of fire, *mais vous n'êtes pas de si froide composition*.

We don't visit the Common constantly because of the East wind; nothing turns round the Point. Mrs. Brett says you must come in, were it only to build her a new chaise,[1] which is to be done as soon as you will give orders for it. I think when you are building you'll build one for me too, since (notwithstanding the badness of the times) I must really have one if I live at Level's Grove[2] next year, unless I could drive myself in a one-horse chair, but you know that I am a *mauvaise conductrice*, which I suppose may be one reason why you never let me *conduct* you, *Monsieur Girard*. *Bien, bien, je ne m'en soucie pas*, and as you do not often contradict my will, I don't see that I have any great pretence to direct yours.

I am diverted with your account of Mr. Osborne's[3] road to the *Tree*. At present, he seems only *en second*. Madame hoists her flag above his, and is much the best steersman, I dare say.

Oh, but I should have told you of Mrs. Colby. Well, what did you do *with* her? *Rien*. To her then? *Rien encore*. But I wish poor Colby isn't affronted with this *rien* of mine. He came to me one morning, soon after I arrived. I received him very cordially and friendly, as usual, but said not one word of Madame, no more than if he had had no such incumbrance. I took leave of him with many good wishes (and all of them sincere), but next day, as we stopped at Miss Bushell's in the

[1] The Admiral, as a Lord Commissioner of the Admiralty, could apparently allow post-chaises to be built in the Dockyard.

[2] Level's Grove, now called Level's Dene, is a house between Hatchlands and Guildford, which Admiral Boscawen was arranging to rent from Lady Onslow while the new Hatchlands was being built.

[3] Probably Vice-Admiral Henry Osborn.

chaise, he went by. I called to him, and then he stopped
and seemed to me very dry and husky—remarkably so. And
it came into my head that I had offended him by not naming
Mrs. Colby and a visit on one side or the other. However,
perhaps I might be mistaken in this conjecture. I hope so, for
though I am *outrageously virtuous* according to some folks, yet
rather than hurt a friend of yours, I would for once have
visited a W——.

10 *p.m.* I hope you have had no return of your headache,
which I am impatient to hear. Pigot[1] (whom I saw at the
Assembly to-night for the first time) assures me that you are
grown fat. I wish I may find it so, for 'tis a sign that you
are in perfect health. Methinks I could keep you so if I had
you once, and I can tell you nothing so true as that I long
to try.

Our Assembly has been rather thin, the dancing men all
marines. Harland's wife safely delivered of a daughter, poor
little woman. I am glad she is out of her pain, for *pains* have
hurt her all this morning, last night and yesterday. She was
brought to bed at 3 p.m. to-day. Pigot seems to be a genteel
man. Came and talked to me about you while I was playing
at Quadrille with Mr. Walter, so I revoked trumps when they
played Spadille, etc., etc., and reserved them to trump their
kings; withal this was not allowed, but served to divert Mrs.
Brett excessively and to set Capt. Pigot to ask pardon and to
go away from the table.

I hear Keppel has taken a prize. I am glad of it, being
inclined to love the said Keppel. Do you know why? It is
because I've a notion he loves you.

30*th October*, 1756. I send you my last advices from Hatchlands, and do not brag how well I have sold your wheat, for
indeed the price shocks me. The poor cannot live if wheat is
£13 a load, and there seems no natural reason why it should be
so; the crops last year and this were fine, and the harvest

---

[1] Captain (later Admiral) Hugh Pigot.

should be good, except 3 weeks this year which affected only those parts that are very early in reaping. I fancy there must be some vile scheme of monopolizing and hoarding,[1] which will demand redress of the legislative power if it goes on, for to have famine added to war, God forbid!

Capt. Proby and Capt. Pigot dined here to-day, together with a very agreeable man with a wooden leg. His name is Scolding—a great friend of Mrs. Brett's. I took to him mightily, for he is very conversible. He was in America last year with Proby, in the *Syren*, and has been describing the irregulars of that country with great humour, and I fancy the life. I'm sure I pity any Commander that is to go to fight with such. The gentleman above named told us that Lord Loudoun has wrote to be recalled, declaring it is impossible for him to carry on the command. If so, I doubt things are in a melancholy way in that country, and will not be amended by the loss of Oswego.

They told us another piece of news, viz.: that Riot Townsend is gone off with Capt. Orme. They were seen together by somebody in the road at Harwich and 'tis supposed they embarked together. What a vile girl! Orme's wife is left in vast distress, they say. I remembered you told me you had met these two last Spring. I am sure you'll be concerned for the death of Lord Drumlanrig,[2] which you read in the enclosed newspaper. I doubt it is too true, and am heartily sorry for it.

A few days after this letter was written, news arrived that the Admiral was at last returning, and a week later he and his wife were home again at Hatchlands.

Awaiting Fanny's return was a characteristic letter from her friend, Mrs. Montagu:

---

[1] A month later Parliament forbade the export of grain and allowed foreign grain to be imported duty free; "but," says Smollett, "the Commons would have still improved their humanity had they contrived to punish those unfeeling villains who, by hoarding . . . had created this artificial scarcity." Smollett, IV, 43.

[2] Charles, Earl of Drumlanrig, younger son of 3rd Duke of Queensberry, died 24th October, unmarried.

SANDLEFORD.
6th November, 1756.

There is no form of confession equal to my guilt in not writing to you, my sorrow when I did not hear from you, or shame when I did. But no traitor was I to any of the warmest and tenderest sentiments of friendship, so I hope you will not order me to be hung, drawn and quartered. . . .

You ask me what I think of the times. I should despair, absolutely despair of the safety of our poor country, if the uncertainty of human events, and the fallaciousness of appearances, did not tell me that one should never hope confidently, nor despair absolutely; and that, for the mind, *motley* is the only wear; but after all, my heart is in more than half mourning to see the wretched state of the public. Wars abroad, factions at home, so much ambition among the great, such discontents among the people! ah, poor England!

I rejoice that Mr. Boscawen is returning to you; in these days of discontent, all are pleased with *him*, and I assure you it will discredit any new administration if he is excluded his share in it. No! that cannot, shall not be; it would put the very ocean in a storm, and the large continent of Cornwall into a rebellion. So let what will happen, I shall hear my coach ordered to the Admiral*tree* as usual.

Mrs. Montagu's prophecy, as we shall see in the next chapter, was fully justified.

CHAPTER XV

THE TRIAL OF ADMIRAL BYNG

WE have seen in Fanny's letter of the 4th October that she and her husband had already decided that, owing to the uncertainty of the Admiral's movements, their household should not move up to London till after Christmas. But scarcely had they returned from Portsmouth to Hatchlands when Boscawen was snatched away to London in connection with the Cabinet crisis. There he learnt that the Duke of Newcastle's resignation had been officially accepted, and that a new administration was forming, with the Duke of Devonshire at the Treasury and William Pitt as Secretary of State. Lord Anson, who, as Chancellor Hardwicke's son-in-law, had for years been a staunch supporter of the Newcastle Whigs, had been dismissed from the Admiralty and, with the sole exception of Boscawen himself, the whole Admiralty Board had been turned out of office. Lord Temple, Pitt's brother-in-law, who had never yet held a Government appointment, had been made First Lord of the Admiralty, but was at present ill in bed. The only other naval member of the new Board was Rear-Admiral Temple West, a cousin of Lord Temple's, who had been second-in-command to Byng at Minorca.

It is plain, therefore, that Boscawen's hands were full. In all but name he was for the moment First Lord of the Admiralty, and much though he would have preferred, while England was still at war, to be actively employed at sea, his presence at the helm was now needed in Whitehall. Luckily, Fanny was near enough to London to be able to spend a few

days there now and again, for owing to pressure of work at
the Admiralty, her husband's week-ends at Hatchlands—when
he managed to take them at all—were of the very briefest
description. Even at Christmas, which fell that year on a
Saturday, he could not leave Whitehall till the morning of
Christmas Day. But by starting from London at cock-crow,
and arranging that the horses from Hatchlands, which were to
bring him the last stage of the journey, should meet him at
Epsom (eighteen miles from Whitehall) at seven o'clock in the
morning, he was able to get home in time for Christmas
breakfast with the children. Yet, on Monday the 27th he was
back again in his office, a performance in no little contrast to
the habits of the twentieth century, when a Christmas holiday
in Switzerland is regarded almost as a necessity, whatever the
state of affairs.

Despite the calls upon his time, however, the Admiral was
not too busy, when he first arrived in London, to perform an
act of kindness to one of his wife's friends. To Mrs. Montagu,
chained to her home in the country, and thirsting for news of
the recent political changes, he wrote on 16th November:

Last week the Duke of Newcastle resigned, and Mr. Fox;
and the following are those that come in: The Duke of
Devonshire, Mr. Legge, Mr. Nugent, Lord Duncannon and
Mr. James Grenville for the Treasury; Lord Temple, Mr.
Boscawen, Mr. West, Mr. John Pitt, Dr. Hay, Mr. Hunter,
Mr. Elliot of Scotland for the Admiralty; Lord Bateman,
Treasurer of the Household; Mr. Edgcumbe, Comptroller of
the Household; Lord Berkeley, the Band of Pensioners; Mr.
George Grenville, Treasurer of the Navy; Sir Richard Lyttle-
ton, the Jewel Office. These have all kissed hands. Mr. Pitt,
having the gout at Wickham, is not yet Secretary of State.
Mr. Amyand is to be a Commissioner of Customs. Sir G.
Lyttleton and Lord Hillsboro have both kissed hands for
peerages.

Writing to her husband in the North of England the following day, Mrs. Montagu repeated some of this news, and her characteristic letter, for all its chaffing vein, gives a clear picture of the general uneasiness in England in November 1756:

November '56.

All honest people wish the public interest in this time of danger were allowed to prevail over every private view. France threatens us with an equal Navy by the spring; there is a great demand for forces in America; and God knows where all this will end. As the weather is so sharp, I do not stir from my dressing-room fire, for indeed I must not hazard my health, which, like Great Britain, is in a tottering condition. If we were in as great danger of being conquered by the Spaniards as the French, I should not be very anxious about my continuance in the world; but the French are polite to the ladies, and they admire ladies a little in years, so that I expect to be treated with great politeness; and as all laws are suspended during violence, I suppose that you and the rest of the married men will not take anything amiss that happens on the occasion; nor indeed should it be a much greater fault than keeping a monkey, if one should live with a French Marquis for a quarter of a year.

Some say Admiral Byng[1] should be hanged for his cowardice and others that he should be knighted for his gallantry. The people in general choose that he should be hanged.

Fanny's existing letters belonging to this period also begin on 16th November, and there is a sly allusion to the corruption that had existed in the Duke of Newcastle's government:

HATCHLANDS PARK,
Tuesday, 16th November, 1756.

The weather is so cruel bad that I don't think I can ask Mr. Westbury to betake himself to Guildford a second time to-day, so you will not have this letter, my dear Sir, till

[1] Admiral Byng's case had not yet been disposed of.

227

Thursday morning—nor miss it in the meanwhile. On the contrary, you cannot have read half the scrabble you have received from the same hand—a hand always devoted to your service!

I had a letter from Mrs. Brett, who says Pigot is going to India, which I'm sorry for, because you like him. I would have him belong to your Squadron. Besides, I think we should keep him at home to produce to the shore-people as a sample of sea-Captains—the first Regiment of Guards can't produce a genteeler man. Mrs. Brett says J. Cleveland and the Willetts are in great trouble lest their father should be out. I hope a few days will set them at rest.

As the taste of the times is to make strict enquiries into the conduct of an administration, the application of public money, etc., etc., I'm determined to be beforehand with any inspection of my conduct, and send you enclosed a faithful account how I have administered the money you left me. It is almost gone already, having paid Mrs. Whaley this morning £17.8.8.

Not the least bit of a walk to-day, and, of course, no manner of stomach for my dinner, which is almost ready. Your son William seems to revenge himself upon his chaise, which rolls its thunder all over the house.

Wednesday, 1 *p.m.* Farewell walking, for the country is rotten. Provided I can get out of doors, I am pretty well satisfied, but yesterday was indeed pitiable, and you did right to pity me. I read as much of Chilperic, Clovis and Charlemagne as filled up the measure of my own stupidity.

I think 'tis an age that you have been gone. I waked myself with talking aloud to you—*enfin, je vous aime un peu trop, et je regrette une absence si longue, après une absence si longue.*

As to the rest, I do very well here when I can walk, as I have done to-day till past 12 o'clock, and, if I could but see you once or twice a day, I defy all the rigours of winter and cold weather. But whether I am of an age to confess myself still *in love*, I leave you to determine. Too true it is that if you don't come on Friday, I shall fret myself more than I'll own. You will come if you can, and if you don't I shall be candid enough to believe it is not your fault.

228

I have given orders about Snip—he is gone to be shod and will be trimmed and ready for Capt. Moore's servant. Pray give my compliments to Capt. Moore if you see him again, and say I shall be glad of his company and Mrs. Moore's here, if they come this way.

I am vastly glad you liked the appearance of your daughters so well. I must take to myself some credit about their improvement, for in the 4 months they were with me, 'twas manifest to everybody how much they improved, both in person, manner, speech and behaviour. As to their Geography, indeed *Jemmy Mocque* with you—nevertheless, 'tis true that Mrs. Frances has a taste for the abstruse Sciences, and I believe would learn the mathematics if she thought 'twould make her appear *womanly* and *clever*. Not so Mrs. Bess. She seems conscious of powers within herself and her own majestic personage that renders all foreign acquisition unnecessary. They are fine infants indeed; God be praised for them, and make them good.

Et toi, mon cher, il faut que je te quitte. The glazier is impatient for my letter. I am excessively so to see you, so come as soon as you can!

HATCHLANDS,
Wednesday, 1st December, 1756.

A short letter from my love to-day and well off too that I have any at all.

I am glad that you went to the Birthday and hope the Princess was gracious.

Here is your son's letter. You see the poor creature has been wasting himself in expectation that you would go to Eton to see him, all founded upon a supposition that you could not be worse than your word. But for once I fancy you will take the liberty to shirk Mr. Edward, for I don't see how you can do otherwise now Lord Temple is ill and *vous êtes le maître*. But you see, your son expected that you would dedicate your Sabbath to him—poor fellow, I pity him. The short, broken sentences of his letter are very expressive of his longings and disappointment.

I had a letter to-day from Mrs. Montagu, dated in Hill Street (doubtless to her great joy). She has not forgot the obligation of your letter, but expresses so much obligation towards you that, methinks, it behoves me to look sharp lest it grows into a softer sentiment. She says Mr. Pitt's administration is attacked before he has administered.

In every leaf that falls we expect to see Capt. Moore and lady, whom you have announced to us. It would be much better if you would help us to receive them, and I rejoice in the expectation of seeing you on Friday, which is a day sooner than I durst promise myself.

Adieu, très cher.

Here is your son's letter, to which I answered *sur le champ*, that whenever he came, it should be upon his bay horse straight hither, for as he don't want clothes, what should he do in London.

I have thought of an honourable match for Colonel J. to give him his desired independence.[1]   I'll tell you it when we meet. 'Tis an ancient virgin; vastly preferable to a battered harridan.

The letter from Mrs. Montagu which Fanny mentions is of interest as showing, as clearly as a letter can do, the difference in the characters of these two devoted friends—Mrs. Boscawen, the greatly loved and loving mother and wife, whose home was the centre of her life, and whose natural gaiety and charm was that of a limpid stream on a summer day; Mrs. Montagu, the sophisticated London hostess and woman of the world, whose polished wit had the hardness as well as the brilliance of a diamond:

From Mrs. Montagu to Mrs. Boscawen.

HILL STREET,
30*th November*, 1756.

I shall not think I am quite happy till you come to town, for methinks I want my best half. Lady Frances Williams told me

---

[1] Col. John Boscawen's wife, Thomasine Surman, had died on 7th January, 1750, in childbirth, after only thirteen months of marriage.

on Sunday evening that you had been in town the foregoing week. *Quel contretemps!* Now you are a country gentle-woman, and I am the fine town lady, and the daily news I begged of you, you may request of my charity.

Mr. Pitt, the great Atlas of the state, can support it only with one arm, having the gout in the other; but he will be well enough to be at the House of Commons on Thursday, and if you have not curiosity enough to see the opening of so great a scene you are as great a philosopher as Diogenes, who chose rather to see the sun than Alexander the Great. So pray, Madam, be not too cynical, but come away to town, and leave the sun to raise the snowdrops and crocuses in your garden.

Lord Temple has a grievous cold and keeps house, and though time and tide wait for no man, the Navy of Great Britain may be more complaisant, and wait his Lordship's health and leisure.

I must tell you of an infinite *politesse* of your Admiral's, for which I desire you to thank him, though I have already done it, but I think your thanks will be many per cent better than mine. You must know, finding in my letter to you that I was hungering and thirsting after the news of the times, he sent me a complete list of who was in, and who was out. You may believe I was very glad he agreed to stay in the Admiralty; setting aside all private considerations (and such as affect you weigh much with me), yet for the public too, it is very right, and every man in this country ought to assist the government in this time of danger.

There is a lively sort of paper who has begun to attack Mr. Pitt's administration before he has ministered or administered . . . which I think not altogether fair. The paper is called the *Test*. . . . I would have the people bestow all their anger, all their virulence and whatever courage they have to spare on our enemies the French; but truly they are for the sport of domestic feuds. I never knew the world so absurd, and these times do not give leisure to be foolish at a small expense. Our country is in danger of ruin, and little factions tear it to pieces.

I hear that Mrs. Spencer is with child, which will make her completely happy. What an absurd thing have I said. Who was ever completely happy in this world? The first created pair you will say; but they were soon tired of it, and if people are happy, yet there is some apple, a golden pippin or a red streak, which they fancy necessary to their feast; and if it be out of reach, or not ripe, or forbidden, they have no stomach to the rest of their delicate and sumptuous banquet.

After his next week-end at home, the Admiral, apparently, again left Hatchlands at cock-crow, for Fanny wrote that day:

HATCHLANDS.
Monday, 6th December.
3 *p.m. and dinner quite over.*

After you was gone, I dreamed I had a small, but very fine, bantling to dress in swaddling clothes and, the said bantling much resembling an eel (in motion), whilst I knew little of my business, it never failed to chuck off its case as fast as I rolled it on, much to my trouble. And this fruitless labour, like Sysiphus's stone, would have lasted for ever perhaps, had not *wakeful* Mrs. Mary ventured to disturb me at 9 a.m. So disturbed, I soon perceived that, though I could not dress my child, 'twas very fitting I should dress myself, which I did, reflecting that my dream might be prophetic and that the bantling might come since my unskilfulness to dress it was there ready. *Le voulez-vous? Si VOUS le voulez, je le veux aussi. Si non c'est beaucoup trop de peine pour plaire seulement à ma bonne amie,* Lady Smythe.

The first inspection I made of the weather gave me to lament that you had to ride through so thick and disagreeable a fog. I wish it did not give you cold.

I breakfasted in your dressing-room, and then betook myself to write at your bureau while Wakeham new listed the door, the former list being worn off and the wind entering at pleasure. Thus occupied, I was agreeably surprised with a visit from your nephew Bisshopp, who told me his wife meant to have come with him to wait on me, but his post-chaise was

232

broke. We visited the foxes, and the hog under Mr. Wood-roffe's knife, and I earnestly invited him to try whether it might not yield good griskins. But he had promised to dine with Mrs. Bisshopp, and would not fail her, which I could not but honour him for.

Au reste, my dinner was ready precisely at 2. Having given a lecture to Mr. Faesch,[1] which he took very respectfully, your son dined with me and we had Admiral Boscawen's health *à plusieurs reprises*. Since which, my gentleman is retired to Becca and to romps, and I to scribble all manner of stuff to those who have least time to bestow on such nonsense.

Ah ça, je les quitte donc, et je m'en vais voir quels espèces de menteries me dira Monsieur de Voltaire.

Bon soir donc, très parfaitement cher.

Monday, 13th December, 1756.

We have had an absolute May day, so warm, so soft, so bright, so fair, that 'tis not in words to express how much I have wished, longed, sighed, pined for your company to enjoy it in our Park. You, that have not enjoyed MAY on *terra firma* these three years, that you should fly from it to London smoke this heavenly day is most vexatious. The birds sang, the hounds were in full cry; and Billy and his faithful Becca disported themselves in the wood. Thither Van and I repaired the instant we had breakfasted, and returned not till toward the hour of 2. But all of us together, in full chorus joined, can never describe to you all the beauty and softness of this day, to which there was nothing wanting but your presence.

The chase of Messrs. William and Edward[2] was like the story of the bear and fiddle, for it broke off in the middle by means of a horse-shoe which was found wanting on Sir William's horse's foot. So they returned about 11 a.m.—the one betook himself to navigation in the horse pond, the other to crow-shooting in the Park. If the first succeeded, I cannot

---

[1] The Swiss chef, who went to America with the Admiral in 1755, was now chef at Hatchlands.

[2] Her younger and elder sons.

tell, but I assure you the latter did not, and that you are not a crow the worse for all his malice.

Miss Botham rode here and took a walk with us in the kitchen garden, but would not dine. At which we neither joyed nor grieved; but judge you whether it was with the same indifference that I saw your place vacant at dinner, when we had 5 successive plates of hot sprats—not to say a word of our good company, which the weather has so enlivened that you do not suspect how clever and agreeable we are.

Au reste, mon cher, I beg as much of your time as you can spare me, and as quick a return as you can afford me.

Fanny's next letter is of particular interest, for she had heard that morning of the imminent publication of the order for Admiral Byng's trial:

Tuesday, 14th December, 1756.

I return my dearest love many thanks for his kind letter. The events you impart to me give me so much curiosity for those which you could not recollect that I was vexed with the interruption (whatever it was) that hindered your writing all that you had in your mind to tell me. As Mr. Fox's plan is to oppose, is he not much *déconcerté* at the defection of his great Duke of Bedford,[1] whose choice of a Secretary I admire? You will say, do I know the bold R?[2] Why, certainly not, yet one cannot help forming to oneself ideas of people that one has seen and heard. My idea, then, of this gallant personage is that he may be well calculated for pleasure, but is not at all fit for business. At least, he will not "*réformer les moeurs des Irlandais,*" we may venture to affirm.

I rejoice extremely at Keppel's[3] taking a small French Man-

[1] John, 4th Duke of Bedford, had been appointed Lord Lieutenant of Ireland.

[2] Richard Rigby, secretary to the Duke of Bedford, when Lord Lieutenant of Ireland, was subsequently Paymaster-General of the Tories, and on his death it was said that he left "near half a million of public money." F. B. had obviously no high opinion of him.

[3] Captain Keppel, commanding the *Torbay*, seventy-four guns, captured the *Chariot Royal*, thirty-six guns, laden with stores and clothing for Louisburg, and carrying 160 soldiers.

of-War: next time I hope 'twill be a great one. Store ships sound likewise well.

Si messieurs les Ministres s'amusent à quereller, le Renard en profitera, and if Lord Temple has no thoughts of removing into Tree, methinks it looks as if he did not take very fast hold of it. *Hébien, nous verrons.*

The Court Martial will become the object of my attention. I hope Buckle will be of it, because he is brave. Won't West be summoned for an evidence? I hope he will for *plusieurs raisons. Je ne dirai pas les noms.* The President is not, to my mind, stern enough. *Je crains la lénité de monsieur,* but if all the members are of one mind, I suppose the President may be vainly of another. If he should be condemned, I fancy our Royal Master will not exert his prerogative of mercy, but leave him to the law. Well—I pray God give his judges sense, the capacity to think aright and the courage to avow it. I don't know that Van and I shall be satisfied unless he's hanged, or shot, but, luckily for him, we are not his judges—he has those who are less prejudiced and more enlightened, 'tis to be hoped. I am heartily glad and very thankful that you have nothing to do with this affair.

Thus far, you see, I have lived upon your letter; indeed, I have little of my own to present your honour, no event having happened to us since I wrote you yesterday, only a message from Lady Onslow to desire our company to-morrow morning. To which humble request we have graciously condescended, and shall set out when our Captains[1] start for Portsmouth. To say the truth, I think myself well off that my Lady does not expect me to return her visits in kind, viz.: of an afternoon, but I have made such profession of my aversion to *groping* that at length I seem to have obtained a dispensation never to visit in the dark, and I'm sure I rejoice therefor.

Having just paid Mrs. Whaley's book, I am extremely of the opinion which you so honourably pronounced upon me, viz.: that I keep a good house. Butchers' bills 2 weeks—£7, besides a sheep and a hog.

[1] Captains Moore and Geary, both members of the court-martial, were to visit Hatchlands *en route* to Portsmouth.

The printed letter you have sent us is not only impudent, but senseless; and if the new Ministry do but once think of *vox populi*, they will act as incoherently and absurdly as ever did their most pelted predecessors, for the people now are more clamorous than ever, and more nonsensical—they don't know what they would be at, and they change oftener than the tide. They must have a Militia,[1] but it must not be exercised on Sundays—that is, it must not be exercised at all. Indeed if our great men worship the populace, I shall have no respect for them or their measures, but I hope Mr. P—— is above courting the vulgar, which yet it is impossible for anybody to please three months.

But I abuse your time (or rather, your want of it), in amusing myself with my simple dissertations.

Adieu donc, très cher. Je souhaite votre retour, car je suis votre très affectionnée servante. Pray remember the *want* of Madeira.

F.B.

Fanny's allusion to her delight that her husband will not be officially concerned with Admiral Byng's trial, makes a convenient place at which to complete the story of that very melancholy affair.

Admiral Boscawen had always hoped to be in no way concerned with the trial of his brother Admiral; and it was a bitter blow when, on returning to England in November, he found that Byng was still a prisoner at Greenwich, and that these hopes had vanished. He realized that in these circumstances it would be for the new Administration to decide on the course to be taken with the prisoner; and if he was to be tried by court-martial, it would be for the new Admiralty Board to frame the charges and appoint the members of the Court.

[1] The Militia Bill was introduced by Pitt in December of this year and provided for 60,000 men to be chosen by lot from Parish lists, to serve for three years, drilling one day a week from April to October. Originally it was intended the men should be drilled on Sundays, but this was abandoned in deference to various dissenting sects.

The situation in regard to Admiral Byng was in every way distasteful to Boscawen. The friends of the Old Administration were apparently anxious for Byng's conviction in order to prove that the late Government was in no way to blame for the shameful loss of Minorca. For the opposite reason, the new Administration were apparently anxious to prove that their predecessors were just as blameworthy as Byng. To a man of Boscawen's single-mindedness and fearless sense of duty, political manoeuvres of this nature were utterly repugnant.

By the end of November the trial of Byng had been decided upon, and on 3rd December, speaking from his place in the House of Commons, Boscawen had had to inform the house that "the King and the Admiralty Board, having been dissatisfied with the conduct of Admiral Byng in a late action in the Mediterranean, and for the appearance of his not having acted agreeably to his instructions for the relief of Minorca, he, the said Admiral, is now in custody, in order to be tried." But from that moment Boscawen's one aim and object was to ensure that fearless justice should be done, in accordance with the existing law, and without partiality, favour, or affection. There must be justice for the prisoner, whose case had been most outrageously prejudged by the populace, who had been kept so long a close prisoner, and whose effigy had been burnt in every town in England. There must be justice for the Navy, of whose honour Boscawen was fiercely proud; and there must be justice for the Country, in whose service, as everyone knew, he was ever ready to sacrifice his own life.

When, therefore, it came to selecting the members of the court-martial, Boscawen saw to it that none were included but officers of proved integrity and wide professional knowledge. Amongst those chosen were Rear-Admiral Holburne, who had served with him in America; his old and trusted friends, Harry

Norris and Francis Geary; Captain Augustus Keppel; and another old friend called Captain Moore. With all the other members of the Admiralty Board, Boscawen signed the order for the court-martial, which was published on 14th December. But there his personal connection with the trial ended; for early in the new year, owing to the necessity of infusing more life into Portsmouth Dockyard, where many ships were being completed and fitted out for the operation in the coming spring, he himself left London and assumed the duties of Commander-in-Chief at Portsmouth.

The trial opened at Portsmouth on 27th December and continued for a whole month; and the proceedings were followed throughout the country with wide interest, the bias of the general public being strongly in favour of a conviction and a death penalty. Executions, it should be remembered, were far more lightly inflicted in the eighteenth century than they are to-day, and the general public was far more accustomed to hearing of them, and even to seeing them, than we of the present day can understand. Death, indeed, was as often the penalty for an offence which to-day would get off with a caution, as for a murder of the most bestial kind. At Exeter, for instance, in 1755, three prisoners were condemned to death on the same day: one for murdering his wife, one for "shoplifting," and the third for stealing £20 in gold.

The interested, if very uninstructed, attention which the public paid to Byng's trial is reflected in a letter from Mrs. Montagu to Mrs. Boscawen, written on the 12th January. A few days earlier, the evidence had been heard of Captain A. J. Hervey,[1] who had commanded a small frigate in the action, and whose task had been to remain near the flagship, and, watch in hand, to record and repeat all signals hoisted by the Admiral.

[1] See footnote, page 87.

Mrs. Montagu commented:

I admire Captain H——y's method of watching the battle. I have known people boil an egg with a watch in their hand, counting the minutes, but I never heard we were to do so when we basted the French. . . . By this noble gentleman's evidence, I conceive Mr. Byng's to have been the most bloody engagement that ever happened. The Blakes, Van Tromps, and de Ruyters, though men of some courage, must strike the flag to Admiral Byng. I do not believe we shall lose this brave commander by any untimely death. He has abused the late Ministry, which I take to be an antidote against ugly accidents.

At this time, moreover, farces, lampoons, and other pamphlets, deriding the Admiral's conduct at Minorca, were finding a ready sale, and the following lines, published in the *Evening Advertiser*, are typical of the general feeling:

> "With 13 ships to 12, cries Byng,
> It were a shame to meet 'em;
> And then with 12 to 12, a thing
> Impossible to beat 'em.
>
> When more's too many, less too few,
> And even still not right,
> Arithmetick must plainly show
> 'Twere wrong in Byng to fight."

In order to gain a proper understanding of this trial, it is important to realize the conditions under which a recent change had been made in the Twelfth Article of War, in accordance with the new reading of which the Admiral was eventually condemned. Twelve years earlier, in 1744, this particular Article laid down that every person in the fleet who "through cowardice, negligence, or disaffection" did not do his utmost to destroy the enemy's fleet in battle, should, on conviction by a court-martial, suffer death, *or such other punishment as the*

239

court should judge fit. In that year, a fleet under Admiral Matthews, with Vice-Admiral Lestock as second-in-command, fought an inconclusive and inglorious action with the combined French and Spanish fleets off Toulon. In the course of this action, Admiral Matthews made a tactical mistake, from the fatal results of which Admiral Lestock, his subordinate, could have rescued him by going to his assistance. Admiral Lestock, however, was on bad terms with his superior. He recognized that a mere technicality, connected with the fighting instructions, offered him a sufficient excuse for refusing to intervene; and, placing his personal enmity before the good of his country, he unworthily snatched at this excuse, with the result that a victory was lost. The incident led to the court-martialling of both officers. Admiral Matthews was cashiered for his mistake. Lestock, pleading his unworthy excuse, was unanimously acquitted by a court of which Admiral John Byng was one of the senior members.

A storm of criticism was aroused by these verdicts; and in 1748, in view of a widespread feeling that there had been several cases in the course of the late war, where naval commanders in action had fallen short of the traditional fighting spirit of the British Navy, it was decided to amend the Twelfth Article of War, by making death the unalterable punishment for conviction, and deleting the clause which gave a court-martial the discretionary power to inflict a lesser penalty. It happened that Admiral Byng was the first officer to be tried under the amended Act.

The Court sat for a month, and examined a cloud of naval and military witnesses, including the gallant old General Blakeney,[1] the late Commander of Minorca. Finally, they adjudged that though the Admiral had not been guilty of "cowardice" or "disaffection," he had, in effect, been guilty of

[1] General Blakeney was created a peer for the defence of Minorca.

"negligence," in that he had not done his utmost to destroy
the enemy's fleet or to succour the beleaguered garrison. In
these circumstances, as the Twelfth Article of War allowed
them no alternative, they regretfully sentenced the Admiral
to be shot. But, in view of the fact that his misconduct did
not arise either from cowardice or disaffection, they unanimously and earnestly recommended him to mercy. And in
a special letter to the Admiralty they repeated that "for our
own consciences' sake, as well as in justice to the prisoner, we
pray your Lordships, in the most earnest manner, to recommend him to His Majesty's clemency."

There can be no possible doubt that, with such a recommendation to mercy, the Court can never have imagined that
their prayer would not succeed. But when the court-martial
proceedings arrived in London, the Admiralty Board, well
aware of the powerful influences that were seeking Byng's
destruction, apparently decided that a better way to save him
than forwarding the recommendation to mercy would be to
petition the King to ask the twelve judges whether the sentence
pronounced by the court-martial was legal. This was done;
but on 14th February the reply was given that the sentence was
perfectly legal. Thereupon, two days later, Lord Temple and
three other members of the Admiralty Board signed the
warrant[1] which required and directed the unfortunate Admiral
Boscawen, as Commander-in-Chief at Portsmouth, "to carry
the sentence of the said court-martial into execution."

Some of the members of the court-martial then did all in
their power to save Byng by appealing to Parliament; and
William Pitt himself did all that he could to obtain the King's

---

[1] The signatories of the warrant were Lord Temple, Dr. Hay, T. O.
Hunter and G. Elliot. Admiral John Forbes refused to sign, owing to dis-
agreement with the severity of the sentence; and for a similar reason
Admiral Temple West refused to accept a seagoing command that was
offered him.

pardon. But the influences of the old Administration, which were thrown into the opposite scale, made all these efforts vain. "You have taught me," said the King to Pitt, "to look for the sense of my subjects in another place than in the House of Commons."

Thus, on 14th March, Admiral Byng was shot by a squad of marines on his own quarter-deck. Throughout the long trial he had borne himself with dignity and calm; he met his end with cool unflinching bravery; and it has been truly said that "Nothing in his life became him like the leaving of it."

From almost every point of view, Byng's death was a tragedy. Yet, as Mr. Laird Clowes remarked, in his *History of the Royal Navy*, the sentence, in those far-off days, may in one respect have been productive of good. "*Dans ce pays-ci,*" jibed Voltaire,[1] "*il est bon de tuer de temps en temps un amiral, pour encourager les autres*"; and perhaps there was more than a grain of truth in his characteristic cynicism. Perhaps it was well to point the lesson that the failure of an admiral, or a general, to do his utmost to defeat the enemy in battle, may lead to the needless sacrifice of thousands of his fellow-countrymen.

[1] *Candide*, Chapter XXIII.

CHAPTER XVI

WILLIAM PITT SUCCEEDS TO POWER

Up to 1752 the English calendar, as in Russia till 1918, was several days behind the new-style calendar in use in Scotland and most of the European countries. In that year, however, the Gregorian, or New Style, calendar was adopted, and the date of the month in England was brought into line with other countries by the simple expedient of skipping eleven days, and calling the day which followed 2nd September the 14th September. It is interesting to notice, however, that in the case of anniversaries of events previous to 1752, it was customary to add eleven days to the new-style date, in order to celebrate the anniversary on exactly the right day. Thus, in the next batch of Fanny Boscawen's letters, we shall see, as in some of her earlier ones, that though the anniversary of her wedding was 11th December, she now celebrated it eleven days later, or on 22nd December. But the change of the calendar increased the difficulty of remembering the date of your wedding, and on this occasion, at least, Fanny forgot hers till after it had passed:

HATCHLANDS PARK,
Thursday, 23rd December, 1756.

Thanks to my dear love for his kind letter, but no thanks for changing Friday to Saturday. Not that I accuse you of voluntary inconstancy, but I must lament the effect, whatever be the cause, for 'tis not that I prefer you to solitude, but that I prefer you to all the world. A strange, old-fashioned sentiment this, to confess to a fine gentleman, but it escaped me, and you must not betray me. For a wife to prefer her husband's company to all the world—ah *fi, c'est de la dernière bourgeoisie. Gardez bien donc le secret.*

Yesterday was our wedding day, and neither of us remembered it, or paid any sort of respect to a day which has and will (I trust) be the source of much happiness to us and our posterity. God grant we may enjoy many more TOGETHER, in that harmony and friendship which are doubtless the sweetest ingredients in the cup of life. I promise my share of love and amity to my dearest partner, and have as little doubt of the performance of his, whose esteem and kindness towards his little wife makes her vastly happy.

Methinks you do Mrs. Hayward's beauty too much honour when you compare it with that of the Countess of Pembroke,[1] who is surely *la plus belle dame d'Angleterre.* How is it that these young ladies can parade away so, after having been married 9 months? But you say Lady Euston[2] was not to dance— I hope Lady Pembroke will soon keep her in countenance.

You have been very good in going to Bond Street[3] so often, and indeed I believe that seeing you gives my father more pleasure than anything else can do.

I really think Mrs. Whaley a good sort of housekeeper. Why may not t'other be so too, for you know the style is the same, viz.: those that have never been in service. However, I begin to see very plainly that, if we don't like Mrs. Darby, we may have Mrs. Whaley again, for this faithful Dolorida has wept daily ever since she came to the resolution of quitting us, and yesterday she gave me to understand that, if my new housekeeper did not please, she hoped I would command her again, if she was at liberty, though it should be only till I got one more to my mind; and, as you observe, never could we have more leisure to break in housekeepers than at present.

I am vastly glad the affair of Level's Grove is settled so much to your satisfaction.

[1] Elizabeth, daughter of 2nd Duke of Marlborough. Married Henry, 10th Earl of Pembroke, 13th March, 1756.

[2] Hon. Anne Liddell, daughter of Henry Lord Ravensworth. Married, January 1756, Augustus, Earl of Euston, who succeeded his father as 3rd Duke of Grafton, 1757. Afterwards divorced.

[3] Her father's house.

The infantry present their duty. It is holiday this afternoon,
for the ladies, having achieved 5 towels this morning, have
freedom for the rest of the day, and have chose to play at
"My Lady's Hole." Now I, pleading my profound ignorance
of this game, have got myself excused, and the scene of action
is transferred to Mrs. Farr's room, Mrs. Farr herself being an
adept at the game in question. Mr. Wakeham also pretending
to understand it well, and Mrs. Cable having confessed that
she understood it in her young days, these are to instruct Mr.
Faesch and my son Edward (who declares he knows nothing
of my Lady's Hole). By this time, I fancy they have instructed
one another, for I remain unmolested in profound solitude and
tranquillity, whereas I should be probably appealed to *en dernier
ressort*, if any difficulty or misunderstanding arose.

I protest to you, I cannot write any more with these
Admiralty pens—it is quite a pain—so must bid you good
night. But first, as I trust this will be the last time of your
going to London this year, I must add a few commissions by
way of more last words to William, of which I enclose a list,
and remain (in the hope of seeing my dearest on Friday noon)
his very affectionate and devoted

F. B.

Please to remember a new suit for Mr. Edward Hugh.
The horses, the same as before, shall be at Epsom at 7 a.m.

Tuesday, 28th December, 1756.

I return you thanks, my dear love, for your kind letter
received this morning. I send this by Jn. Postillion, who is
going in the curricle-cart to Ripley to fetch Mrs. Susan Darby.

Mr. Evelyn[1] departed this morning, universally regretted
by both great and small. I imagine the hopes to see his love
might have some share in the attraction. I agree with you
that 22 is a most improper age to marry and settle, and consequently that 'tis a misfortune for him to think of it—but
then, when I study the personage, and consider how apt he is
to fall in love, I rather am inclined to grant a dispensation for
this missey, lest a worse should ensue, for I have entertained

---

[1] Fanny's elder half-brother. He was engaged to a Miss Borret.

a high opinion of his present choice. I am sure she has not been educated in all the nonsense that fills a modern missey's head and heart. I expect her modest instead of bold, and sober instead of being a rake. In short, I think it a desirable thing, except in one single instance—that same 22. Please not to mention my opinion of it in Bond Street.

Au reste, mon cher, yesterday was a very eventful day. Hessians[1] in the morning; company at dinner; a ball at night. But, to be more explicit, I must tell you that 5 Companies of Hessians passed us about 10 a.m. and, as we had seen their forerunners, who said they were near, I caused to be carried up to the gate some bottles of your American raspberry rum, and some brandy, with glasses. John Smith, Tom, Wakeham, and many others ready to pour, they offered it to the men that went first, but they shook their heads, looked wishfully, pointed at their pockets, as much as to say, *personne au logis,* and marched on, without being convinced of their mistake. This, however, did not last, and they presently began to find out *de quoi il s'agissait.* As soon as any of them got a glass full, they ran and presented it to an officer, who drank it off with pleasure, and made me a bow afterwards. And so most of the officers drank a glass and many of the men. The waggoners all brought to, for their part, and, having drank themselves, recommended it to the ladies in the waggon, who drank likewise. They all seemed much pleased, and very thankful, and indeed it was peculiarly proper, for it snowed all the time they passed.

Bowell came for money, but when I looked in my bag, expecting to find 50 pieces, behold there was only 22, of which I was obliged to give 6 to Mr. Spratley. This tends to tell you that you will bring some more *guineas,* also *oranges* seville, also *wax candles,* Hannah[2] having sent me 12 candles, instead of a dozen pound, which I meant. Also *half a firkin of good salt butter and a gallon of spirits.* This last I care little about, as it is just as good at Guildford.

[1] One of Pitt's first acts was to send back the Hessian troops, who had been in England since March.
[2] The Boscawens' housekeeper at the Admiralty.

Adieu, très cher. I must conclude lest I make Madam Darby wait.

Je suis toute à vous,   F. B.

Good salt butter will be a vast conveniency, for we are perpetually distressed for that commodity.

For the past few years, Mrs. Boscawen and her husband had been planning to invest some of the Admiral's prize-money in building the house of their dreams; and though the Admiral's expedition to North America, and the subsequent outbreak of war, had delayed the start of the work, they had now decided, despite the continuance of the war, to let it wait no longer. Most of the plans were ready; the money was lying idle at "Mr. Child's shop"; Level's Grove, a convenient near-by house, had been rented from Lady Onslow for the family's occupation while the work proceeded; and when peace should come at last, the new home would be waiting with out-stretched arms to receive them. And so it happened that, soon after Christmas, Mrs. Boscawen and her children said good-bye to their first Hatchlands home, and the old Tudor house, which had become much too small for them, began to make way for the friendly red brick mansion which stands in its place to-day.[1]

Beyond a casual reference to utilizing the plan of "Lady Essex's house,"[2] Fanny Boscawen's letters throw no light on the designing of the new Hatchlands, nor on the name of its first architect. This, however, is of no great importance, for the new house had scarcely been completed in 1758 when she happily chanced to meet the young Robert Adam, fresh

[1] In 1770, nine years after the Admiral's death, the Hatchlands Park estate, much increased in size since the Admiral purchased it, was sold to W. B. Sumner, Esq. From his family it was bought by the late Lord Rendel; and Lord Rendel left it to his grandson, H. S. Goodhart-Rendel, Esq., the present owner.

[2] See page 151.

from his studies in Florence. Fascinated at once by the ideas of that enthusiastic young artist, she promptly enlisted his help, and offered him his first commission for interior decoration.[1] Robert Adam accepted it. Level's Grove was consequently rented for a further period; Adam spent the next eighteen months in altering and decorating Hatchlands; and the exquisite mantelpieces, ceilings and carved wood-casings, which adorn the house to-day, are amongst the finest examples of his earlier work in existence. Some of the panels are allegorical of Admiral Boscawen's career, with representations of Neptune and Fame, Victory and Justice, and trophies of weapons and flags. And on a plaque on one of the mantelpieces is the study of an old dog, which, though probably not Adam's handiwork, is as likely as not, a portrait of Billy Boscawen's faithful playmate Becca.

But to all who take a pride in what remains of London's eighteenth-century architecture, Mrs. Boscawen's early recognition of Robert Adam's genius has a wider significance than has ever yet been realized. At the end of 1759, when Adam was completing the decoration of Hatchlands, it became necessary to reduce the size of the forecourt in front of the Admiralty, in order to make room for the widening of Whitehall. This entailed the demolition of a small and insignificant wall, and it was decided to replace it by a higher and handsomer wall, with a more imposing gateway. The work was entrusted to Robert Adam, and his accepted design, dated May 1760, for the lovely screen that is standing there to-day, hangs in a small frame in one of the Admiralty corridors. Admiral Boscawen, crowned with laurels for the two great victories—Louisburg and Lagos Bay—which had made Walpole prophesy that his name would be the talk of future ages, resumed his duties as Lord Commissioner of the Admiralty in the autumn of 1759.

[1] Compare Bolton's *Architecture of R. & J. Adam.*

ADMIRAL BOSCAWEN'S DINING ROOM AT HATCHLANDS

(Country Life)

And as he and his wife were living at the Admiralty when the new wall was decided upon, there can be little doubt that it was to their influence that Adam owed his commission, and that Londoners ever since have owed their possession of that very graceful screen. It has been well described as "one of Adam's best known and most loved works"; and, for my part, as Mrs. Boscawen's biographer, I like to think of it as London's forgotten memorial to her heroic husband's half-forgotten fame.

This, however, is a digression; and we must get back to the story of 1757.

Fanny Boscawen's hopes of joining her husband in London at the beginning of the new year were doomed to disappointment. First she was delayed by building troubles at Hatchlands, for on 12th January Elizabeth Montagu wrote to her: "If you have not hands enough to pull down your house, let me come, for I am so enraged at its detaining you, I believe I should be as boisterous as Samson."

But more important than labour troubles was the sudden appointment of the Admiral as Commander-in-Chief at Portsmouth. This put an end to Fanny's winter season, and for the next few months she remained at Level's Grove.

Meanwhile, both at home and abroad, the situation was black indeed. William Pitt, the people's favourite, had succeeded to place, but had not succeeded to power. Constituted as Parliament then was, the favourite of the people could not depend on a majority in the people's own House, and most of its members in 1757 were loyal to their old patron, the Duke of Newcastle. The King, moreover, detested the new Administration. As early as February he confided to Lord Waldegrave that he disliked Pitt's long speeches and pedantic letters; and that as for Temple, at the Admiralty, he disliked him even more—that he was "pert, troublesome, and ignorant of his duties." This situation could have but one ending, and early in April, Temple and Pitt were both dismissed from office. The whole of the Admiralty Board, with the exception of Boscawen and Elliot, were turned out at the same time, and Lord Winchilsea again became First Lord of the Admiralty.

For the next three months, though Parliament was sitting and a war raging, England was without a Ministry, and the situation grew from bad to worse. Pitt's dismissal had met with a storm of resentment throughout the country. The City of London presented him with its freedom; most of the other big cities followed suit; and in the words of Horace Walpole, "For some weeks it rained gold boxes." The Duke of Newcastle, whom the King summoned to St. James's, was afraid to form a government without the help of such a popular rival. The King, on the other hand, was violently opposed to Pitt's return. Pitt himself, though ready, for his country's good, to sink his personal feelings, and assume office with Newcastle, would only do so on certain stated terms, which the Duke, for the moment, was determined not to accept. In June the King attempted to ignore both men, and persuaded Waldegrave to attempt the formation of a government without them. But this, it was found, was a sheer impossibility.

Finally, in July, and just in the nick of time, Newcastle and Pitt came to terms, and the King gave his very unwilling approval. Newcastle, at the Treasury, would be nominal head, and would resume control of patronage with secret-service money. Pitt, as Secretary of State, would be in charge of foreign policy and of the supreme direction of the war.

At the Admiralty, the Board was again entirely reconstituted. Lord Anson, as part of the bargain with Newcastle, returned to his old position as First Lord; and, once again, Boscawen and Elliot were the only two of the old members who retained their seats. Boscawen, however, was not in England at this time. In the spring of this year the work of blockading the French coast had been so inadequately performed that three French squadrons had succeeded in leaving port with reinforcements for Louisburg. For this reason, Boscawen himself had sailed for Brest at the beginning of June to take command of the main blockading fleet.

In power at last in the early days of July, William Pitt bent all his tireless energy and lofty brain to the herculean task of saving his country from the increasing dangers with which she was now surrounded. "I know," he had said, earlier in the year, "that I can save this country, and I know no one else that can." With Newcastle's sanction, he now took upon himself the entire direction of the war, and issued his orders direct to the fighting services. He had already decided that England's correct role was to make all the use possible of her money and her sea power. She must fight France at sea and in America, in India and West Africa; but on the continent she must work for France's downfall by subsidizing an army to protect Hanover, and by giving Frederick of Prussia all the financial support of which he stood in need.

But before any improvement could be expected in England's conduct of the war, it would first be necessary for Pitt to imbue the fighting services, and especially the Army, with his own indomitable spirit. In America, in particular, owing to the inefficiency of officers in high places, added to the apathy of the colonial governments, and the apparent impossibility of getting the thirteen colonies to work in unison for the common good, there had already occurred a long chapter of reverses, and the dismal story had not yet come to an end.

Lord Loudoun, the Commander-in-Chief in America, was proving his right to the nickname of "St. George of the Inn signboards: always on a horse, and always standing still"; for since his arrival in America he had accomplished literally nothing. In 1756 it had been decided that the three necessary operations were (i) the capture of Fort Niagara, between Lakes Ontario and Erie, in order to cut the French communications between Canada and Louisiana; (ii) the capture of Forts Ticonderoga and Crown Point, on Lake Champlain, to protect the frontier of New York, and (iii) the capture of Fort Duquesne, to free the Ohio valley and safeguard the frontiers of Pennsylvania and Virginia. Pending the arrival of Lord Loudoun, nothing had been done to set these plans in motion, and, after his arrival in June, so much time was lost in discussions that nothing was done at all. The season ended, as already noticed,[1] with the disaster at Oswego, and all thought of an English offensive was postponed till the following year.

But now, in 1757, the sorry tale was the same. In the previous December it had been decided, instead of launching an attack on the French posts on Lake Champlain, to begin the year with the siege and capture of Louisburg. Pitt himself had approved this plan; 7,000 men were collected in America; 5,000 more, and a strong squadron under Admiral Holburne, were sent from England to co-operate; and the whole force was assembled at Halifax in July. Meanwhile, the French, quicker off the mark than the English, had eluded the Brest blockade, and reinforced Louisburg; but their fleet was rotten with scurvy, and the garrison was short of rations and in no condition to fight. These facts, however, were not known to Loudoun; and shortly after his arrival at Halifax, he received so gloomy a tale of the enemy's strength that he abandoned the attack, re-embarked his troops, and returned to New York. There he learnt that, during his absence at Halifax, the Marquis de Montcalm, the new French Governor-General, had

1 See page 215 and sketch map facing page 154.

marched south from Lake Champlain, captured the frontier fort of William Henry, and allowed his Indians to butcher the English garrison while the French troops looked on.

Nor was this the only disaster of the year. In September, after being reinforced by four more ships of the line, Holburne returned to Louisburg, hoping to induce the French to venture out and fight him. But his squadron was struck by a violent hurricane; two of his ships were wrecked; eleven more were dismasted; others had to throw their guns overboard in order to keep afloat; and the total damage was so severe that the squadron was obliged to return to England to refit.

From other parts of the world the news was equally grim. From India, earlier in the year, there had arrived the news of the loss of Calcutta, and the shocking story of the "Black Hole," where, of the 147 prisoners, crowded into a dungeon measuring eighteen feet square, only twenty-three were alive the following morning. On the Continent, Frederick the Great, after a victory at Prague in May, had been heavily defeated in June at Kollin; King George's younger son, the Duke of Cumberland, in command of the allied army in Hanover, had been beaten by the French at Hastenbeck on 25th July, and, with the King's own connivance, had signed, on 8th September, the Convention of Closterseven, by the terms of which 38,000 Hanoverians laid down their arms.

Even before the long tale of these disasters was completed, public confidence in a successful end to the war had disappeared. Writing to the Duke of Newcastle on 22nd July, Lord Hardwicke had said: "For God's sake let us push for a peace, and all channels be tried for it with discretion, for I look upon this nation as on the brink of ruin." And as an example of the depression that was seizing the general public, Mrs. Montagu wrote to her husband on 1st August: "Perhaps this is the last summer I may ever be an idle traveller through a peaceful country—the best we can hope is to be tributary vassals to France."

Pitt's first attempt to stem the tide of adversity was an effort to paralyse the French offensive on the Continent by means of a strong raid on Rochefort. But this scheme was spoilt by the King's insistence on the military command being given to Sir John Mordaunt, who was quite unfitted for an enterprise of that nature. On the naval side, Pitt placed Admiral Hawke in command of the escorting fleet, and Boscawen was recalled to England to go as his second-in-command. Here, however, there was a sudden change of plan, doubtless due to the fact that Boscawen, at that time, was not on good terms with Anson, who had just returned to power. When Boscawen arrived at Portsmouth he was ordered to the Admiralty for duty, and, to his great disgust, the post of second-in-command was given to Charles Knowles.

As events turned out, however, Boscawen lost nothing by his disappointment, for the expedition was a complete fiasco. Arriving off Rochefort towards the end of September, the situation was very favourable for a most successful raid. But after a council of war Sir John Mordaunt decided that it would be unsafe to disembark his troops; and to the disgust of the whole country the expedition sailed straight back to Portsmouth. "And there," succinctly commented the youthful James Wolfe, the future hero of Quebec—"and there ended the reputation of three bad generals."

Colonel James Wolfe, then only thirty years old, was already recognized as one of the most earnest and brilliant young officers of his day, and had held an important position on Mordaunt's staff. He knew, therefore, better than anyone, the reasons for the tragic failure of the enterprise, and in a deathless letter to a friend, written a few weeks afterwards, he laid down the principles which should invariably govern the landing of troops in the face of an enemy. That letter has often been repeated; but as the non-observance of its principles led not only to the fiasco at Rochefort in 1757, but also to the failure of the vitally important landing at Suvla Bay a century and a half later, it may well be repeated again:

BLACKHEATH, *5th November, 1757.*

DEAR RICKSON. . . . I am not sorry that I went, notwithstanding what has happened; one may always pick up something useful from amongst the most fatal errors. . . . Experience shows me that, in an affair depending upon vigour and dispatch, the Generals should settle their plan of operations, so that no time may be lost in idle debate and consultations when the sword should be drawn; that pushing on smartly is the road to success, and more particularly so in an affair of this nature; that nothing is to be reckoned an obstacle to your undertaking which is not found really so upon trial; that in war something must be allowed to chance and fortune, seeing it is in its nature hazardous, and an option of difficulties.

In the next chapter we shall see how splendidly Wolfe himself put those principles into practice when he accompanied Boscawen to the famous siege of Louisburg.

A little light on the events at Rochefort, and on the Admiral's disappointment at not accompanying that expedition, is thrown by Fanny's next letters, addressed to her husband at the Admiralty.

LEVEL'S GROVE,
Tuesday p.m.
20th September, 1757.

I return my dear love many thanks for two kind letters. Lady Smythe had a letter from her spouse this morning, entirely upon your subject. He flatters himself, he says, that you will no more resign than he did, when a junior was put over his head (meaning Sir Robert Henley).[1] He charges her to prevail with you to come to Bounds and join one more Cincinnatus at the plough. He is so earnest on this subject that were you to see his entreaties, I think you could not be deaf to them. Besides, you know there are many pretty misses upon the Pantiles in his neighbourhood[2] and these, you acknowledge, are *to you* irresistible.

Wednesday, the 21st Sept., 1757.

The weather, impatient of your absence, will stay no longer for you. And, since you would not come when the roads were good, the weather fine and the country pleasant, you will now have bad roads, rainy weather and only my dull company. To all which I beg you surrender yourself with as good grace as you can to-morrow, for indeed, my love, having DEPENDED upon Thursday, I can by no means digest Friday. I try to submit to your sentence, but I cannot —Thursday must be the day. Why should it not? The board has had your attendance ever since Monday se'ennight, the news is all come, read and digested—for, as to news from Hawke, you cannot persuade me you wait for that, when I know that with this north-east wind none can come. *Enfin, mon cher, cher, ayez pitié de votre pauvre solitaire,* for if you spend all your life in London I shall begin to think that you have found something there, something very unworthy of your interest! Jesting apart, I will not doubt of your coming to-morrow, unless it should really be extremely inconvenient to you.

I have agreed for 50,000 bricks brought in from Peas Marsh at 25 sh. pr. thousand, which is a shilling cheaper than I expected to get them. I assure you there are affairs here as well as in London that require your presence, so that there is no need I should put in the balance the very earnest desire of your affectionate, faithful,

F. B.

[1] Sir Robert Henley, afterwards 1st Earl of Northington, was appointed Lord Keeper (the last) in 1757, when Sir Sidney Smythe expected the appointment. Smythe was made Lord Chief Baron in 1772.
[2] I.e., Tunbridge Wells.

I am as well as you left me, and slept well. When I can give you an account of *un petit* more lively than Mr. Billy, I'll be sure to let you know. *What can I say more?* Why, wish you health, and pleasure and success. I do—*et tendrement.*

The sequel to this last postscript was the birth, at the beginning of the following May, of the little Benjamin, upon whose arrival, as Fanny's previous letters have shown, she had set her heart so long.

Immediately after the Admiral's next week-end at Level's Grove, Fanny drove to Sandleford to spend a fortnight with her friend, Mrs. Montagu; and there is a charming pen-picture of her in a letter which Elizabeth Montagu wrote to her sister a few days after Fanny had returned home. To the casual observer, Mrs. Montagu may have appeared as a woman whose head was a great deal bigger than her heart; but this impression was very far from the truth. For those who could penetrate the protective armour of slightly venomous wit with which she faced the world, there was a heart of warm sympathy and rich understanding. Yet, of all Mrs. Montagu's friends, there was probably no one who could bring to the surface so much of the best in her character as Fanny Boscawen; and there was consequently no one of whom she was quite so fond. Certainly none of Fanny's friends can have appreciated her more than Elizabeth Montagu did, and nobody ever drew such a vivid and understanding portrait of her as is contained in this letter:

SANDLEFORD,
14th October, 1757.

I am indeed deprived of my friend, Mrs. Boscawen; she left me on Tuesday last. I was very happy in her company, and we really looked very foolish at parting. She is in very good spirits, and sensible of her many felicities, which I pray God to preserve to her. But her cup is so full of good, I am always afraid it should spill. She is one of the few whom an un-bounded prosperity could not spoil. I think there is not a grain of evil in her composition. She is humble, charitable, pious, of gentle temper, with the finest principles, with a great deal of discretion, void of any degree of art, warm and constant in her affections, mild towards offenders, but rigorous towards offence, and speaks her mind very freely to young people in regard to the fashionable levities. She intends to ask Miss Williams to go with her into Surrey, to stay till she comes to London again, and I wish Lady Frances[1] may send her, for Mrs. Boscawen tells her very roundly sometimes of the mis-conduct of our fine ladies, and even of some who are the Miss's intimates. And as she has a great deal of cheerfulness in her manner, what she says does not look like the lessons of severity.

Fanny returned straight home from Sandleford, and her next letters to the Admiral complete the story of Charlotte Williams's arrival:—

LEVEL'S GROVE,
Wednesday, 12th October, 1757.

Lady Frances Williams returns me a thousand thanks and expresses the highest satisfaction in "putting her daughter into my hands," for that is her phrase; and on Monday I go to Epsom to fetch Miss Williams. Lady Coningsby[2] intends to bring her so far. I think I have been very clever in mustering for myself so agreeable a companion so soon.

Van seems vastly sorry to resign her share of me, and begs I will yet fetch her from Sunbury, whither she intends to go for

[1] Lady Frances Williams, daughter of Thomas, Earl of Coningsby, was the wife of Sir Charles Hanbury-Williams, K.B. This daughter (Charlotte) married Captain the Hon. R. Boyle Walsingham. Her elder daughter, Frances, was already married to William, 4th Earl of Essex, and died in 1759. Captain Walsingham was lost on board H.M.S. *Thunderer* in a hurricane in the West Indies in October 1779.

[2] Viscountess Coningsby, elder sister of Lady Frances Hanbury-Williams became Viscountess Coningsby on the death of her father, the 1st Earl, in 1729. She died, unmarried, in 1761, when the title became extinct.

the purpose, as soon as THE GUESTS have left Shottesbrook. But perhaps Miss Williams will stay till we go to London, or near it. Not that I shall be in a hurry to settle there. On the contrary, I am willing to keep house for your hunting a week or two after the meeting of the Parliament if you please. But meantime I have thought of going up to the Birthday if I am well and my garment succeeds.

I have been let blood to-day, which I fancy was very necessary. I am very well, but was so tired with my 33 miles yesterday[1] that I went to bed at 8 p.m.

Your son has galloped to Hatchlands this morning. Says it is very high, the last scaffolding up and looks just ready for the roof.

EPSOM,
Monday, 17th October, 10 a.m.

I have very little to add to-day to a very long epistle I wrote my dearest love yesterday. Only I forgot an injunction which I had resolved to give YOU and which you *must obey.* It is to betake yourself to-morrow evening to the hundreds of Drury (an odd command for a wife to give, you'll say—and such a wife!) but you may trust her. She does not mean *the Balcony above stairs,* but the stage box below, where she requires and directs you to be stationed during the performance of *The Author,*[2] a farce. Mr. Foote performs Cadwallader and it is also to be hoped that Mrs. Clive[3] will favour you with poor, simple, foolish Becky. Foote is going to Ireland, which makes it absolutely necessary for you to go. But why the stage box, you'll say—well, I would place you where you'll be best entertained. In the front, believe me, you will not hear. Why? Because Mr. Foote in the person of Mr. Apreece gives you a torrent of words, more rapid and more violent than an April shower of hail. Nor is it possible to distinguish

[1] Her journey from Sandleford.
[2] Produced by Foote in February 1757, at Drury Lane, *The Author* was a skit on Mr. Aprice, a man of fortune, whose peculiarities were made the butt of Foote's mimicry in the part of Cadwallader. Aprice, who was actually a friend of Foote's, eventually persuaded him to stop the play, as too unkind a joke.
[3] Kitty Clive, the famous actress.

it into words unless you are near him. Therefore a second row in the stage box, nay even a place in the first, though it should be between two fine ladies, is the station I would choose for you. *Voyez un peu je suis généreuse*, but did you ever know me otherwise *quand il s'agissait de votre plaisir?*

LEVEL'S GROVE, 4 *p.m.* Miss Williams arrived at Epsom before I had made the tea and we are both arrived safe here, the sun very kindly gilding our way. She seems to have brought good health, good spirits and good humour, which, being the three necessary qualifications toward cottage life, I hope she will be pleased with her abode. She is gone upstairs to write to Lady Frances, an attention that I approve mightily.

Adieu, très cher. I long to see you. Come as soon as you can and, lest you should not be welcome, fill your pockets with money.

LEVEL'S GROVE.
Wed. 19*th October*, 1757.

Heavenly weather, my love. Come and enjoy it, 'tis lost upon you in London. What signifies bright, clear, delightful sunshine in a place which is covered with clouds, the fogs, the storms of politics and public distress.

But now I have your letter. How grieved I am, dearest love, to find you vex yourself at your present inactive situation! *Pour Dieu, mon cher, consolez-vous.* I would not have you do your enemies, your enviers, so much honour as to let them vex you. I cannot, meantime, agree with you to lament that you were not on the expedition, unless you can prove that your noble spirit would have been caught by the General, with whom, no doubt, you would have had some sharp dispute.[1] Think of three hardy men of war, escorted *safe* home by 14 of ours. Should you have done so, do you think? And now, considering the advanced season, not to mention the fatality of all our undertakings (which I own has made me

---

[1] All England, at this time, was blaming the conduct of the English General at Rochefort. Even Mrs. Montagu, writing to a civilian friend, said, on 26th October, "Tell me all you hear of our sad and dire disgrace at Rochefort."

(*From an old photograph*)

HATCHLANDS, NEAR GUILDFORD

superstitious) I cannot look for much success. Therefore, think you are reserved for better days, and be content to pass these in a home where you are sure to find all the tenderness and all the affection that can render every part of that home agreeable.

After this sermon of resignation, I am glad you have once more sounded your wrongs in the ears of Mr. Newcastle, who I suppose in twenty friendly squeezes of the hand, assured his *dear Admiral* that he was the best officer in the King's service.

I have left directions in writing with Waite, but for better security shall creep over to the planting at Hatchlands the moment I am up. The holes for the pines were dug yesterday. I shall mark the places for the laurels to-morrow. I know partly already where I shall place them. Two caroline poplars I am also to have.

The box of scarlet acorns you cannot bring, because of Miss Williams' guitar, but it (the box) may come next week by Daws.

Adieu, très cher. Ever and entirely yours,

F. B.

This last letter had scarcely been dispatched, when, in great excitement, the Admiral himself arrived at Level's Grove, with the news that he had been given a sea-going appointment, and must start next morning for Portsmouth. His complaints to Pitt and Newcastle of his recent supersession (for so he apparently regarded it, despite the fact that Admiral Knowles was his senior in date of rank) had at last borne fruit. He had been appointed second-in-command to Hawke, who was proceeding to sea at once; and their task was to intercept the French fleet on its way home from Louisburg. Early next morning, with Fanny waving him a brave good-bye, he started off again in his coach-and-four; and two days later the whole fleet set sail from Spithead.

To the Admiral himself, fretting at the hard fate which chained him to an office desk in the middle of a European war,

261

his new appointment was like a reprieve from prison. But to Fanny, bracing herself to face this new and unexpected anxiety, in her delicate state of health, the sudden change in her husband's fortunes did not appear in quite the same light. Her friend, Elizabeth Montagu, thoroughly understood this; and as soon as the news arrived, she wrote her a letter of loving and helpful sympathy:

SANDLEFORD.
25th October, 1757.

You are very obliging on every occasion, and was it not excessively kind, as my letter, on Sunday morning, ended with wishing Mr. Boscawen in employment, you should begin a letter which I received on Sunday evening, with telling me he was actually in commission. I am a little uneasy lest the surprise should have hurt you; satisfy me in that matter, and my imagination will then sit down and weave laurel garlands for your husband's head, and I will rejoice in the advantage which I hope his country will reap from his arms; but think me not ignoble if I own, glory is but as bright moonshine when compared to your welfare, and think me not below the standard of true patriotism if I confess it is for the sake of such as you my country is a name so dear.

I know you are too reasonable to wish Mr. Boscawen might avoid the hazards of his profession. The Duke of Marlborough, his kinsman, lived to old age, and survived, perhaps, all the cowards that were born on that same day; the accidents of life are more than the chances of war. Be not afraid, but commit it all to the great and wise Disposer of all events. A firm hope and cheerful reliance on Providence I do believe to be the best means to bring about what we wish, and that such confidence does it far better than all our anxious foresight, our provident schemes, and measures of security. I remember with sorrow and shame I trusted much to a continual watching of my son; I would not have committed him to a sea-voyage, or for the world in a town besieged; I forgot at whose will the waves are still, and who breaketh the bow and snappeth the spear asunder. What was the reward of this confidence of my own care, and diffidence of His who only could protect him? Why, such as it deserved! I lost my beloved object, and with him my hopes, my joys, and my health, and I lost him, too, not by those things I had feared for him, but by the pain of a tooth.[1] Pray God keep you from my offence, and the punishment of it.

I do not mean that you should be void of anxieties in time of hazard; but offer them up to God every night and sleep in peace; the same every morning, and rise with confidence.

I will own that I have had a great desire to see Mr. Boscawen's name on most honourable record for some great victory before this war is at an end, that when the annals of our time are read, his countrymen, his friends, and his family may glow with pride for him, while they must often for others blush with shame. I am much pleased with his Majesty's well placed confidence in Mr. Boscawen. The Duke,[2] it seems, is gone to plant cabbages. As soon as these great folks are disgusted, they go into the country: the indignant statesman plants some trees, upon which he wishes all his enemies hanged: his occupations are changed, but his passions are not altered. The angry warrior rides a-hunting, "*mais le chagrin monte en croupe et galope avec lui,*" nor can the hounds and horn "that cheerly rouse the slumb'ring morn," content the sense that wants "th'ear-piercing fife and spirit-stirring drum." How often have these men, who have accustomed themselves to the loud uproar of the world, reason to wish, as Pope says we should, if stunned by the music of the spheres, that Heaven had left them still "the murmuring zephyrs and the purling rill." Indeed it is a great misfortune to have set one's mind above the key of ordinary life; how often does it make these great performers play out of time and out of tune?

I suppose Lord Halifax is going to be Secretary of State: he has behaved so well in his office, I wish him a greater, and that he may not be reduced to the pacific delights of rural life, for which I presume his mind may be a key too high. I think one

[1] Her only son died when 12 months old of convulsions brought on by teething troubles.
[2] After his defeat and subsequent disgrace at Closterseven.

should put one's son apprentice to a gardener before he goes into the House of Commons, that when he is an unsuccessful politician he may retire to his garden with some pleasure and skill to boot. They are seldom so lucky as Boileau's antagonist, "*qui, de mauvais médecin devint habile architecte.*" These chiefs out of war, and statesmen out of place, generally make an absurd figure in the country.

Pray make my compliments to your amiable guest. I expect a cargo of Morgans and good folks from Newbury to dine here; I always endeavour to depart the country in odour of civility, and I think I bid them adieu with easy grace and agreeable freedom, which ever accompanies the movements of the heart. Not so did I take leave of my friend this day fortnight! Pay me for that parting pang by bringing yourself to London in good health.

> I am,
> My dear Madam,
> Most affectionately yours,
> E. MONTAGU.

On this occasion, however, Fanny's anxiety did not last long. After cruising off Brest for some weeks in cold and boisterous weather, the English fleet was caught by a severe storm, and blown away from its station. The returning French squadron, still weak with fever, and a very easy prey, ran into the tail end of the same storm. But by good luck it succeeded in reaching Brest before the English fleet had reassembled, and when this was discovered by Hawke he sailed back to Portsmouth. Boscawen landed on 15th December, and a few days later he and his family moved up to London for Christmas.

CHAPTER XVII

THE CAPTURE OF LOUISBURG

IN any future war, when not only the Generals and their staffs, but even the men in the trenches, will probably be in less danger than their mothers and sisters and wives and little children, the fighting man will experience, in addition to the normal discomforts of active service, a new and unbearable fear for the safety of his friends at home. Before the days of bombing aeroplanes, the Army and the Navy had few such cares to perplex them. In the comparatively gentlemanly days of the eighteenth and nineteenth centuries, and even in France in 1914, it was the women, and not the men, who paid, with mental anguish, the bitter price of war. And in 1757, after months and years of torment, Fanny Boscawen's peace of mind at her husband's safe return only lasted a week.

One of the first visits that the Boscawens paid on returning to London was to the Pitts' new house at 10 St. James's Square, the building which now, as Chatham House, is the home of the Royal Institute for International Affairs. And there, after dinner, while Fanny, in all probability, was being shown the house by her friend, Lady Hester, William Pitt told the Admiral that he would be wanted to return to America almost immediately, and gave him a brief outline of his plans for the coming year. Pitt had decided that the whole energy of the country must first be directed to safeguarding the American colonies, and that this could only be done by the destruction of the French power in Canada. Lord Loudoun was being recalled, and though the King insisted on his place being taken by General Abercrombie, the senior officer on the spot, Pitt was sending out Lord Howe, the most talented officer of the day, to act as his second-in-command. These two would be responsible for securing the wholehearted co-operation of the colonies in the coming spring; and three operations would be set on foot at the earliest possible moment.

In the south, there would be an expedition to capture Fort Duquesne. In the centre, a large force under Abercrombie would capture the French forts on Lake Champlain, and then advance on Montreal. Thirdly, and most important of all, a combined force was to be fitted out for the capture of Louisburg, that strong fortress at the mouth of the St. Lawrence, which Pitt regarded as the key to the conquest of Canada. For this operation Pitt had gained the King's permission to nominate all the commanders. Boscawen would be given the chief naval command, and he must be ready to sail at a very early date. An attack on Quebec would follow, but whether it could be attempted in 1758 would depend on the time occupied in reducing the fortress of Louisburg.

There were to be no half measures this time. While the ships and troops for Admiral Boscawen's operation were being assembled in England and America, redoubled precautions were to be taken to prevent the sailing of French reinforcements. Pitt believed in youth: the military command of the expedition was to be given to Colonel Jeffery Amherst, then only forty years old, with the rank of Major-General; and Colonel James Wolfe was to be the Senior Brigadier.

Promoted Admiral of the Blue at the early age of 46, Boscawen set out for Portsmouth on 5th February, leaving Fanny at their house at the Admiralty. Glowing pride at her husband's selection, and choking anguish at his departure, were fighting out their battle on the day she said good-bye to him. She was expecting the birth of her child at the beginning of May.

Arriving at Portsmouth on 7th February, Boscawen found that the troops to accompany him from England were already embarking; but continual westerly gales delayed his departure, and it was not till 19th February that his squadron put to sea. During this time of waiting he first made the acquaintance of James Wolfe, and no one who reads Wolfe's letters[1] can doubt the confidence and regard which the Naval Commander-in-Chief and the young Brigadier immediately began to feel for each other.

Wolfe had first heard of his appointment in the middle of January, and it would be hard to read the letter which he wrote to his mother at that time without a feeling of keen admiration:

"I don't deserve so much consideration as my father and you are so good as to express for me. He wishes rank for me, and you my preservation. All I wish for myself is that I may at all times be ready and firm to meet that death we cannot shun, and to die gracefully and properly when the hour comes." Little did his parents realize how soon and how abundantly that wish would be fulfilled. It was on 13th September in the following year that the hero of Quebec succumbed in the hour of victory.

The voyage across the Atlantic was dogged by evil luck. Within half an hour of leaving St. Helen's, one of the Admiral's best ships, missing stays, ran herself aground on Bembridge ledge and became a total wreck. Arriving off Plymouth, the squadron had to shelter from a fierce gale. Thereafter there was such a succession of contrary winds that they had to touch, in turn, at Madeira, the Canaries, Bermuda, and Sable Island; and the voyage to Halifax occupied eleven weeks. Eventually, however, with all the troops in good health, the squadron anchored at Halifax on 9th May. At home, three days earlier,

---

[1] *Life and Letters of James Wolfe,* Beckles Willson.

Fanny had given birth to her third son;[1] but the news that all was well with her did not reach Boscawen for another two months.

The troops from New York also began to assemble at Halifax on 9th May, and the next three weeks were occupied by Boscawen and Wolfe in final preparations. Amherst, meanwhile, had not arrived, for, sailing a few days later than the Admiral,[2] his voyage had been even slower. On 28th May, as the General's ship had still not put in an appearance, Boscawen decided to wait no longer, and the whole fleet headed for Gabaras Bay, a few miles south of Louisburg. The military force amounted to 12,000 men, with several batteries of artillery. Coming out of Halifax harbour, Amherst's ship was encountered, and the General at once transferred to the Admiral's flagship.

A characteristic example of Boscawen's solicitude for his men was given in one of Wolfe's letters at this time. "There is not," he wrote, "an ounce of fresh beef or mutton contracted for, even for the sick and wounded, which, besides the inhumanity, is impolitic and absurd. But Mr. Boscawen has taken the best precaution in his power by ordering 600 head of cattle for the fleet and the army the moment he arrived."

Of the troops, Wolfe commented at the same time that while some of them were "very good" battalions, and Fraser's Highlanders "very useful soldiers, commanded by the most manly corps of officers I ever saw," the majority of the regiments were "very undisciplined." "No nation in the world but this," he remarked, "sends soldiers to war without discipline or instructions." Nor was it only to the provincial troops that these remarks referred, for speaking of the garrison

[1] George Evelyn, subsequently succeeded his uncle as 3rd Viscount Falmouth.
[2] General Amherst (created Baron Amherst in 1788) was in H.M.S. *Dublin*, Captain (afterwards Admiral Lord) Rodney.

GEORGE EVELYN, 3RD VISCOUNT FALMOUTH
In the uniform of the Irish Dragoons
(*From the painting at Bill Hill*)

at Portsmouth, a few weeks earlier, he had written, "the condition of the troops that compose this garrison (or rather dirty vagabonds that stroll about in dirty red clothes from one gin-shop to another) exceeds all belief. There is not the least shadow of discipline, care, or attention."

Louisburg, the goal of the expedition, and the strongest fortress in North America, was situated at the northern end of Cape Breton Island, facing south-east, and was described by contemporary writers as the Gibraltar of the New World. It possessed a considerable land-locked harbour, with a single narrow entrance, protected by a group of small islets in the middle of the channel. The town and fortress had a civilian population of about 4,000, and there was a garrison of over 3,000 regular troops and a number of Indians, in addition to some 3,000 sailors from the eleven warships anchored in the bay. The well-designed fortifications were protected by over two hundred pieces of artillery; and several weeks' warning had been given of the impending attack. Added to these advantages, the adjoining coast-line was rocky, and protected by a heavy surf; and the French General Drucourt had utilized his breathing space of five weeks by constructing trenches and redoubts at every possible landing-place.

During the voyage from Halifax to the rendezvous, Bos-cawen's fleet was dispersed by another storm; but the whole force assembled in Gabaras Bay on 2nd June. Even then, the landing had to be postponed four times in succession, on account of heavy seas; but on 7th June, though the wind was still high and the surf heavy, the Admiral took his courage in both hands and decided to wait no longer. Shortly after day-break, the boats were lowered, and, while feint attacks were made in three other places, the main covering force of twelve picked companies, led by the intrepid Wolfe, were steadily rowed ashore, covered by the guns of the fleet.

So heavy a fire met the boats as they neared the land, that Wolfe hoisted a signal on the mast of his small boat, intending the attack at that point to be abandoned. But his mast was shot away; and the boats on the extreme left, finding it possible to gain shelter from a small projecting cape, rowed with all their might to that point, and Wolfe quickly followed them. Some of the boats were smashed to pieces on the rocks, and a number of men were drowned. But thanks to the help of that small projecting rock—and precisely as happened in the Great War at the first landing at Helles—a handful of men on the left established themselves ashore. This helped the landing in other parts of the beach; and Wolfe, with only a cane in his hand, charged the enemy's position at the head of his troops.

The main body, with the necessary guns and stores, could now land in safety. The fortress was gradually invested, and after a siege of seven weeks the French garrison of 6,000 men surrendered. The co-operation between the army and the navy had been in every way exemplary. "The Admiral and the General," wrote Wolfe, "have carried on public service with great harmony, industry, and union. Mr. Boscawen has given all and even more than we could ask of him, and is, I must confess, no bad fantassin himself, and an excellent back-hand at a siege . . . and all the officers of the navy have given us their utmost assistance, and with the greatest cheerfulness imaginable." This was generous praise from the young officer who, as the Navy well knew, had been the very spearhead of the operations on shore.

With the surrender of Louisburg, the whole of Cape Breton Island fell into English hands, and the capture of St. John's (now Prince Edward's Island) inside the gulf was completed a few days later.

Very unfortunately, however, Boscawen's success was not

shared by Abercrombie's column, which a few weeks earlier had attacked the French position at the south of Lake Champlain. There, on 6th July, by cruel mischance, Lord Howe had been killed in an unimportant skirmish, and Abercrombie, attacking the French next day with little skill, had been beaten back with very heavy loss. In view of this reverse, General Amherst embarked for New York with reinforcements, and all idea of attacking Quebec was postponed till the following year.

Of the third operation in America in 1758 it need only be said that, after an initial reverse, General Forbes's column, operating from Philadelphia, succeeded in taking possession of Fort Duquesne in November, and renamed it Fort Pitt, a name that was changed the following year to Pittsburg. To those accustomed to-day to the easy journey by train from Philadelphia to Pittsburg, it is strange to read of Forbes's difficult march through "a prodigious tract of country, very little known, destitute of military roads, and encumbered with mountains, morasses, and woods that were almost impenetrable."[1] Yet Wolfe's agile brain had already foretold the future. Writing to his mother a fortnight after the fall of Louisburg, he predicted that the American colonies "will some time hence be a vast empire, the seat of power and learning. Nature has refused them nothing, and there will grow a people out of our little spot, England, that will fill this vast space."

In England, the news of Boscawen's notable victory, closely following the report of Abercrombie's defeat, was received with tumultuous rejoicings, for it marked the turn of the tide, and the first important success of the war. Gigantic bonfires were lighted in every village and town; Boscawen and

[1] Smollett, IV, page 311.

Amherst were acclaimed as national heroes, and the captured French colours, escorted by horse and foot, were carried in procession from Kensington Palace to St. Paul's, amidst the roar of cannon and the cheers of a frenzied multitude. But fame is a fickle goddess. To-day the name of Louisburg is all but forgotten, and the student alone remembers the importance that once attached to that vanished fortress, of whose proud defences and busy streets the only remaining trace is a few sandy mounds and tufts of arid grass on a bleak, deserted shore. Yet at the time of the Seven Years' War no other event—not even the capture of Quebec—was the cause of such widespread joy.

There is, however, one memento of Louisburg in the heart of the West End of London upon which a forgetful country might surely place a plaque for the sake of the passer-by. Opposite No. 2 St. James's Square, which till recent years was the ancestral town house of Admiral Boscawen's family, is a street lamp-post, the base of which is one of the French guns from the captured fortress. The silencing of that gun was one of the steps which led to the foundation of the Dominion of Canada. In its entirely suitable environment, at the portal of the house that was inherited by the Admiral's son, it should conjure up, for all who pass that way, a proud picture of Wolfe's assaulting columns and Boscawen's thunderous fleet. Yet it stands neglected and forgotten, in the heart of the British Empire, besmeared and disfigured with Council lamp-post paint—and not one soul in a thousand of those who pass it by is aware of its epic history.

Needless to say that Fanny, who was staying at Mrs. Clayton's house near Marlow when the news of her husband's triumph first arrived, was inundated with letters of congratulation. To her old friend and cousin, Julia Sayer, she wrote:

HARLEY FORD,
NEAR MARLOW,
25th August, 1758.

My dear Cousin's letter of congratulation, for which I heartily thank her, being accompanied and followed by at least forty more, I am unable to write more than a very few words.

My joy is without alloy, for Mr. Boscawen assures me of his perfect health, and I think I may appeal to the Nation for the *perfection* of this glorious conquest, which has not been bloody, thank God, nor taxed with any grievous loss either public or private.

Pray send me your news, direct to the Admiralty. Not but that I go into Surrey from hence, but, wherever I am, I have a daily dispatch from the Admiralty.

I must now return to the innumerable letters which friendship and civility require at the weary hand of
Your ever sincere and affectionate
F. BOSCAWEN.
Best respects to my Aunt and a kiss for Fanny.

The Fanny mentioned in this postscript was Julia's two-year-old daughter, Frances Sayer, who was Mrs. Boscawen's goddaughter, and in later years became her constant companion. And as it was she, who, after her godmother's death, collected the volumes of her letters which are now in the library at Nunwell, she may fairly be claimed as the godmother of this story.

Ten days later, Fanny Boscawen was again writing to Julia:

LEVEL'S GROVE,
5th Sept., 1758.

DEAR COUSINE,

Tho' I have not a moment's time to write to-day (having all things to settle previous to a journey into Kent) yet I will not defer telling you that I had the pleasure of a letter to-day from Mr. Boscawen, dated the 10th of August. He had been saluted from the walls of *the English town of Louisburg*, which must doubtless have been music to his ears. And he had entertained on board the *Namur* Monsieur Drucourt and all the principal officers of the garrison and French navy. He had also been in the Town to return their visit and to wait on the ladies.

I send Fanny enclosed a leaf of a rose that grew at Louisburg. My blessing to her and respects to my Aunt. Direct if you please to Ed. Boscawen at the Admiralty, and

      Believe me always

           Your affectionate *Cousine* and sincere friend.

                              F. B.

Leaving a portion of his squadron to winter at Halifax, Boscawen sailed for home at the beginning of October, with James Wolfe as his passenger, and often, throughout that voyage, they must have fought their battles over again. Their passage across the Atlantic was a rapid one, but nearing the English Channel on October 27th, the squadron became separated in a stormy sea, and on the afternoon of that day, with only two other ships and two frigates in his company, the Admiral encountered a French squadron of five large ships of the line, a frigate, and a captured British East Indiaman. The enemy ships were on the contrary tack; and passing Boscawen very close to leeward, they discharged their broadsides in passing. Some of the English ships replied, but the wind was blowing so hard that most of the vessels could not open their lower ports, and little damage was done. Boscawen, ever ready for action, immediately changed his course and ordered a general chase. Darkness soon fell, and the night was black and stormy, but at daybreak the French squadron was still in sight. Boscawen had by this time lost sight of his frigates, but greedy of honour, he held on in pursuit. The French, however, refused to accept battle, and though the captured East Indiaman was recovered, the English ships could make no impression on the faster sailing Frenchmen. At midday on the 28th, therefore, Boscawen again headed for England—much, we may believe, to the joy of his officers and men—and dropped anchor at Spithead on 1st November. From thence, with Wolfe beside him, he crossed in his barge to Portsmouth, where Fanny and a huge concourse were waiting on the jetty to greet him.

After a hurried visit to Hatchlands to see the new house—to say nothing of the new baby, who was now six months old —the Admiral and his wife returned direct to London. There, on every side, from the King downwards, he was universally honoured and acclaimed; and on 12th December, dressed in his Admiral's uniform, he received in person the culminating honour of the thanks of the House of Commons. On that occasion, his remarks punctuated by applause from every part of the house, the Speaker addressed him as follows:

"Admiral Boscawen,

"The house has unanimously resolved that their thanks should be given to you for the services you have done to your King and country in North America, and it is my duty to convey their thanks to you.

"I wish I could do so in a manner suitable to the occasion, and as they ought to be given to you, now standing in your place as a member of this house.

"But were I able to enunciate and set forth in the best manner, the great and extensive advantages accruing to this nation from the conquest of Louisburg, with the Islands of Cape Breton and St. John, I could only exhibit a repetition of what has already been and is the genuine and uniform sense and language of every part of the Kingdom.

"Their joy, too, has been equal to their sentiments upon this interesting event, and in their sentiments and joy they have carried their gratitude also to you, Sir, as a principal instrument in these most important acquisitions.

"You are now, therefore, receiving the acknowledgments of the people, only in a more solemn way—by the voice, the general voice, of their representatives in Parliament—the most honourable fame that any man can arrive at in this, or any other country. It is on these occasions a national honour, from a free people, ever cautiously to be conferred in order to be the more esteemed—to be the greater reward; and which ought to be reserved for the most signal services to the State.

"The use, I am persuaded, you will make of this just testimony and high reward of your services and merit will be the preserving in your own mind a lasting impression of what the Commons of Great Britain are now tendering to you, and in a constant continuance of the zeal and ardour for the glory of your King and country which have made you deserve it.

"In obedience to the commands of the House, I do, with great pleasure to myself, give you the thanks of the house for the services you have done to your King and country in North America."

Admiral Boscawen's modest reply is also on record, and was typical of the man:

"Mr. Speaker,
"I am happy in having been able to do my duty, but have not words to express my sense of the distinguishing reward that has been conferred upon me by this house. Nor can I enough thank you, Sir, for the polite and elegant manner in which you have been pleased to convey to me the resolution of the house."

CHAPTER XVIII

DEATH OF THE ADMIRAL

THOUGH force so often triumphs over reason, and nothing is so fallacious as an attempt to foretell the duration of any war, it is safe to predict that prophets will always prophesy, and will almost invariably be wrong. The civil war in Spain, it was confidently asserted, could last but a few months. The great war that began in August 1914 was all to have been over by Christmas. Every economist agreed that it was economically impossible for a European conflict to be prolonged over two harvests. And in Mrs. Boscawen's day it was just the same. In the spring of 1759, when the Seven Years' War had still four years to run, Horace Walpole was writing: "This summer, I think, must finish all war, for who will have men, who will have money to furnish another campaign?"

In India, no less than in America, the year 1758 had witnessed the turn of the tide, and Clive's epic victory at Plassey was beginning to be recognized as the foundation of an eastern empire. On the continent of Europe, however, the power of France was still immensely strong, and she now decided upon a new effort to destroy her Island rival by striking a blow at the heart. Renewed preparations were begun to invade the southern counties, and the main operation was this time to be supported by simultaneous descents upon the coasts of Scotland and Ireland. The first essential of success was to obtain a temporary command of the English seas, and with this object a large armament was fitting out at Toulon, to reinforce the main fleet at Brest.

In England, apparently, or at least in the heart of London, where balls and assemblies continued to engross the attention of the *beau monde*, the threatened danger was not taken too seriously. "I have not announced to you," wrote the same Walpole on 1st June, "in form the invasion from France . . . nor do I tell you every time the clock strikes. . . . Yet I believe there are people really afraid of this—I mean the new militia, who have received orders to march." Pitt, nevertheless, had already formed his plans; and Boscawen, his most trusted Admiral, had again put out to sea. "When I explain my projects to other Admirals," said Pitt, "they always raise difficulties: Boscawen alone always finds expedients." And this, perhaps, is the highest praise that any commander can receive.

Leaving his wife and family at Level's Grove, where Fanny could find her best distraction in watching the work of Robert Adam at Hatchlands, Boscawen sailed from Portsmouth early in April to assume the chief command in the Mediterranean. His special task was to blockade the Toulon squadron in its home port, and to prevent at all costs its junction with the northern squadrons. True to his principles, the Admiral had allowed no difficulties to be looked upon as insuperable. But his task was not an easy one. His instructions were confused; his squadron was none too strong; and many of his ships were so foul that they were quite unfit for prolonged operations.

Following the loss of Minorca, it was no longer possible for an English fleet to maintain itself for any length of time in the Mediterranean; and after three months at sea Boscawen was compelled to raise the blockade of Toulon and return to Gibraltar to refit. Seizing their opportunity, the Toulon squadron made a bold dash for the Atlantic, and on the evening of 17th August the French Admiral de la Clue, with fifteen sail, was descried by an English scout, approaching the Straits of Gibraltar, close to the Barbary shore.

Boscawen was supping ashore when the news was brought to him about eight o'clock in the evening; and with one bound he was out of the house and rushing down to the quay. His squadron was not yet ready for sea, and his own flagship, the *Namur*, had not a sail bent. But a few minutes later the harbour was throbbing with activity, and by ten o'clock the first division of the squadron, led by the Admiral himself, had weighed anchor and started off in pursuit. The second division followed before midnight.

During the night, three of the French ships deserted their admiral, and ran for safety to the neutral port of Cadiz. The remainder, holding their course, were sighted by the English at daybreak, and, after a stern chase, a running fight began in the afternoon, and ended next morning with the total destruction of the French in the battle of Lagos Bay. In the early part of the action, Boscawen's flagship, hotly engaged with the three sternmost French ships of the line, had her mizzenmast shot away and both of her top-sail yards, and began to drop astern. Thereupon the Admiral at once ordered out his barge, flung himself aboard the *Newark*, hoisted his flag in her, and again continued the pursuit. "Never before," says Sir Godfrey Callender, "was battle like the battle of Lagos; never was one that counted more to the growing British Empire."

Boscawen had again covered himself with glory, and his return to Portsmouth with his prizes at the beginning of September was again a scene of wild popular rejoicings. Summoned immediately to London, he was met with a public ovation. The King received him with every mark of esteem; he was sworn a member of the Privy Council, and promoted General of Marines with a salary of £3,000 a year.

Nor was it only in official circles that Boscawen's praises were sung. Every bookseller in the country was doing a thriving trade in tracts and poems extolling the Admiral's

fame; and of these "An Ode occasioned by the success of
Admiral Boscawen, by a Gentleman of the University of
Oxford," may perhaps be taken as a very fair example. This
particular ode, a copy of which enriches the British Museum,
consists of twenty-two verses, but it will perhaps be enough for
honour if we quote the last two:

"Tell them, my sons, to smite the sounding lyre,
　To brave Boscawen tune their noblest lays.
His deeds shall every manly breast inspire,
　Each infant tongue shall lisp the Hero's praise.

Wake, then, O wake to Glory, wake to Fame,
　Nor sighing say such splendid scenes are past;
The verse that flows with great Boscawen's name
　With time itself, and his renown, shall last."

There is, moreover, another interesting proof of the evident
esteem in which the Admiral was then held, in a letter written
by Edmund Burke to Mrs. Montagu. Burke was trying in
1759 to be appointed Consul at Madrid, and he wrote to ask
if Mrs. Montagu would help him with letters of recommendation. Could she write to Mrs. Boscawen? "The Admiral," he naïvely suggests, "has such great merit with the
Ministry and the nation that the want of it will be the more
readily overlooked in any person for whom he may be induced
to apply."

But for Fanny Boscawen, the joy of her husband's safe and
triumphant return was sadly clouded over by a reawakened
anxiety. There could no longer be any doubt that even his
constitution could not endure for ever the mental and physical
strain of unending active service.

After a very short leave in the country, Boscawen returned to
the Admiralty, and for the next three months he resumed the
routine of five days' work in London and the Saturday to

Monday at home. The few existing letters from Fanny which date from that period are mostly domestic scraps of no interest, but one or two of them throw a little light on her daily life. Early in November, though Adam's decorations were still far from complete, she and her family took up their residence in the new house at Hatchlands, and it was apparently about this time that she wrote to her husband:

HATCHLANDS PARK.
Thursday, 10 *p.m.*

Peradventure my dear love and I have spent our day very differently—you in the populous city midst the busy hum of men, I in the woods all alone, midst the rustling of falling leaves. What is more, I shall go to bed *first* to-night. Let me only give you the *bon soir*, and I am gone.

However, lest you should entertain too mean an opinion of my solitude and obscurity, 'tis fit you should know that I have been visited both morning and evening—first by a Justice (of the Quorum, aye and rotilorum, too, for aught I know), and secondly by a Right Honourable Peeress. But, to deliver myself more like a woman of Surrey, I should say that I have been visited by Mr. Weston[1] and Lady Onslow,[2] not forgetting the jovial Benny. All rejoiced with me on my Admiral's safe return, and I assure you my Lady was quite eloquent upon the occasion. She called you the Staff of the Nation. I liked the term, for I believe indeed the nation may lean and rest upon you without fearing to find a broken reed. We talked little politics, for she is very backward, as you may believe when I tell you she really thought you was the Head of the Admiralty, and she rejoiced therefor. I was forced to take this joy from her, lest she should impart it, and then we talked of marriages and their contraries.

I have seen the cloak bags here. Tom[3] says "Squirrel hab

[1] A descendant of the famous Sir Richard Weston, of Sutton, which is only a few miles from Hatchlands.
[2] Widow of the 2nd Lord Onslow.
[3] The Negro page, now growing up.

eat 'em a little at Lebel's Grove," but I have sent 'em to Bob Hides to be cobbled.

Girls present humble duty: they look very handsome.

Please to bring me a small cargo from the milliner's. She'll send it to the house. I'm quite vexed that we cannot find your pocket book. Pray comfort me with your letter. I long to hear from you. More to see you again; and if you could bring me from London, by way of fairing, ½ oz. of good memory, you would make me a much more useful animal than I can now pretend to be.

Sealing-wax wanted. Sand wanted. The waggon is come safe and cargo in the hall.

Meanwhile, for England, the war was still prospering, and every month was bringing its crop of victories. In America, in July, the forts of Niagara and Ticonderoga had both fallen; in August, on the continent, there had been the great triumph of Minden; in September, Quebec had been captured, though the gallant Wolfe had died in the hour of triumph. Rodney had raided Havre and destroyed the enemy's flotillas of flat-bottomed boats; and best of all, on 21st November, the Brest squadron was totally destroyed by Hawke in Quiberon Bay. The fear of invasion had now come to an end.

But it was still essential to blockade the French coast and harass French trade; so early in January 1760 Boscawen was again appointed to command the Western fleet, in relief of Admiral Hawke. And here a succession of minor misfortunes was in store for him. Leaving Portsmouth, he encountered such severe storms that he had to put back to St. Helens and wait for better weather. Sailing once more in February, he again ran into violent gales on his passage down Channel, and was forced to run for shelter. One of his biggest ships was lost with all hands, and the rest of his squadron returned to Plymouth in such a disabled condition that it took them a month to refit. In March, however, he at last arrived in

Quiberon Bay, which was now regarded almost as an English anchorage, and there he lived for the next five months a life of drab monotony, unrelieved by any major excitements.

During these months, the Admiral interested himself, as always, in the health of the lower deck; and, far ahead of his time, he took possession of the small island of Vannes, for the sole purpose of growing green vegetables for the use of his sick in hospital. It is surely a sign of the affection with which he was regarded in the fleet, that one of the sailors' ditties of that year—a ditty which dwelt on the joys of the coming peace —ended with the refrain:

"That day, then, jolly buck, we'll set the taps a-flowin'
    And drink rest and good luck to Admiral Boscawen."

Rest, indeed, was what Boscawen needed, and when, in September, he returned home to England his health was so run down that he was relieved of all duty, and retired to Hatchlands to recuperate. There, in the heart of his family, in the comfort and delight of his new exquisite home, and in the tender care of his deeply-devoted wife, he seemed to begin to mend. But his years of unsparing exertions, in all climates and all seas, at a time when, even for an admiral, a life at sea meant a life of continual hardship, had utterly destroyed his power of recuperation. It was in this condition that, early in December, about six weeks after the sudden death of the King, he was struck down with a fever, which his lowered vitality found it hard to fight.

From Fanny, who was always with him at this time, there are no letters to describe those last few weeks—weeks to which she had looked forward with such excited pleasure, and which were now filled with such anxious, nameless dread. But from Mrs. Montagu's letters we are able to reconstruct a few details of the scene. About the middle of December she wrote to her husband:

I told you in my last that Admiral Boscawen was ill of a fever; I hope he is out of danger. The noble Admiral does not fight so well with a fever as he does with the French; he will not lie in bed, where he would sooner subdue it. Poor Mrs. Boscawen is very anxious and unhappy about the Admiral, and indeed the loss to her and her children would be as great as possible.

In a letter written to her friend, Elizabeth Carter, whose famous translation of *Epictetus* had recently been published, Mrs. Montagu repeats the same sad story, in words which disclose her deep attachment to Fanny. Fanny and Miss Carter had often met at Elizabeth Montagu's house, and were soon to become intimate friends:

My health is very good, but my mind has been in an uneasy state for this fortnight for Admiral Boscawen, who has had a very bad fever; he is now, we hope, out of danger; the letters yesterday brought an account of his amendment. Mrs. Boscawen's happiness and the welfare of her children depend on the life of the Admiral, so you may believe it is a great object to me, and I could not settle my mind to anything while the alarm was strong. Thank God we have better hopes than we had; but it would be too much to say he is out of danger.

For the next few days the news continued good, but two days after Christmas Mrs. Montagu was writing again:

His fever still hangs upon him; his strength is quite subdued; any sudden attack, any degree more of fever, and my good friend loses a good husband, her children a good father, their situation in life will suffer a grievous alteration, and the public will be deprived of a man who serves it with zeal and ability and is always more tender of the honour of his country than of his own person.

On New Year's Day the Admiral had a relapse, and Mrs. Montagu, as soon as she heard of Fanny's renewed distress, rushed to Hatchlands to help her. But to avoid frightening the Admiral, he was not allowed to know of her arrival, and she slept in the house of a neighbour; and after a few days, as the Admiral could not bear Fanny out of his sight, and Mrs. Montagu could never see her for a moment, she returned home to London.

A few days later the Admiral began to realize how desperately ill he was, and sending for his sister, Lady Frederick, he begged her to stay with Fanny, and, if the worst should happen, to get her away to London as soon as possible. The next morning he died.

Fanny, utterly dazed, was led away from his room, and taken with his children to London. But despite the repeated attempts of Mrs. Montagu to persuade her to stay at Hill Street, she insisted on remaining as long as she could in her old Admiralty home. Elizabeth Montagu, a real friend in need, was seldom absent from her side; and a week after the Admiral's death she was able to write to her husband:

I thank God her mind is very calm and settled; she endeavours all she can to bring herself to submit to this dire misfortune. I know time must be her best comforter, so that I oppose her lamentations rarely and gently, but when they continue long, I set before her the merit of her five children, the want they will have of her, and the comfort she may derive from them.

As soon as arrangements could be made, the Admiral was taken with simple dignity to Cornwall, for burial in the Boscawen family church of St. Michael Penkivel. And there, on a tomb designed by Robert Adam, can be read the noble and deeply-moving epitaph which Fanny herself composed:

SATIS GLORIAE SED HAUD SATIS REIPUBLICAE

Here lies the Right Honourable Edward Boscawen, Admiral of the Blue, General of Marines, Lord of the Admiralty, and one of his Majesty's Most Honourable Privy Council.

His birth tho' noble, his titles tho' illustrious, were but incidental additions to his greatness.

History, in more expressive & more indelible Characters, will inform latest posterity with what ardent zeal, with what successful valour he served his country! And taught her enemies to dread her naval power.

In command he was equal to ev'ry emergency—superior to ev'ry difficulty.

In his high departments masterly and upright. His example form'd, while his patronage rewarded merit. With the highest exertions of military greatness he united the gentlest offices of humanity.

His concern for the interest, and unwearied attention to the health, of all under his command, softened the necessary exactions of duty and the rigors of discipline by the care of a guardian, and the tenderness of a father.

Thus belov'd and rever'd, amiable in private life as illustrious in public; this gallant and profitable servant of his country, when he was beginning to reap the harvest of his toils and dangers, in the full meridian of years and glory, after having been providentially preserved through ev'ry peril incident to his profession—died of a fever on the 10th Janry, in the year 1761; the 50th of his age, at Hatchlands Park in Surrey,—a seat he had just finished at the expense of the enemies of his country, and (amidst the groans and tears of his beloved Cornishmen) was here deposited.

His once happy wife inscribes this marble—an unequal testimony of his worth and of her affection.

Summer, indeed, had passed.

INDEX

Abercrombie, General, 266, 271.

Abergavenny, Lord, 32 n.

Adair, Mr., 177.

Adam, Robert, 247, 248, 249, 286.

Admiralty House, Portsmouth, 196.

Admiralty Screen, Whitehall, 249.

Aix-la-Chapelle, Treaty of, 82, 116 n.

Alcide, Boscawen's capture of the, 183.

Alexandria, Virginia, 156.

Alleghanies, The, 153, 156.

Alton, Hants, 213.

Amelia, H.R.H. Princess, 162.

America, The French in North, 153.

American War of Independence, xii.

Amherst, General Jeffery, 266, 268.

Amyand, Mr., 226.

Angel Inn, Oxford, 112.

Anne, Queen, 7.

Anson, Admiral Lord, 37, 38, 39, 40, 41, 70, 86, 92, 166, 182 n., 209, 225, 250.

Anson, Elizabeth Lady, 70, 124, 206.

Anstey, Mrs., 171.

Aprice (Apreece), Mr., 259.

Argyll, Archibald, 3rd Duke of, 71 n., 90, 91, 103.

Ascot Races (1748), 101.

Audley Street, Fanny's house in, 65, 69, 163 n.

Austrian Succession, War of the, 16.

Author, The (Foote's farce), 259.

Bank of England, run on in 1745, 18.

Barham, Mrs., 84.

Barrington, Hon. Shute, Bp. of Durham, 87 n.

Barrington, William Wildman, 2nd Viscount, 87.

Bartholomew, Miss (Lady Geary), 25 n.

Bateman, Dicky, 86.

Bateman, Lord, 86, 87.

Bath, Lord, 86 n.

Bath, Order of the, 48.

Bathurst, Lord, 212.

Beaconsfield, Waller's House at, 100, 103.

Bear, Mrs., of Kensington, 172.

Beauclerc, Lady Diana, 87.

Beaufort, Elizabeth, Duchess of, *see* Elizabeth Boscawen.

Beaufort, Henry 5th Duke of, xii.

"Beauty and I were never acquainted," 96.

Beck, or Becca, an old dog, 150, 248.

Beckford, William, 212.

Bedford, Duchess of, 79.

Bedford, Duke of, 48, 71, 79, 81, and n.

Belle Isle, Straits of, 184.

Bellenden, Mr., 89, 90.

"Bells of Ouseley" Inn, 96.

Bemish, Lt., R.N., 124.

Berrisford, Mr. (theatre ticket agency), 77.

Berwick, Duke of, 8.

Best, Mrs., 32, 38.

Beuvregny, Fanny's butler, 62, 73, 109, 134.

Beverstock, Mr., 160.

Bill Hill, xiii.

Birthday, the admiral's, celebrated, 102, 192.

Bisshopp, Sir Cecil, 31 n., 38, 86.

Bisshopp, Charlotte, 89.

Bisshopp, Lady (Hon. Anne Boscawen), 31, 35, 49 n.